AF125497

William T. Preyer, Henry W Brown

The mind of the child ... observations concerning the mental

development of the human being in the first years of life

William T. Preyer, Henry W Brown

The mind of the child ... observations concerning the mental development of the human being in the first years of life

ISBN/EAN: 9783742896698

Hergestellt in Europa, USA, Kanada, Australien, Japan

Cover: Foto ©ninafisch / pixelio.de

Manufactured and distributed by brebook publishing software (www.brebook.com)

William T. Preyer, Henry W Brown

The mind of the child ... observations concerning the mental development of the human being in the first years of life

CONTENTS.

	PAGE
PREFACE BY THE EDITOR	v
PREFACE TO FIRST EDITION	ix
PREFACE TO SECOND EDITION	xvi
INTRODUCTION BY PROFESSOR G. STANLEY HALL	xxi

FIRST PART.

DEVELOPMENT OF THE SENSES.

CHAPTER

I.—SIGHT 2

Sensibility to Light, 2. Discrimination of Colors, 6.
Movements of the Eyelids, 22. Movements of the Eyes,
34. Direction of the Look, 41. Seeing Near and Distant Objects, 50. Interpretation of what is Seen, 60.
Sight in New-Born Animals, 66.

II.—HEARING 72

Deafness of the Newly-Born, 72. First Sensations
and Perceptions of Sound, 76. Hearing in New-Born
Animals, 91.

III.—FEELING (OR TOUCH) 96

Sensibility of the Newly-Born to Contact, 96. First
Perceptions of Touch, 108. Sensibility to Temperature, 111.

IV.—TASTE 116

Sensibility to Taste in the Newly-Born, 116. Comparison of the Impressions of Taste, 123. Taste in
New-Born Animals, 127.

V.—SMELL 130

Capacity of Smell in the Newly-Born, 130. Discrimination of Impressions of Smell, 133. Smell in New-Born Animals, 136.

CHAPTER   PAGE

VI.—EARLIEST ORGANIC SENSATIONS AND EMOTIONS . . 140

     Feelings of Pleasure in General, 141. Unpleasant
Feelings in General, 146. Feeling of Hunger, 152. Feeling of Satiety, 157. Feeling of Fatigue, 158. Fear, 164.
Astonishment, 172.

VII.—SUMMARY OF GENERAL RESULTS 176

SECOND PART.

DEVELOPMENT OF WILL.

VIII.—MOVEMENTS OF THE CHILD AS EXPRESSIONS OF WILL . 188

     Recognition of the Child's Will, 188. Classification
of the Child's Movements, 195.

IX.—IMPULSIVE MOVEMENTS 201

X.—REFLEX MOVEMENTS 211

XI.—INSTINCTIVE MOVEMENTS 235

     Instinctive Movements of New-Born Animals, 235.
Development of the Power of Seizing, 241. Sucking,
Biting, Chewing, Tooth-Grinding, Licking, 257. Holding the Head, 263. Learning to Sit, 267. Learning to
Stand, 269. Learning to Walk, 271.

XII.—IMITATIVE MOVEMENTS 282

XIII.—EXPRESSIVE MOVEMENTS 293

     The first Smiling and Laughing, 294. Pouting of the
Lips, 301. Kissing, 304. Crying and Wrinkling of the
Forehead, 307. Shaking the Head and Nodding, 311.
Shrugging the Shoulders, 317. Begging with the Hands,
and Pointing, 318.

XIV.—DELIBERATE MOVEMENTS 325

XV.—SUMMARY OF GENERAL RESULTS 334

INTRODUCTION TO THE AMERICAN EDITION.

IF one would train and break horses, however unmanageable, like Willis J. Powel, who perhaps excelled all others in this art before or since, he must, like him, study long and patiently the nature of the horse. If one would raise sheep with greatest success, he must, like the English herdsman who said that he and his family were Cotswold people and knew nothing whatever of Southdowns, serve a long apprenticeship in learning the habits, instincts, and all the conditions that affect sheep development favorably or unfavorably. The principle has long been a commonplace with breeders and trainers of domestic animals, although many naturalists now believe that for him who will long and patiently study and think and feel his way down and back into the soul of a particular animal, there are possibilities both of scientific discovery and of control and modification of brute instinct undreamed of before. The trained agent of charity organizations, who labors among the poor, must prepare himself for efficiency by careful study of the way in which individual poor people, and even beggars, think, feel, live, and act. The modern prison-keeper studies criminals till he becomes an expert in the psychology of crime. The missionary first studies the existing beliefs and superstitions of the savage races among whom he is to labor, or, if not, his work is but little more effective than if he did not take the trouble to learn their language.

Teachers as a rule do not study the nature of the children they instruct in any such way, and that for the following reasons : First, their business, as too often viewed, is not to educate or unfold, a process to which all have a right, but to instruct, or infuse set courses and sums of information to which the nature of the child may or may not have a right. Secondly, many think they have all the knowledge of childhood they require, from memory of their own childish years. This is wrong. Mental and moral growth necessarily involves increasing oblivion of everything of childhood save mere incidents, and even these are, other things being equal, remembered inversely as the degree of development to fullness of maturity. What remains from this source often misleads and has no regulative value for the teacher. Thirdly, many think a course in a text-book in psychology supplies this need. This is probably the gravest mistake of all. All such books I know are far too abstract and schematic, too much devoted to definition or in some cases even controversy, too commonplace and traditional in their subject-matter, so as to be sometimes an impediment to the fine tact and instinct that, in minds of finest fiber, divine, perhaps half unconsciously, the needs and individual nature of children.

The living, playing, learning child, whose soul heredity has freighted so richly from a past we know not how remote, on whose right development all good causes in the world depend, embodies a truly element-ary psychology. All the fundamental activities are found, and the play of each psychic process is so open, simple, interesting, that it is strange that psychology should be the last of the sciences to fall into line in the great Baconian change of base to which we owe nearly all the reforms, from Comenius down, which distin-guish schools of to-day from those of the sixteenth century. It is a striking fact that nearly every great teacher in the history of education who has spoken words that have been heeded has lived for years in the closest personal relations to children and has had the sympathy and tact that gropes out, if it can not see clearly, the laws of juvenile development and the lines of childish interests.

Among all the nearly fourscore studies of young children printed by careful empirical and often thorough-ly scientific observers, this work of Preyer is the fullest and on the whole the best. It should be read by teach-ers and parents even of older children, as the best ex-ample of the inductive method applied to the study of child-psychology. The development of each sense, and the unfoldment of the power of voluntary motion, are traced with great fullness; and still more attention is devoted to the growth of the ability to speak, with a suggestive co-ordination of the progressive stages of decay of the linguistic centers in aphasia and allied forms of disease.

A work on the whole so good awakens a desire for still further advance along the same lines. Not only does Preyer not continue his studies into school age, but he has not attempted, like Perez, to trace the unfoldment of sentiments and emotions, nor, like Herbart and Ziller, to tabulate the spontaneous interests of children. The most hopeful effort yet made in this direction was begun three years ago in the institution with which the translator of this work is connected, and may be described as follows, as characterized substantially in the words of the principal, E. II. Russell: Systematic observation of children is made a part of the regular work of this normal school, with a view of enlarging the scope of the ordinary study of psychology, to render it more objective and useful, to bring the prospective teachers into closer and better relations to children, and to gather a store of facts whereby in time to increase and rectify our present unsatisfactory knowledge of child-nature. The method is : First, to explain to the students, at the beginning of the second half-year in school, how to improve their opportunities on the street, at home, in families of friends, of noticing minutely the spontaneous, unconstrained activities, bodily and mental and physical, of children of all ages, at play, study, or work, etc. Then, at the earliest convenient moment, concise record is made on blanks with printed headings, and colored—e. g., white for personal observation, red for second-hand facts, etc. The records, now some five or six thousand in number, are classified, so far as can be, under memory, imagination, deceit, ignorance, mechanical construction, moral sense, etc., etc. Precisely what the value of this material will be it is now too soon to say, but as to its good effects on the powers of observation, tact, psychologic knowledge and interest of those who make them, there can be no question whatever. The students soon become more interested in children and their ways, and more skillful in dealing with them; and some acquire much ingenuity in following out the more complicated and obscure processes of child-life. They also acquire right habits of observation and investigation generally, learning in some degree the caution, discrimination, and veracity required in studying nature. It is so interesting that students must be rather restrained than impelled to the work; and graduates are believed to be distinctly guided toward best success and pleasure in their vocation by these studies, and display intelligence and sympathy in dealing with troublesome children. Many of the essays of the graduating class are based on this work.

While commending this book to American teachers generally, the writer desires to commend the Worcester method of psychogenetic study to the careful attention of principals of normal schools.

G. STANLEY HALL.

JOHNS HOPKINS UNIVERSITY, *January 7, 1888.*

EXPLANATION OF ABBREVIATED CITATIONS.

Kussmaul: "Untersuchungen über das Seelenleben des neugeborenen Menschen" ("Investigations concerning the Mental Life of the New-Born Human Being"), 1859 (38 pp.); and "Störungen der Sprache" ("Disturbances or Obstructions of Speech"), 1877.

Genzmer: "Untersuchungen über die Sinneswahrnehmungen des neugeborenen Menschen" ("Investigations concerning the Sense-Perceptions of the New-Born Human Being"), 1873 (reprinted 1882, 25 pp.).

Sigismund: "Kind und Welt" ("The Child and the World"), 1856.

Gustav Lindner: in Twelfth Annual Report of the "Lehrerseminars in Zschopau," 1882, and in the periodical "Kosmos," 1882.

Frau Dr. Friedemann; Frau Professor von Strümpell; and Herr Ed. Schulte—to these the author is under particular obligation for MSS.

All other references, sources of information, and names of authors are given without abbreviation.

THE MIND OF THE CHILD.

FIRST PART.

DEVELOPMENT OF THE SENSES.

THE foundation of all mental development is the activity of the senses. We can not conceive of anything of the nature of mental genesis as taking place without that activity.

Every sense-activity is fourfold in its character: First, there is an *excitement of the nerves;* then comes *sensation;* and not until the sensation has been localized in space and referred to some point in time, do we have a *perception.* When, further, the cause of this is apprehended, then the perception becomes an *idea.*

The adult human being is a person who is responsible, who acts according to his own pleasure, and is capable of independent thought. For our understanding of his psychical states and processes, it is of great importance to know what is the condition of things as to the above stages of sense-activity, in the newly-born, and in the infant, who is not responsible, who does not act according to his pleasure, and does not think at all.

I have therefore instituted many observations concerning the gradual perfecting of the senses at the

beginning of life, and I commence with a description
of them. In these observations I have had especially
in mind the prominent part played in the mental development of the child, at the earliest period, by the sense
of sight.

CHAPTER I.

SIGHT.

THE observations with regard to the development
of the sense of sight during the first years relate to
sensibility to light, discrimination of colors, movements
of the eyelids, movements of the eyes, direction of the
look, seeing of near and distant objects, and interpretation of what is seen. To these are attached some statements concerning sight in new-born animals.

1. Sensibility to Light.

My child's sensibility to light, when he was held
toward the window in the dusk, five minutes after
birth, did not seem unusually great. For he opened
and shut his eyes, with alternate movement, so that the
space between the lids was about five millimetres wide.
Soon after, I saw in the twilight both eyes wide open.
At the same time the forehead was wrinkled.

Long before the close of the first day, the child's expression, as he was held with his face toward the window, became suddenly different when I shaded his eyes
with my hand. The dim light, therefore, undoubtedly
made an impression, and, to judge from his physiog-

nomy, an agreeable one ; for the shaded face had a less contented look.

On the second day the eyes close quickly when a candle is brought near them ; on the ninth, the head is also turned away vigorously from the flame, when the candle is brought near, immediately after the awaking of the child. The eyes are shut tight. But, on the following day, the child being in the bath, when a candle was held before him at a distance of one metre, the eyes remained wide open. The sensitiveness to light is, therefore, so much greater at the moment of waking than it is a short time afterward, that the same object causes at the one time great annoyance and at the other time pleasure.

Again, on the eleventh day, the child seemed to be much pleased by a candle burning before him at a distance of one half a metre, for he gazed at it steadily with wide-open eyes, as he did also, later, at a shining curtain-holder, when the bright object was brought into his line of vision, so that it was in the direction in which he seemed to be gazing. If I turned the child away, he became fretful and began to cry ; if I turned him to the light again, then his countenance resumed the expression of satisfaction. To verify this, I held the child that same day at the same distance before a burning candle, once immediately after his waking, and again after he had been awake some time in the dark. In both cases he shut his eyes.

That he liked moderately bright daylight was apparent from the frequent turning of his head toward the window when I turned him away from it. This twisting of the head became the rule on the sixth day ; on the seventh it was often repeated, and every time that the face was turned toward the window the expression of satisfaction was unmistakable.

I have repeatedly made the observation that, when the light falls upon the face of sleeping infants they suddenly close the eyes more tightly, without waking, and this from the tenth day on.

In the case of my child, I found the pupils in ordinary daylight for the most part more contracted than is the case in adults—certainly less than two millimetres in diameter; and the lessening of the space between the lids, at sight of a bright surface of snow or of a shining summer cloud, was likewise more frequent and more persistent than with adults, during the whole period of observation.

Brightly-shining objects, appearing in the field of vision, often produce, from the second month on, exclamations of delight. But other highly-colored objects also easily rouse the attention of the infant. In the tenth month he is pleased when the lamp is lighted in the evening; he laughs at the light, and reaches after the bright globe.

Of the observations of others concerning the sensibility of new-born human beings to light, the following are to be mentioned :

1. Fully-matured children just born shut the eyes quickly and convulsively when exposed to bright light. Individuals, also, among children born two months too soon, distinguish between light and darkness on the second day.

2. In the very first hours the pupil of the eye contracts in a bright light, and expands in light less bright.

3. If one eye of the new-born child is shut while the other is open, then the pupil of the latter expands.

4. Infants from two to four days old, sleeping in the dark, shut the lids tightly, and even awake with a start when the bright light of a candle comes very near their eyes.

To these statements of Prof. Kussmaul, the first of which, in particular, I can confirm, Dr. Genzmer adds that the eyes of the newly-born, when suddenly exposed to bright light, make a movement of convergence; and that sensitive infants are brought into a state of general discomfort and made to cry, by a sudden glare of light, or by a quickly-changing, dazzling light; this I can confirm. The alternate shutting and opening of the eyes, that is often to be seen in infants exposed to bright light, was seen by Genzmer even in a sleeping child two days old—a remarkable observation, which waits confirmation. On the other hand, I never saw a new-born child bear dazzlingly bright light quietly with open eyes. Assertions of an experience contrary to this may, perhaps, rest on the observation of children born blind.

From all the foregoing statements we conclude that, with fully-matured new-born human beings, sensibility to light is normally present either directly after birth, or a few minutes, or at most a few hours, after birth; that light and darkness are discriminated in sensation; further, that the reflex arc from the optic nerve to the *oculomotorius* already performs its function—especially is this true of the filaments that contract the pupils. Here, then, we have an inborn reflex, and that of a double sort, since both pupils contract when the light reaches one of them. Further, at the beginning,

3

sensibility to light on awaking, or after being awhile in the dark, amounts to an aversion to light; yet a dim light is already sought, and therefore is not unpleasant. Finally, we infer that after some days ordinary daylight, or a brilliant and brightly-shining object, excites cheerfulness, the aversion to light disappears, and the head is turned oftener to the window.

2. Discrimination of Colors.

At what age the child is capable of distinguishing colors, at least red, yellow, green, and blue, it is hard to determine. In the first days, it is certain that only the difference of light and dark is perceived, and this imperfectly; moreover (according to Flechsig), the *tractus opticus,* which in the matured child is still gray at first, does not get its nerve medulla, and with that its permanent coloring, till three or four days after birth. And even then the differentiation of simultaneous bright and dark impressions proceeds slowly.

The first object that made an impression on account of its color, upon my boy, was probably a rose-colored curtain which hung, brightly lighted by the sun but not dazzlingly bright, about a foot before the child's face. This was on the twenty-third day. The child laughed and uttered sounds of satisfaction.

As the smooth, motionless, bright-colored surface alone occupied the whole field of vision, it must have been on account either of its brightness or of its color that it was the source of pleasure. In the evening of the same day, the flame of the candle, at the distance of one metre, caused quite similar expressions of pleasure when it was placed before the eyes, which had been gazing into empty space; and so did, on the forty-second day, the sight of colored tassels in motion, but in this case the movement also was a source of pleasure.

In the eighty-fifth week, when I undertook the first systematic tests, with counters alike in form but unlike in color, no trace of discrimination in color was as yet to be discerned, although without doubt it already existed. Different as were the impressions of sound made by the words " red," " yellow," " green," " blue " (these were certainly distinguished from one another), and well as the child knew the meaning of "give," he was not able to give the counters of the right color, even when only "red" and "green" were called for. We are not to infer from this, however, an inability of the eye to distinguish one color from another, for here it is essential to consider the difficulty of associating the sound of the word "red" or "green" with the proper color-sensation, even when the sensation is present.

At this time, before the age of twenty-one months, there must have been recognition not only of the varying intensity of light (white, gray, black), but also of the quality of some colors, for the delight in striking colors was manifest. Yet in the case of little children, even after they have begun to speak, it can not be determined without searching tests what colors they distinguish and rightly name.

In order, then, to ascertain how the separate colors are related to one another in this respect, I have made several hundred color-tests with my child, beginning at the end of his second year. These I used to apply every day in the early morning, for a week; then, after an interval of a week, again almost every day, but in a different manner—as will be shown directly.

In all these tests I made use of the colored ovals
which Dr. H. Magnus, of Breslau, gives in his "Tafel
zur Erziehung des Farbensinnes" (1879), ("Chart for
the Training of the Color-Sense").

After the names "red" and "green" had been repeatedly pronounced while the corresponding colors
were presented, then these two colors were simply presented and the questions, "Where is red?" and "Where
is green?" were put, always in alternation. The trials
were absolutely without result in the eighty-sixth and
eighty-seventh weeks. After an interval of twenty-two
weeks, on the seven hundred fifty-eighth day, I received
eleven times a right answer, six times a wrong answer.
On the following day the answers were right seven
times, wrong five times; on the day after that, nine
times right, five times wrong. From this it seemed
probable, already, that the two colors were distinguished, either on account of their quality or on account of their brightness, and that the right names were
often associated with them. To my surprise, however,
on the seven hundred sixty-third day the answers were
right fifteen times and wrong only once, and on the following day ten times right and not once wrong. The
child had therefore firmly grasped the connection of the
sound-impressions "red" and "green" with two different light-impressions. For such proportions as those of
the above numbers exclude the possibility of chance.

I carried the test further. To red and green I added
yellow, and when the three colors were lying near one
another, each one was rightly pointed out in answer to
the question where it was. Then came a disinclination
on the part of the child to continue, such as often makes

color-tests impossible in children so young. When the
trial was repeated, he was inattentive, and he confounded the three colors with one another. On the following
day, the seven hundred sixty-fifth, green especially was
confounded with yellow. The answers on five days of
the one hundred tenth week were :

	Right.	Wrong.
Red..	26	10
Green................................	24	7
Yellow............................	23	5
Total	73	22

Blue was now added as a fourth color. The answers
in eight trials, during the time from the end of the one
hundred tenth to the beginning of the one hundred
twelfth week, were:

	Right.	Wrong.
Red............................	32	14
Green	31	8
Yellow..............................	34	2
Blue................................	27	12
Total	124	36

Often, especially on being asked "Where is blue?"
the child would consider long, observe the four colors
attentively before deciding, and then give me the color
quickly. It appears evident that yellow is recognized
more surely than are the other colors. Yellow seems to
be the easiest to distinguish, and hence the easiest also
to retain in memory. I made other tests of the same
sort, which showed the superiority of yellow. Then
violet was added as the fifth color, called " lila," as easier
to speak, and a different way of conducting the experiment was adopted.

I laid each color separately before the child and asked, "What is that?" He answered, *rroot* [Eng. pronunciation *wrote*] (for *roth*, red), *delp, depp, gelp* (for *gelb*, yellow), *rihn, ihn* [Eng. pr. *reen, een*] (for *grün*, green), *balau* (for *blau*, blue), and *lilla* (for *lila*, violet).

In the one hundred twelfth week the answers in four trials were:

	Right.	Wrong.
Red	10	2
Yellow	9	0
Green	9	1
Blue	5	7
Violet	11	1
Total	44	11

Here, too, yellow is foremost; it was named correctly nine times, not once wrongly named. Blue comes last. It was confounded especially with green and violet. If the child's attention failed, I broke off.

Afterward the tests were continued in both ways combined; but these proved to be great consumers of time. It often happens that the child takes no interest in the colors. Sometimes, from roguishness, he *will* not name the color he knows, and will not point out or give me the one I ask for. At other times he himself brings the box that holds the color-ovals, and says *wawa* = "Farbe" (color), in expectation of a lesson. The trials in which the attention is undivided are, however, not numerous.

Gray is added. In the one hundred twelfth and one hundred thirteenth weeks five tests yielded the following answers:

	Right.	Wrong.
Red	16	3
Yellow	22	1
Green	14	5
Blue	10	15
Violet	18	1
Gray	10	2
Total	90	27

Yellow maintains the first place, being rightly named in twenty-two instances, and wrongly only once. The judgment in regard to blue is the worst; fifteen wrong judgments to ten right ones. It is noteworthy that in this series, as in the preceding, violet is rightly named oftener than green.

I now bade the child, repeatedly, to place together the ovals of the same color. After much moving hither and thither, he succeeded with yellow, red, rose, green, and violet, but very incompletely. The expressions "light" and "dark," before the names of the colors, were beyond the child's understanding. So the saturated and the less saturated colors, the light and the dark, were, as before, indicated by the common name of the quality alone. Four trials with the colors mixed, during the time from the one hundred fourteenth to the one hundred sixteenth week, resulted as follows:

	Right.	Wrong.
Red	15	1
Yellow	13	0
Green	4	7
Blue	3	10
Violet	11	2
Gray	6	0
Brown	4	0
Rose	1	2
Black	2	0
Total	59	22

Blue was especially confounded with violet, also with green. All very pale colors were confounded with gray, all dark ones with black. The order in which the colors were recognized, i. e., rightly named, is now the following: Yellow best of all, then red, violet, green; and worst of all, blue.

On other days I laid before the child, as I had done previously, a single color, with the question, what it was, and marked the answer wrong if it were not given right immediately. The colors are now called by the child *rott, delp, drün, blau, lila, grau, swarz, rosa, braun.*

Four trials in the one hundred fourteenth and one hundred fifteenth weeks yielded the answers:

	Right.	Wrong.
Red...........................	13	0
Yellow.......................	11	0
Green.........................	7	9
Blue..........................	5	13
Violet........................	10	3
Gray..........................	1	3
Brown.........................	4	1
Rose..........................	3	3
Black.........................	4	0
Total.......................	58	32

For the first five colors this trial gives the same order of succession as above. Blue and green are very uncertain; blue is called *drün* (meant for grün) and *lila* (violet), green is called gray; and, oftener still, neither blue nor green is named at all; while yellow, and red, and black, are given correctly and quickly.

I now let the child take out of the box of colored ovals one after another of them, at pleasure, name it, and give it to me. At the first trial he seized at random; at the second he sought his favorite color, yellow.

Two trials in the one hundred fifteenth week:

	Right.	Wrong.
Red..	6	0
Yellow.	8	0
Green	1	2
Blue.	0	5
Violet.	4	1
Gray.	1	5
Brown.	0	1
Rose.	3	2
Black.	2	0
Total.	25	16

The result is the same as above. Red, yellow, and black are the only colors that are surely recognized.

I now made no more trials for two months. The child spent the larger part of the day in the open air, with me, on a journey; the greater part of the time was spent in the neighborhood of Lake Garda.

In the one hundred twenty-first week, an occasional examination showed a greater uncertainty than before. Blue was scarcely once named rightly, in spite of the most urgent cautions. When the trials were resumed, after our return, the result was bad. I took the colored counters in my hand and put questions. At the very first questioning, yellow was indeed named rightly three times, and not wrongly at all; but red was twice wrongly and not once rightly named.

I got the following answers in the one hundred twenty-fourth week, in the first four trials with all the colors after the interval:

	Right.	Wrong.
Red.....................................	17	0
Yellow..................................	22	0
Green..................................	0	18
Blue....................................	0	13
Violet..................................	9	4
Gray....	0	5
Brown.................................	4	3
Rose...................................	3	4
Black..................................	3	0
Orange.................................	0	2
Total............................	58	49

Here it is still more evident than before that red and yellow are already more surely recognized and more correctly named than green and blue. On the eight hundred sixty-sixth day the child, without being constrained, took colors out of the box and gave them to me, naming them as he did so. The colors that were mistaken for one another were rose, gray, and pale green; brown and gray; green and black; finally, blue and violet.

In the following experiments, also, the child every time took the colors out of the box and gave them to me, telling the names at the same time, without the least direction. Five trials out of the one hundred twenty-fourth and one hundred twenty-fifth weeks gave:

	Right.	Wrong.
Red.....................................	29	1
Yellow.................................	16	0
Green.................................	0	4
Blue...................................	0	6
Violet..................................	14	0
Gray...................................	0	8
Rose	14	5
Brown..................................	7	2
Black..................................	0	2
Orange.................................	0	6
Total............................	80	34

Red and yellow are eagerly sought and almost always rightly named; blue and green avoided and always named wrongly (e. g., as *lila*, *swarz*). I now removed all the red and yellow colors from the collection, and let the child give to me, and name as many of the remaining ones as he could on a stretch. Now that red and yellow are wanting, however, he shows from the first a less degree of interest, and in the case of green he says "Papa tell!" In all other cases he had a name for the color he took. If that was wrong, it was always corrected by me, often by the child himself; but it was always entered in the record as wrong, if the first answer was wrong. In the one hundred twenty-fifth and one hundred twenty-sixth weeks six trials were made in which this method was strictly observed and the following judgments were registered:

	Right.	Wrong.
Green	2	19
Blue	6	20
Violet	20	3
Gray	0	6
Rose	19	6
Brown	15	0
Black	7	2
Orange	11	7
Total	80	63

The brighter colors were at first selected. The child confuses orange (*oroos*, as he calls it) with yellow, blue with violet, green with gray, black with brown.

I tried repeatedly to induce the child to place together the colors that seemed to him alike, but it was a total failure. Then I asked for single colors by their names, but the results of this procedure were likewise

poor. (This on the eight hundred seventy-ninth day.)
Finally, I took a single color at a time and asked, " What
is that?" In four trials in the one hundred twenty-
sixth, one hundred twenty-seventh, and one hundred
twenty-eighth weeks, the answers were:

	Right.	Wrong.
Red............................	11	(1)
Yellow............................	11	0
Green............................	1	14
Blue............................	1	11
Violet............................	12	1
Gray	6	1
Rose	11	2
Brown............................	10	0
Black............................	6	1
Orange............................	6	2 and (1)
Total........................	75	34

For green and blue—which are confounded with
gray when they are light, and with black when they
are dark—there is probably a less degree of sensibility,
certainly a less interest. Blue is still called *lila*. Besides, it is very difficult to direct the attention persistently to the colors. The child, although tested only in
the early hours of morning, seeks now other means of
entertaining himself. Now and then he makes a mistake in speaking. (Errors of this kind are indicated by
parentheses). But on the eight hundred ninety-eighth
day every color was rightly named—green and blue, to
be sure, only after some guessing. In six trials in the
one hundred twenty-ninth, one hundred thirty-fifth, one
hundred thirty-sixth, one hundred thirty-seventh, and
one hundred thirty-eighth weeks the child took the colors
and gave them to me, naming them. The answers were:

	Right.	Wrong.
Red......................	27	1
Yellow.....................	27	0
Green......................	2	14
Blue......................	2	13
Violet.....................	15	2
Gray......................	5	1
Rose......................	10	3
Brown.....................	14	0
Black......................	5	1
Orange.....................	12	3
Total.....................	119	38

There is confounding of colors as before. The only thing new is the designation *garnix* (for *gar nichts*, " nothing at all ") for green and blue. Unknown colors are now often named green—e. g., blue. In a bouquet of yellow roses these were designated as yellow, but the leaves were obstinately called *garnix*, and so likewise were very whitish colors, whose quality is, however, recognizable at once, in a moderate light, by adults acquainted with colors.

On the nine hundred thirty-fourth day there was this remarkable utterance when green and blue were placed before the child: *grin blau kann e nicht, grosse mann kann grin blau*, which meant (as appeared from similar utterances), " I can't give green and blue rightly; a grown person can." Green was mostly called gray; very rarely (inquiringly) it was called red; blue was named *lila*. In the one hundred thirty-first and one hundred thirty-fourth weeks I made three trials, asking for colors which I laid out; in the one hundred thirty-eighth and one hundred thirty-ninth weeks, in three trials, sometimes the child took the colors himself, sometimes I put them before him. The answers were:

	Right.	Wrong.
Red.....................................	14	1
Yellow..................................	24	0
Green..................................	4	13
Blue....................................	0	15
Violet..................................	9	5
Gray....................................	5	0
Rose....................................	9	2
Brown..................................	11	1
Black...................................	7	1
Orange.................................	10	1
Total.................................	93	39

Here begins at last the right naming of green, while blue is not yet so often correctly designated. The child took the colors of his own accord and named them in three trials, in the one hundred thirty-ninth, one hundred forty-first, and one hundred forty-sixth weeks, as follows:

	Right.	Wrong.
Red.....................................	19	2
Yellow..................................	13	0
Green..................................	2	2
Blue....................................	2	11
Violet..................................	6	1
Gray....................................	1	2
Rose....................................	3	0
Brown..................................	10	0
Black...................................	3	0
Orange.................................	8	1
Total.................................	66	19

The red twice misnamed was dark. The word "green" was now rightly applied continually to leaves and to meadows, and, before the completion of the third year, blue also was almost invariably designated correctly, if the attention was not diverted.

With regard to the order in which the colors were rightly named up to the thirty-fourth month, the total result is as follows:

	JUDGMENTS.		PER CENT.	
	Right.	Wrong.	Right.	Wrong.
I. Yellow.................	232	8	96·7	3·3
II. Brown...............	79	8	90·8	9·2
III. Red..................	235	36	86·7	13·3
IV. Violet................	139	24	85·3	14·7
V. Black	39	7	84·8	15·2
VI. Rose.................	76	29	72·4	27·6
VII. Orange..............	47	23	67·1	32·9
VIII. Gray................	35	33	51·5	48·5
IX. Green................	101	123	45·0	55·0
X. Blue.................	61	151	28·8	71·2
Total..............	1,044	442	70·3	29·7

Thus, of the four principal colors, yellow and red are *named rightly much sooner* than are green and blue; and yellow first—brown is (dull!) yellow—then red. That the color-sensations, green, blue, and violet, exist in very different proportions, is probably not a peculiarity of the individual. Violet, which was much oftener named rightly than were green and blue, contains the already well-known red, and may appear to the child as a dirty red, or as dark red. For it is in fact probable that blue and greenish-blue were perceived in the earliest period, not as blue and greenish-blue, but as gray and black. That green of every sort is not named rightly till very late, may be owing, in part, to a stronger absorption of light, by means of the blood of the vessels of the retina. Although the place of the clearest vision, in the back part of the eye, is free from blood-vessels, yet the other colors which, like yellow, orange, red, and brown, reach the retina undimmed, in great extension, have, on that account, an advantage over green and blue, which are most easily confounded with gray.

Even in the fourth year, blue was still often called gray in the dusk of morning, when it appeared to me distinctly blue. The child would wonder that his light-blue stockings had become gray in the night. This I observed on three days.

Gray is, without doubt, along with white and black, rightly known long before the first discrimination of colors, but is often wrongly named, for the reason that green and blue are probably perceived as gray. The right naming of it became the rule before the end of the third year, whereas yellow was rightly named, almost invariably, nearly a year earlier. To this color the pigment of the yellow spot is most helpful. Red may also have an advantage, in the fact that in bright daylight, when the eyes are shut, especially when snow is on the ground, that is the only color in the field of vision [i. e., the eyelids are translucent, and we perceive red]; as black is the only one before we fall asleep in the dark.

On the whole we must, accordingly, declare the child to be still somewhat lacking in sensibility to the cold colors in the second year and the first half of the third year; a conclusion with which occasional observations concerning other children harmonize. At any rate, by very many children, yellow is first rightly named and blue last. One boy began, before he had reached the age of four months, to prefer a brilliant red to other colors.* All children prefer, like him, at this

---

* According to Genzmer: "Untersuchungen über die Sinnes-wahrnehmungen des neugeborenen Menschen," 1859.

age and long after, the whitish colors, without regard
to their quality.

The incapacity of the two-years-old child to name
blue and green correctly can not be attributed solely to
his possible inability to associate firmly the names
"blue" and "green" (which he has heard and which
he uses fluently) with his possibly distinct sensations;
for "yellow" and "red" have already been used correctly many months before. If green and blue were as
distinct as yellow and red in his sensation, then there
would not be the least occasion for his giving them
wrong names, and preferring red and yellow to them in
all circumstances. The child does not yet *know* what
green and blue signify, although he is already acquainted with yellow and red. Neither does he yet know
what "green" means when, in the one hundred ninth
and one hundred twelfth weeks of his life, he apparently distinguishes "red" and "green" correctly. Green
is at this time, for him, merely something that is not
red.

I have yet to mention that my child, at the beginning of his third year, moved and handled himself with
surprising sureness and quickness in the semi-darkness
of twilight; he thus discriminated well between light
and dark. And at the beginning of his fourth year he
named correctly all the colors except the very dark or
the pale ones, particularly even the most varying shades
of green and blue, to the astonishment of those who
had been occasionally present at the color-lessons here
described, and who had witnessed his numerous errors.

Other children, with sound eyes, are likewise perfectly sure in their naming of colors at the age of three

4

years, though very uncertain at the age of two years. A boy of two and two-thirds years was impressed by the colors in the following order:

1, dark violet; 2, yellow; 3, red; 4, blue; 5, green. Here the first named was singled out before the others on account of its being dark.*

A boy of four years, who had received no regular instruction in observing colors, was asked by his father what colors he saw in a brilliant rainbow that was just then defining itself sharply upon the gray sky. The child answered slowly, but with decision, " Red, yellow, green, blue "; and he afterward, as I am informed by his father, Prof. Bardeleben, of Jena, always picked out these principal colors easily among paints, whereas the naming of violet, reddish-yellow, and other mixed colors, was difficult for him.

3. Movements of the Eyelids.

The eyelids are not often kept apart long in the first days of life. Newly-born children, even when awake, keep their eyes shut far more than they keep them open. And, when the lids are raised, there appears for the most part a strange asymmetry. One eye remains open while the other is shut. Alternate shutting and opening were seen by me frequently from the first to the eleventh day; afterward more seldom. Yet my child, before the first twenty-four hours were passed, had both eyes wide open, once, at the same time, in the twilight. During the first month the rule was, that when both eyes were open at the same time, they were not open

---

* Frau Dr. Friedemann.

equally wide; this was still strikingly noticeable on the thirty-first day. At this time, too, the occasional keeping open of one eye only had not ceased. Further, even when both eyes were closed, the movements of the left and right upper lids were frequently not simultaneous.

Other remarkable irregular (atypische) movements of the lids were seen in connection with the raising and lowering of the look on one side and on both sides. Especially, in the fifth week, the lids were often raised while the look was directed downward, so that the white sclerotic was visible over the cornea; a movement that an adult imitates with difficulty, and that lends to the countenance an expression almost of a character to cause anxiety. But long before the third month the lid followed the pupil regularly when the look was downward. When, on the contrary, the child, as he lay on his back, directed his glance toward his forehead, which he did without wrinkling his forehead in the least, the lid was not always raised, but it often covered the iris close up to the pupil, sometimes even partially covering the latter; and this I saw repeatedly as late as the eighth week.

The "rolling of the eyes" by sick children, the pupils going upward and the upper eyelid downward, so that only the white sclerotic remains visible in the space between the lids, is an advanced stage of this physiological irregularity, which appears also in hysterical patients. Even toward the end of the third month I saw that when the child looked up (as he was carried on the arm in an upright position), e. g., to a lamp standing high, the eyelid was not completely raised, but here,

too, the pupil was touched by the edge of the lid at a
tangent. At this time the forehead, which, in the first
days, appeared often in horizontal folds, as is the case
with monkeys, was either not wrinkled at all or very
little, and in exceptional cases, when the look was
directed upward. Not till the ninety-eighth day was
my boy's brow wrinkled when he looked upward, and
then not to such a degree as that of an adult, and even
in the eighth month the brow was not wrinkled invariably; but from the end of the ninth month it was regularly so. This co-ordinate movement is therefore acquired, probably because it enlarges the field of vision
when one is looking upward, without making it necessary to bend back the head.

The raising of the lid along with the downward
look was seen in the first days of infant life, up to the
tenth day, by Raehlmann, and Witkowski also, and
they rightly call attention to the fact that the relation
of compulsory dependence between the raising of the
lid and the elevation of the cornea does not yet exist at
the beginning. The muscle that raises the lid can contract at the same time with the lower rectus muscle of
the eye; the upper rectus muscle of the eye may contract without the one that lifts the lid: later, this can
no longer be done. There must be, then, at the beginning, within the province of the oculomotorius, an independence of the separate branches, that is afterward
lost. The co-excitement of the branch that goes to the
elevator of the lid (levator palpebræ), on occasion of
the excitement of the branch going to the elevator of
the glance (rectus superior), in the upper division of the
oculomotorius, is accordingly something acquired—is

learned afresh by each individual human being—on account of the help it gives in the act of seeing. Just so, according to our observations, the perfectly useless excitement of the elevator-branch on occasion of the excitement of the branch that goes to the muscle that depresses the glance (rectus inferior) in the lower division of the oculomotorius, though frequent at first, is so persistently omitted farther on, that adults are hardly able to contract at the same time the lid-elevator and the eye-depressor (rectus inferior), i. e., to direct the look downward with the eye wide open. Consequently, the movements under consideration—of the upper eyelid upward in looking up, and downward in looking down—are not inborn in human beings.

On the other hand, the closing of the lid when it is exposed to a strong light, as well as the contracting of the pupil in light, is inborn. But the case here is one of reflex action of the optic nerve: on the one hand, upon the orbicularis branch of the facialis; on the other hand, upon the *iris* branch of the oculomotorius, not therefore a case of associated movements, but of purely sensori-motor reflexes.

The quick shutting of the eye by a sudden movement of the lid, followed immediately by the opening of it—what is called winking—does not appear, as is well known, in new-born or in very young infants. The fact is well established that they bear the sudden approach of a hand to the eye without moving the lid; whereas, later in life, every one in such circumstances shuts the eye for an instant, or even starts back at the first approach, just as after an actual touch—and this even when there is a pane of glass before the face—un-

less special practice in the control of this reflex movement leads in manhood to the voluntary inhibition
of it.

I have determined the time in the case of my child
at which the first winking occurred as a sign of fright
at any sudden impression, and as an expression of surprise at a new impression made upon the sense of
sight. My experience is as follows:

I put my hand suddenly near the face of the child,
as he lay quiet with open eyes, without the least reaction
on his part, on the sixth, eighth, eleventh, twelfth,
twenty-second, twenty-fifth, fiftieth, and fifty-fifth days.
During this period the softest touch of the lashes, of
the edges of the lids, of the conjunctiva, or the cornea,
occasioned an immediate closing of the lid. The dropping of the lid up to the twelfth day was, however,
decidedly slower than it is in adults. On the fifty-
seventh and fifty-eighth days I noticed that winking
made its appearance for the first time, occurring when
I put my head quickly near the child's face; but, on
repeating the experiment several times, both eyes remained open. On the sixtieth day, the quick, simultaneous shutting and opening of both eyes in case of
fright at a quick approach to the face (just as in case of
a sudden loud sound), is already the rule. At such
times the child often throws up both arms quickly, alike
whether he is lying down or is held in the arms. This
is the case especially as late as the fourteenth week. At
this time, however, there was not observable any starting back with the head, or the upper part of the body,
at the rapid approach of my face to his; whereas the
winking now invariably appears promptly, even when

the approach is repeated several times in close succession. It was the same in the fifteenth and sixteenth weeks. Other children, however (according to Sigismund), do not yet close their eyes in the fourteenth and even the sixteenth week, when you thrust at them with the finger as if you meant to hit them. The difference is probably owing to the fact that the finger occupies too small an area in the field of vision compared with the palm of the hand and with the face. O. Soltmann found that the seventh and eighth weeks marked the first appearance of the lid movement in the experiment of the "attacking hand," and my observations accord with this.

Not till after the first three months did I observe that the eyes were closed when, in the bath, water touched the cornea or even the lashes; in the first days the wetting of the eyes, even when it was repeated, having occasioned no closing of the lid at all. Probably it is experiences of this kind—of disagreeable sensation when the exposed parts of the eye are touched—that caused in the ninth week, for the first time, the closing of the lid when a large object suddenly approached the eye without touching it; for the rapid approach is in itself not pleasing. For the rest, the winking on occasion of a strong, unexpected impression remained, after it had once appeared, as an acquired reflex movement, which returned on every provocation of that sort. Thus, it followed with uncommon quickness upon a puff of wind in the face (e. g., in the twenty-fifth week). The child stared with an inquiring gaze in the direction whence the current of air came, after he had responded to it with the eyelids.

It is not allowable to assume, in explanation of this reflex movement, that the idea of danger must first be formed in order to produce the closure of the eyes, as many suppose. In that case there would be no purely reflex action, but a habit. But the time is too short for the production of an idea along with the volitional impulse to lower the lid, and a child of nine weeks has not yet the idea of danger. He does not know that, with the sudden change in the distribution of light and shade in the field of vision, at the approach of the hand, there may be joined a danger to himself; and he winks just the same at a sudden noise, even on the twenty-fifth day of his life.

Had he the idea of danger, he would start back with the head or the upper part of his body at the quick approach of my hand or my head, as he does later. We should be forced to adopt the auxiliary hypothesis that an experience made by the child's ancestors in a more mature period of life led to a habit which then manifested itself in the descendants early in life as an hereditary habit. This Darwinian view is superfluous, because *the disagreeable feeling* that is connected with every unexpected, sudden, and strong sense-impression, is of itself sufficient to induce the closing of the lid. For so long as the child can not rightly separate his sense-impressions, especially those of sight, so long as he does not plainly discern the rapid changes in a moderately bright field of vision, he can not be disagreeably affected by these changes. But if he is sufficiently developed to observe sudden and important changes, then he will experience a disagreeable feeling, will be frightened, and the immediate consequence of this will be the warding off of that which offends him—he will shut the eyelids. Thus, the shutting of the eyes at the sudden impression of light is seen to be akin to the keeping of them tightly shut when exposed to bright light during the first days of life; and it remains only to explain the difference, that at the beginning the eye remains closed longer, for the newly-born do not wink. This difference, merely quantitative, is probably due to the less rapid propagation of the nerve-excitement, to the greater extent of time involved in the reflex, and especially to the greater intensity and duration of the stimulus. Dazzling light causes to adults likewise a more disagreeable feeling than does the rapid approach of a strange hand. Lightning produces a momentary closing of the lids; a surface of snow, brightly illuminated by the sun, occasions shutting of the eyes and blinking, and even the tight compression of the eyelids.

The lessening of the space between the lids, and the complete closing of the eyes, in shutting them tightly, is effected, upon the whole, by the contraction of the muscle that closes the eye (musculus orbicularis), whereas the dropping of the upper lid in winking is produced by the contraction of the lid-muscles (musculi palpebrales) alone; and blinking, proper, at the sight of a dazzlingly bright object, by the contraction of the external parts of the orbicular muscle (particularly the orbital and cheek muscle). All these orbicular filaments are supplied by the facial nerve (nervus facialis) as their only motor nerve. As the reflex from the optic nerve is perfect from the first day of existence, since bright light causes tight closing of the eyes, it follows that the reflex arc from the optic nerve to this branch of the

facialis, as well as that to the iris branch of the oculomotorius, must be inborn.

The quick shutting and opening of the eye in case
of surprise also becomes more intelligible if we dismiss
the hypothesis of the idea of danger—an idea that is as
yet foreign to the child—and consider rather that every
surprise, even a joyous one, is at the first instant akin to
fright, on account of the unexpectedness it brings with
it—the sudden impression on the senses. Sudden danger is only a special case. Even in adults an unexpected
loud sound occasions invariably the winking movement
of the lids.

On the twenty-fifth day my child fixed his eyes for
the first time upon the face of his nurse, then upon mine
and his mother's, and when I nodded he opened his eyes
wider, and shut and opened the lids several times. The
same movements appeared when I for the first time
spoke to him in a deep voice, as I did on the day mentioned. It was a reflex movement of surprise.

At the end of the seventh month, a green fan being
rapidly opened and clapped together at a distance of
half a metre from his face, my child shut and opened
his eyes quickly every time with an expression of the
greatest astonishment, until I had repeated the experiment a good many times in succession; and even then
there remained a boundless surprise at the disappearance
and reappearance of the large, round surface. This was
discernible in his immovability, following upon previous
agitation, and in the intensity of his gaze. The play
of the lid is also observed in case of other new movements, especially rhythmical ones, as in hearing new
noises; and then the mouth often remains open, and

the eyes are wide open, yet there is no lifting of the eyebrows (in the eighth month).

But not only surprise, strong desire is likewise associated with the keeping of the lids open to the maximum extent. When, in the thirty-fourth week, I took away from the babe his milk, he gazed at it rigidly, and opened his eyes wide, and they took on an expression of indescribable longing. Moreover, sounds of desire were often expressed imperfectly, with closed lips, and this continued as a habit with him in the second year. The eyes were, besides, noticeably more lustrous than usual, when the child was mastered by strong desire, surprise, or joy, which is to be explained as the consequence of an excitement of the secretory nerve of the lachrymal gland (ramus lacrymalis trigemini) accompanying the psychical excitement, rather than as the result of compression of the gland through increased supply of blood.

More important in regard to psychogenesis is the fact, established by me concerning all infants, that from birth they manifest a high degree of pleasurable feeling by wide-open eyes; unpleasant feeling by shutting the eyes and holding them firmly together. In reference to the first, it surprised me that when the child was placed at his mother's breast, and even just before being placed there, the eyes were regularly stretched open, and almost always remained wide open when he began to suck. This was observed in increasing measure on the third, sixteenth, and twenty-first days. But also, in a warm bath of 35° C., the eyes were wide open in the first three weeks, and, although the child did not laugh, his countenance took on a pleasant expression from the widening of the opening between the lids. Audible and visible laughing, which appeared first on the twenty-third day, is simply an advanced stage of this expression of pleasure, in which "the eyes laugh." Certain mild impressions of light also produce a wide opening of the eyes; this was often observed from the first day on, as has been already stated. In the case of another child, which cried out immediately after its head emerged from the womb, I put my finger, three minutes later, into the child's mouth and pressed on the tongue. At once all crying ceased, a brisk sucking began, and the expression of the countenance, which had been hitherto discontented, became suddenly altered. The child, not yet fully born, seemed to experience something agreeable, and therewith—during the sucking of the finger—the eyes were widely opened. All these observations decidedly support the opinion that pleasure is expressed by wide-open eyes, so far as these will bear the light of day—in twilight and moderate artificial light, even from the moment of birth. Equally certain is it that discomfort is manifested by shutting the eyes.

The eyes are generally shut together at the first cry of the child, and later the rule is that all outcry on account of painful or unpleasant feelings, e. g., hunger, brings with it a gripping of the eyes together, or, at any rate, a considerable lessening of the opening between the lids. And the screwing up of the eyes without crying and without any vocal utterance, but often with turning away of the head—e. g., in the second half of the first year, when the teeth are coming or when the gums are examined—is an indubitable sign of discomfort.

Afterward follows the closing of the lids at all sudden strong sense-impressions, because these bring in their train unpleasant feelings; and with feelings of pleasure the eyes are opened. If that inborn expressive movement is frequently repeated, then it takes place with greater and greater rapidity, and becomes at last pure reflex movement, occurring at all sufficiently strong, new, sudden impressions, before feelings of pleasure or of discomfort can be developed.

The already mentioned hereditary reflex from the trigeminus to the orbicular branch of the facialis—the existence of which is manifested on the first day by the closing of the lid when the hairs of the eyelash are touched, or when the conjunctiva or the cornea is touched—this, too, might be, at first, a defense against the disagreeable, an expressive movement of displeasure; since every touch, even the lightest, of the exposed parts of the eye, so abundantly supplied with nerves, is unexpected and disagreeable. The corresponding reflex path is traveled with less swiftness at first, because at this time the feeling of displeasure probably inserts itself between the centripetal and the centrifugal processes—not to mention the less rapid propagation of the nerve-excitation. Later, the reflex closing of the lid will come mechanically, after contact, without previous feeling of discomfort, and even with the appearance of the most deliberate purpose of defense. It is as if one said, " I shut my eye because it might be hurt "—in reality, however, there is no deliberation.

The difference between this hereditary trigeminus-facialis-reflex and the hereditary opticus-iris-reflex shows plainly the difference between reflexes of ancient inheritance (palæophyletic) and reflexes inherited more recently (neophyletic). For the adaptation of the pupil to bright light, which appears at once and invariably in the newly-born, and in animals without eyelids, must have been inherited at an earlier epoch than was the closing of the lid upon the eye's being touched, because the latter does not occur so promptly in the newly-born. But the new-born holds the eyes shut when dazzlingly bright light is thrown upon them, and in general when it feels discomfort, as does the maltreated frog. Out of this act of holding the eyes tightly shut has probably been differentiated the sudden, brief closing of the lid (opticus-facialis-reflex) that follows all sudden sense-impressions, and that still in the present generation, as an acquired reflex, even one that may be inhibited by the will, stands in contrast with the two other hereditary reflexive movements of defense.

4. Movements of the Eyes.

The eye-movements of the newly-born and of infants are of great interest in their bearing upon the history of the origin of the perceptions of space. The contending parties, the Nativists and the Empiricists,* in support of their views, make their appeal expressly to the child that has had no experience. The Nativists maintain that a pre-established mechanism produces from the beginning co-ordinated, associated eye-movements in the newly-born. The Empiricists hold that this is not the case, but that the eye-movements of the newly-born are

---

* See "Elements of Physiological Psychology," by George T. Ladd (1887), for explanation of these terms.

asymmetric and non-coördinated; that the intentional use of the muscles of the eye is learned only through experience, and that binocular vision, such as adults have, becomes afterward possible through the association of the movements of both eyes in "fixating" an object.

My observations show that, with regard to the simple matter of fact, both parties are right. Some new-born children actually make associated, co-ordinated movements of the eyes several times on the first day; others do not. In some cases I saw both these facts in the same child, but I never found in any child co-ordinated movements exclusively.

I saw my child before the close of the first day of his life turn both eyes at the same time to the right, then to the left, frequently, hither and thither, his head being still; then, again, he would do it moving the head in accord. During the whole time his face was turned toward the window, in the twilight. Nay, only five minutes after his birth, when I held him in the dusk toward the window, an associated movement of the eyes took place. And when I began to observe new-born children, it happened that I saw a child thirty-five minutes after birth (January 4, 1869) move his eyes only as an adult is accustomed to do, in accord.

Donders and Hering, also, have perceived such movements of the eyes in the newly-born. The observation requires only patience, because the newly-born spend the first twenty-four hours mostly in sleep, and when awake they cry a good deal, and their eyes do not remain open.

If we were to rest satisfied with noticing such facts as these, we should come to quite erroneous results.

More accurate and often repeated observation of the eye-movements of the child, especially during the first six days, taught me that the simultaneous turning of both eyes to the right or to the left is not co-ordinated with complete symmetry, as it is in adults. In the cases of a child ten hours old, and of one of six days, their eyes being wide open, I saw eye-movements that were associated, and only such, but which showed themselves, on more accurate observation, to be not perfectly in accord. On the whole, I have found that, in the newly-born, one eye very often moves independently of the other, and the turnings of the head take place in a direction opposite to that in which the eyes move. The unintentional character of both movements is plainly recognizable, and the combination of the two is, at the beginning of life, accidental. The turning of both eyes to left and right, also, which is established on the first day, takes on the appearance of accident, coming in as one among all possible movements.

As the other muscles of the body and of the face are contracted, without intention, by the very young infant, so also are the muscles of the eye.

For this reason we may observe all sorts of non-coördinated movements of the eyes accompanying grimaces, wrinkling of the brows, and movements of the lips, in cases where there is no possibility of sight or of sensibility to light, the lids being closed—e. g., on the tenth day—while the child is not crying, but is lying still. Sometimes it falls asleep with eyes half open, as may be known by its regular breathing and by the repose of its limbs, and then also are seen various unintentional movements of the eyes. Among those which attract

notice when the child is awake are movements of decided convergence. The child looks like a squinting
child. But at the beginning of the third week of life
the maximum degree of convergence and the strabismus are by no means so frequent as in the first; the
irregularity of the movements of the eyes, which others
also have observed in many new-born children, is still
clearly pronounced. Schœler saw in the first days, until the fourth, only non-coördinated movements, and until the tenth day no perfectly correct fixation. Here
his observation ceased. On the thirty-first day, in my
child, strabismus was noticed as rare; on the forty-sixth,
as very rare; on the forty-eighth and fiftieth, the same;
and irregular movements in general, as very rare from
the fifty-fifth day on; but they did appear until the
tenth week, while the child was awake. During sleep,
however, he moved his eyes asymmetrically as late as
the sixtieth day in a lively manner, often the lids, too,
on both sides, the eyes being half open and his snoring
uninterrupted. When he had attained the age of three
months, non-coördinated movements of the eyes were no
more to be observed. After this I watched the sleeping child, however, only now and then, and in the ninth
month I noticed an occasional slight irregularity.

This consolidation of the mechanism of the muscles
of the eye does not, however, by any means involve the
cessation of useless co-ordinated movements of the eyes,
as is shown by several experiences. Thus, the gaze of
one child in the twenty-third week was almost regularly
directed toward his forehead. This child, troubled with
an itching eczema on the head, would, at that time, let
his head swing hither and thither when his hands were

5

held, in case anything whatever, were it only a pillow, touched his head.

The eyes of my child easily converged in the ninth month without any assignable cause, and upon objects held before his nose at a distance of one or two inches.

In the tenth month the convergence of the lines of vision seemed disturbed; a very insignificant squinting inward appeared, but this anomaly vanished completely a few weeks later, after I had directed that he should spend more time out-of-doors, in order to favor his seeing at a distance. From that time the movements of the eyes continued to be normal. The readiness with which convergence of the eyes, upon my finger, held at the end of my boy's nose, occurred (as late as the twentieth month), is remarkable, as well as the fact that at the beginning such high degrees of convergence occur along with pupils relatively very wide open, which is not the case with adults.

All these observations are absolutely favorable to the opinion that conscious vision has decisive influence upon the regulation of the eye-movements; that only after discrimination of the light-impressions by the optic nerve-center do harmonious centro-motor impulses proceed from the nerves of the muscles of the eye (the motor oculi, abducens, trochlearis of both eyes), and that at the beginning, before the faculty of sight manifests itself—i. e., so long as only the function of sensibility to light is active—the eye-movements are not associated and not co-ordinated. Even when they are found symmetrical we can not, in face of a majority or of a very great number of irregular eye-movements, infer a pre-established, complete nerve-mechanism, having bilateral symmetry and capable of functioning at birth, such as exists in the case of sucking. For, if man brought such a mechanism with him into the world (as the chicken and other animals do), how could he come to make so many irregular, purposeless movements of the eyes before making permanent use of this mechanism?

The general rule is, that out of concurring non-coordinated movements of the muscles there grow gradually co-ordinated ones; so, here, with the muscles of the eyes. And, after the co-ordinated movements have become confirmed in the act of sight, there takes place, little by little, an elimination of the superfluous ones, a preference of those that are useful for distinct vision with both eyes. Just so the unregulated movements of the legs at the time of learning to walk become more and more rare, and of the co-ordinated ones, the most useful alone are retained, those which do the most service with the least effort.

It is surprising that representatives of the nativistic theory should, notwithstanding, urge in their own support the results of the investigations in regard to the newly-born—e. g., Rachlman and Witkowski, as follows: "As for the character of the eye-movements in the newly-born, they are in some respects similar to those made in sleep, but in many respects not similar. They are so far similar that they are often entirely non-coördinated; sometimes, though more seldom, of one side only; not similar, in that they generally follow much more rapidly, and in a very great majority of cases appear to be of both sides and often co-ordinated. Even at the first spontaneous opening of the space between the lids, following directly upon birth, we saw apparently co-ordinated lateral movements, which, however, in extent and intensity, were of irregular character. The eyes moved for some minutes incessantly hither and thither with a vast range, such as they do not take later in the regulated act of vision. Among these we saw, to be sure, non-coördinated movements enter suddenly, movements in which the principle of association had absolutely no part."

With this my observations are in full accord. And what the observers report of the eye-movements of sleeping children (whose lids were lifted up without their waking) also agrees in many particulars therewith and with the statements of Schœler: "As to the form of such movements we find, first, lateral turnings that are associated—i. e., they take place bilaterally and with seeming co-ordination. These are rare in sleep, yet they seem to occur; at any rate, it may be said decidedly that non-coördinated movements of the eyes are the most frequent ones. We see, e. g., both eyes move slowly to the right; the apparently associated side-movement is, however, not equal on the two sides, but is of varying force, now in one eye now in the other, so that convergences and divergences are introduced alternately.

Moreover, there are frequently quite abnormal, diametrically opposed movements of the two eyes; one eye moves slowly to the right, the other to the left; or the right eye upward to the right, while the left moves upward to the left. Finally, there occur vertical variations of both eyes of such sort that, e. g., while the right eye turns to the left and somewhat downward, the left eye turns to the left and at the same time somewhat upward. The most remarkable observation, however, is that absolutely one-sided movements occur. While, e. g., the right eye seems to fix the observer, the left eye is seen to move sidewise."

Although all these observations relate to the eyes of children (and adults) in sleep, they are all, according to my experience, perfectly applicable to waking infants in their first days.

5. Direction of the Look.

The ability to "fixate" a bright object is utterly lacking in the new-born child, because he is not yet in condition to move the muscles of the eye at his pleasure, and every fixation is an act of will. On the other hand, the ability to turn the head toward a bright object so that this can produce an image on the retina is often present on the first day of life. And the gaze of a new-born child as he lies quiet, with open eyes, is seen directed to the candle that is held before him in passing. But, in fact, the very young babe *stares*, motionless, with a stupid expression of countenance, into empty space, and merely *seems* to "fixate" the object that is brought into his line of vision. For the staring with unchanged position of the eyes does not cease when the object is removed. The look does not yet follow the removed object, neither does the head. Yet the eyes move on the seventh day independently of the turnings of the head, and converge strongly.

It has indeed been observed by Kussmaul that individuals among children prematurely born (two months too soon) lying with head turned away from the window in the dusk of evening on the second day of life, repeat-

edly turned the head to the window and the light when a
change was made in their position; and I have observed
the same thing in the fully-matured infant regularly on
the sixth day; but this is merely a case of desire in a
primitive form, not a case of the gaze following an object. The object that is apparently sought is motionless,
and is not a recognized cause of sensation. The nature
of the experience is rather this: such and such a position
of the body or of the head is associated with an agreeable sensation—in this instance an agreeable sensation
of light—and is therefore preferred; another position,
a disagreeable one, in which the face is shaded, is avoided. Just so the head is turned to the warm, smooth
breast of the mother, and the turning away from it is
felt as disagreeable, even in the dark.

Accordingly, the turning of the head toward a motionless, moderately bright light. that has been noticed in
some children even in the first days, can not be regarded
as a voluntary direction of the gaze. At the beginning
there is nothing but staring when the eyes are opened,
and even on the ninth day the turning away from dazzling light is no sign of knowledge of direction.

Here again I agree entirely with Kachlman and
Witkowski, when they report that they have never seen
movements of real fixation up to the tenth day. "It
may occasionally happen that upon a certain change of
the position of the lighted candle, or through some movements of the child's eyes, the eye is accidentally put in
position for the light; i. e., an image arises on the yellow spot, but this apparently intentional relation of position between the eye and the object is a purely accidental
one, and assuredly is not based upon a conscious fixation."

When Darwin says that on the ninth day the eyes were directed to the lighted candle, the meaning is simply that the flame was placed in the line of the fixed gaze; but when he adds that up to the forty-fifth day nothing has seemed thus to fasten the eyes, it must be that the critical period of the beginning of fixation passed unnoticed.

The second stage is made known by the turning of the head from one motionless, extended, bright surface in the field of vision to another. On the eleventh day my child held his gaze from one to two minutes steadily upon my face, and turned his head toward the light, which appeared close by in the field of vision. In like manner behaved a female child, who on the fourteenth day directed her gaze, which had been fastened upon her father's face, to some one who came up, and at the sight of this person's head-covering the child's gaze became rooted as if with surprise.*

At this time and later it is noticed also that the infant gazes preferably upward toward the white ceiling of the room. But the upward look that grows out of this, through which the human infant is said to be essentially distinguished from the animal, depends without doubt upon his horizontal position in the arms of his mother or nurse. If the babe were never carried in this manner, it would hardly look upward often.

The *third* stage is attained with the following of a bright object in motion, and is characterized by the associated movement of the eyes while the head is motionless.

It was on the twenty-third day of his life that my

---

* Frau Prof. von Strümpell.

child, who was gazing at the candle burning steadily at the distance of one metre before him, turned both his eyes to the left when I moved the candle to the left, and to the right when the candle was moved to the right. As soon as I held the burning candle up, both his eyes were directed upward toward the light, without any movement of the head. At the same time his face suddenly assumed a surprisingly *intelligent* expression, not before observed. When the light was moved sidewise the head was moved, often; but generally the eyes alone moved. It would also happen that the movements of the eyes were accompanied by a slight sympathetic movement of the head. The motion of the candle had to be very slow always, otherwise it was not followed.

Twenty times that day, certainly, I repeated the experiment, the result of which greatly surprised me, as other children do not follow a moving light with their eyes till after many months. I had, to be sure, made the trial almost every day since the birth of my child, and thereby the mechanism of convergence may have got an earlier start.

Two days later, and seven days later, the same trial was made with the slowly-moved candle or with my hand only. Whenever the movement was slow enough, the child followed it with his look, moving sometimes the eyes only, sometimes head and eyes in accord. Every time that both eyes moved with the light, the countenance assumed again the contented, intelligent expression which it had never worn until the twenty-third day. With that day began also active looking (as distinguished from staring). The outstretched hand, the flame of the candle, faces when they came into the field of vision, were looked at, one can not yet say "fixated," because with this word is associated the notion of voluntary, distinct vision. But from this time forth the gaze of the child was actively directed, daily, without any contrived occasion, to bright surfaces in the field of vision such as have been mentioned.

It is to be noted that no part is played in this progress by the cerebral cortex. For Longet removed carefully the cerebral hemispheres of a pigeon, sparing the corpora quadrigemina and the rest of the brain, kept the bird alive for eighteen days, and saw that in the dark not only did the sudden approach of a light produce contraction of the iris and blinking, but also as soon as he moved the burning candle in a circle the creature made a corresponding movement of the head. To this act, then, the cerebrum is not indispensable. But after the destruction of the corpora quadrigemina the trial yields no results.

While by means of such observations the transition from staring to looking could be marked with tolerable accuracy, the passage from looking to observing and "fixating" objects was not so sharply defined. In the fifth week the Christmas-tree, with its many lights, was looked at with pleasure; in the seventh the child followed with both eyes a lamp carried by some one, a glittering gold chain, or the movements of his mother's head, much more quickly and exactly than before. When looking persistently at a face quite near, his mouth is pursed in a remarkable manner, as is often seen to be the case in adults when there is a great strain of the attention.

A week earlier even, on the thirty-ninth day, the

swinging movement of tassels close in front of the child's face would elicit a pleased expression and a cry of delight. It happened also that the child, when he had been moving actively in his bed, and so had unintentionally shaken it, suddenly became still, and laughed when the blue tassels over his face were set swinging in consequence of the shaking.

In the following weeks, gilded picture-frames, that shone brightly as they reflected the light of the lamp, were looked at for minutes at a time, and the gaze was lifted accordingly. Such strong impressions of light produced gayety, just as swinging objects did. On the sixty-second day, for example, the child looked for almost half an hour at a swinging lamp hanging from the ceiling, with continuous utterances of pleasure. The eyes did not, however, in this case, follow closely the separate oscillations. Both eyes, indeed, often moved simultaneously to the left or to the right, but not in time with the lamp. His pleasure manifested itself by movements of the arms, and by sounds such as are made by a child only when he is pleasurably excited; his interest was shown by an unwavering gaze.

The day before, the child had looked upon the friendly face of his mother for some minutes and then given a cry of joy. It was as if for the first time he had discovered his mother. The face of his father, too, which always exerted a quieting influence on the child when "worrying," became at this time—before the tenth week—an occasion of gayety. In the case of a little girl, the same thing took place in her sixth week.*

* Frau von Strümpell.

All these facts indicate that motionless images on the retina are distinguished from moving ones, although distinct sight is not yet attained; accommodation, indeed, is still wanting.

With this the fourth stage is reached, marked by the ability, which is retained from this time forth, to direct the eyes toward an object. Right and left, above and below, are distinguished, and very soon the most extended use is made of this ability. For now the child *seeks* with his eyes untiringly for new objects, when he is awake and well. This seeking, i. e., primarily the endeavor to give *a definite direction to the look* and to hold it there, dates back to the first three months. In the tenth week, a girl-child looked for the face of the person calling her, although it was with difficulty that she held her head erect. On the other hand, a boy of the same age,* who was lying on his back, could not follow with his eyes a cane that I moved hither and thither before him, but simply stared at it.

A third child began, after the end of the sixteenth week, to look at its hands, and in the twenty-third week carried to its mouth the finger of another person that had been put into its hand.†

When, on the eighty-first day, at a distance of about one metre from my child, I rubbed with my wet finger a tall drinking-glass, and produced high tones new to the infant, he immediately turned his head, but did not hit the direction with his gaze; sought for it, and, when it was found, held it fast. From this time forth he followed with a more animated look, much more accurate-

---

* Frau von Strümpell. † E. Schulte.

ly, even without movements of the head, an outstretched hand not in rapid motion. When the hand was moved very quickly, however, the eye did not follow at all (thirteenth week). What the child seemed to like best of all to follow with his eyes, was a person walking back and forth in the room; he would turn the head more than ninety degrees, and look attentively after the moving figure (fourteenth week).

On the one hundred first day a pendulum, which was making just forty complete oscillations to the minute, was for the first time followed surely and with machine-like regularity. This proves that less than three eighths of a second is needed for the lateral movement of the eye. But for the present such quick movements are not preferred. When, in the sixteenth week, the infant went with us on a journey by rail, he directed his gaze, not at the images that were swiftly passing by the windows, but persistently and attentively at the sides and ceiling of the carriage, and (after our arrival) at the new, motionless objects in the room into which he was brought. The persistent gazing at the ceiling with head leaning back, peculiar to many infants, was especially frequent at this time and in the nineteenth week (p. 43). Yet it is becoming easier for him all the time to follow objects moved quickly. When I have been occupied with the child, if I suddenly get up to leave the room, the child always turns his head round exactly toward me very quickly, and looks after me with great eyes, one might almost say with thoughtful, inquiring eyes (fifth month). But it was not till the twenty-ninth week that I saw the child look distinctly, beyond all doubt, after a sparrow flying by.

But a much longer time passed before objects thrown on the floor, playthings which had served to amuse for a time, were followed with the eyes. Inasmuch as the point concerned here is of a discovery made afresh by every individual human being, viz., that bodies are heavy, and fall if they are not supported, I directed my attention particularly to this, and I give here some observations concerning it in the case of my child :

30th week.—The child very often lets fall to the floor objects held a short time in the hand, but up to this time he has not once looked after them.

31st week.—If the child sees or hears anything fall, he sometimes turns his gaze in the direction where the fall took place.

33d week.—The falling and letting fall of an object make no impression, although objects moved slowly downward are followed with especially close gaze of both eyes.

34th week.—The child but rarely looks after an object that falls out of his hand.

36th week.—Objects thrown to the ground are not yet followed by the child regularly, or with any expression of attention, whereas he fixes his gaze with the greatest interest on any slowly-moving objects that he can hold in view, e. g., tobacco-smoke.

43d week.—The child looks after objects thrown on the floor, oftentimes as if in wonder.

47th week.—The child throws down objects of all sorts that are put into his hands, after busying himself with them some moments, and frequently looks after them. Once he threw a book on the floor eight times in succession, with eager attention, which was manifested by the protruding of the lips.

63d–65th weeks.—Very often the child throws down objects that displease him, or with which he has played awhile, and generally looks after them.

78th week.—The throwing away of playthings is rare (giving up of the habit).

124th week.—Throwing the ball, of all plays, yields by far the greatest pleasure, and the gaze follows the ball with special precision.

The knowledge that bodies are heavy would begin, according to this, in my child, with the forty-third week, when for the first time the fall of an object previously held in his own hand causes astonishment. It would be interesting to know how it is with other children in this respect. Darwin observed that a child, even in the eighth month, could not properly follow with his gaze an object swinging only moderately fast; on the other hand, at the age of thirty-two days, this child perceived his mother's breast three or four inches away; for without touching it he protruded his lips, and his eyes were "fixed" (cf. p. 32), just as happened on the forty-ninth day at sight of a brightly-colored tassel, which made him stop moving his arms when it appeared in the field of vision.

6. Seeing Near and Distant Objects.

The approach of the flame of a candle or of a shining metallic surface to the face of an infant that has not yet moved its eyes, produces, in the first two to six weeks, convergence of the lines of vision and strabismus. This convergence seems to be associated with a strain of the muscle of accommodation, as Genzmer ascertained

by observation of the lens-images. He examined one
eye while the other was alternately brightly lighted and
shaded, and he concludes that a previously-formed connection exists between the position of convergence and
the strain of accommodation. This conjecture is, in
fact, very probable. For the ante-natal existence of the
reflex arc from the optic nerve to the motor oculi is
proved by the contraction of the pupil exposed to light
immediately after birth. Now, the motor oculi,
through the excitement of which the pupil is contracted,
is also the nerve of accommodation, which strains the
ciliary muscle when near objects are seen, and is at the
same time the nerve which supplies the internal rectus
muscle of the eye and so the muscle of convergence.

When a bright object approaches the eye, accordingly, through the mere excitement of the motor oculi
from the retina outward, the whole machinery of adaptation, accommodation, and convergence is at once set
in action. Contraction of the pupil, thickening of the
lens, and looking inward, occur together when a light is
brought near the child, without justifying the supposition of the least choice or intention in the case, solely
through the reflex excitement of the motor oculi from
the optic nerve outward. At any rate, vision is introduced through the concurrence of these three processes
with the sensation of brightness. Indistinct as the muscular sensation of the ciliary and convergence muscle
may be, it will associate itself with the sensation of
light the more perceptibly the oftener a bright object
approaches the eye. The contraction of the pupil, moreover, does not invariably take place along with convergence in the newly-born (p.38).

But thus far the conditions are not fulfilled for securing a sharply-defined image on the retina, nor if such an image were to arise could the object be distinctly seen as a bounded surface.

For, as to the first point, it is evident that only seldom does the flame of the candle (or any bright object whatever) come directly within the distance at which the child's eye sees plainly. The infant seems to recognize distinctly, earliest of all, the face of his mother or nurse, since this is light, pictures itself oftenest on his retina, and is at the same time so near that it comes most frequently within the range of distinct vision. In this way the difference between a faint retinal image (of objects distant or too near) and sharply-defined images is impressed upon the child. The diffusion circles must assert themselves less when the moderately bright object is at a certain small remove from the eye; at all other distances they make their appearance.

As to the second point, it is certain that in the first days or weeks, even if the diffusion images should be utterly wanting, still the form of the object can not be plainly seen; the only distinct sensation is that of brightness. All experiences with people born blind, but after some years operated on successfully, point in this direction. And although learning to see is with such persons a different thing from what it is with normal infants, because the long repose of the central organs of the sense of sight causes a partly quicker, partly slower, functional development of these, yet no radical essential difference between the two developments of the process of sight can be established if the operation is

performed during childhood. Even the experiences of
space gained through seizing and touching can not be
directly made available at the first attempt at accommodation by one born blind and gaining sight late in life.
By him, as by the infant, among the countless retinal images must be preferred above all others, those which are
of moderate brightness and those in which the diffusion
circles amount to a minimum. For very great brightness is disagreeable, like every over-strong nerve excitement, and the dark involves a weaker nerve excitement
than the moderately bright, and thus seems less adapted
to arouse the attention of the eye. Of the images of
medium intensity of light, that which is sharply defined
is observed before all others, for the reason that this one,
apart from the pleasurable feeling it causes, is distinguished from all others—precisely through its sharp
outlines—the relative position is better ascertained, and
the object is more easily recognized when seen again.
Thus when the retinal images all appear together the
brighter and sharper ones are preferred; these impress
themselves first and most enduringly upon children, the
others being consequently neglected. In this way the
function of accommodation is set in operation. Then the
eye can fixate, one after another, objects that are at unequal distances from it.

Still the step, from the reflex accommodation at the
approach of an object to the eye in repose to the voluntary accommodation at the sight of two unequally distant objects, remains obscure. Probably it is first taken
upon the ground of a logical process, after the child has
moved himself, or at least his head and his arms, toward
the object. Then first will the knowledge dawn upon

him, "I do not need to be nearer the object in order to see it plainly."

This experience can not, however, be turned to account before the development of the power of choice. For "fixation" is the *voluntary* bringing of an illuminated point on the place of clearest vision, the yellow spot, to a distinct image. The child that for the first time gazes at the flame of the candle has no power of choice; for him, therefore, fixation is not possible. He simply stares spell-bound by the new sensation.

Binocular fixation must, however, be inexact long after the first voluntary act of accommodation, because irregular movements of the eyes are still frequent. Fixation, properly speaking, does not in any case take place before the day on which for the first time a moving object is voluntarily followed with the gaze—not before the close of the third month (according to my observations and those of Cuignet).

But for a long time after this critical point, the perception of objects unequally distant from the eye, as also the estimate of distances, remains imperfect. How slowly the third dimension of space gets established in perception, in spite of daily practice, appears from the following observations, separated by great intervals of time, made in regard to my boy, whose sight was afterward very keen.

In the ninth week the apparatus of accommodation was already in action. At least I inferred so, from the fact that, while head and eyes were motionless and the amount of light remained unvarying in good daylight, the pupils expanded and contracted alternately several times, although this was done also even when my face remained at the same distance from that of the child. He was evidently experimenting here, letting his eyes converge more and less strongly, allowing my face to become distinct and less distinct before them.

17th week.—Objects accidentally seized are moved toward the eyes. The child often grasps at objects which are twice the length of his arm away from him; indeed, at the same object several times in succession.

18th week.—Reaching too short for the distance is very frequent.

44th week.—New objects are no longer, as was the case earlier, carried to the eyes (and to the mouth), or, at any rate, only rarely; on the other hand, they are attentively regarded and felt with the hands, the mouth being pursed. When the child regards a stranger near him (in the seventh month) his countenance takes on an expression of the greatest astonishment, mouth and eyes being wide open, all the muscles becoming suddenly rigid in the exact position they were last in. The new retinal image must therefore be quite clear, to be so easily distinguished from other retinal images of human faces—i. e., the accommodation is perfect.

47th week.—Playing with a single hair (a woman's), on which the eyes were long fixed, proves the same thing.

51st week.—Some men sawing wood, at a distance of more than one hundred feet, attract the attention of the child and give him pleasure. His sight, therefore, is keen at a distance, as it is for near objects. But that things plainly seen are at unequal distances he has not yet comprehended; for, in the—

58th week.—The child grasped again and again, with

great perseverance, at a lamp in the ceiling of a railway-carriage in which he was passing some hours, and was unusually merry over it.

68th week.—He continues to come short, very often, in his attempts to seize objects; he also reaches too far to the left or to the right, and too high and too low.

96th week.—I stood at the window in the second story and threw a piece of paper to the child, who was in the garden below. He picked it up, looked at it, and held it toward me a long time, with uplifted arm, expressing his desire that I should take it—a convincing proof how little he appreciates distance.

108th week.—Looking at small photographic likenesses of persons known to him, the child at once knows whom they represent; he must, therefore, have good power of accommodation, since only in well-defined retinal images can be perceived the differences, often slight, by which human faces are recognized.

113th week.—Articles of household furniture known to the child are also recognized at once when represented in the picture-book, and at a distance of three inches, and of three feet.

It follows from these observations that the accommodation is perfect long before the perception of distance begins—i. e., the child is able to see plainly objects at very unequal distances from the eye without knowing how unlike their distance is, nay, even without any knowledge of their being at unequal distances. He becomes acquainted with distance only at a later period, probably through the movement of his body toward the object seen, and through the failure of his attempts to seize what lies at a distance.

Yet, for all children, probably the correct estimate of distance is first established by this very act of seizing, because in this there is abundant experience, the number of the attempts being great. On the contrary, by the act of offering things to others a correct estimate of distance is not formed till much later, because there is a lack of experience at the beginning. *Giving* makes its appearance much later than *taking*.

In any case the child is much longer in getting his bearings in space, even after he has the power of visual accommodation, than are many animals, e. g., the chicken, which, after a few hours, correctly perceives the distance of a grain of corn at which it pecks (p. 67). The human being must *infer*, by a roundabout way, from many individual experiences, the third dimension of space, whereas those animals inherit a nervous mechanism which makes this appear by no means a thing to be learned. In man, right and left, over and under, are given by means of the arms and legs, as these are separated from one another; but extent from before to behind is not thus given, because the child does not see or feel itself behind. For the knowledge of extent from front to rear, i. e., of the dimension of depth, there is need of movements, especially of seizing; hence, this is not acquired until later.

The old, much-mooted question, whether the child supposes the objects it first sees distinctly (but not yet as at unequal distances from the eye) to be *in* the eye or outside of it, is answered by John Stuart Mill (1859), according to the Berkeleyan theory of space-perception, for he says that a person born blind and suddenly enabled to see would at first have no conception of *in* or *out*, and would be conscious of colors only, not of objects. When, by his sense of touch, he became acquainted with objects, and had time to associate mentally the objects he touched with the colors he saw, then, and not till then, would he begin to see objects.

The correctness of this view is shown by all the earlier and later reports of oculists in regard to blind children who learn to see after being operated upon. The same thing is true of newly-born children that have their sight; for, whenever two impressions belonging to different departments of the senses occur together in our experience, then from the presence of the one we infer the other. The knowledge of *outness* is hence much earlier awakened and established than that of the unequal distances of objects from the eye. "At the age at which a child first learns that a diminution in brightness and in apparent magnitude implies increase of distance, the child's ideas of tangible extension and magnitude are not faint and faded, but fresh and vigorous." In the beginning, however, the perception of distance, as well as perception by touch, does not exist at all, and the former is still utterly lacking when the latter has reached a comparatively advanced stage. For the experiences with persons born blind that have afterward learned to see, show that some of these patients supposed the objects seen to be touching their eyes, as objects felt touch the skin. Here Stuart Mill is quite correct in saying, "That the objects *touched* their eyes was a mere supposition which the patients made, because it was with their eyes that they perceived them." From their experiences of touch, perception of an object and contact with it were indissolubly associated in their minds. The patient would certainly not say, however, that all objects seemed to touch his eyes, if some of them appeared farther off than others. Cases of this sort, therefore, fully prove that children are at first incapable of seeing things at unequal distances. But because the patients show great zeal in learning to judge of impressions of sight by means of the sense of touch, they must also learn to judge of distances.

One question more belongs here: Are newly-born children oftener myopic (near-sighted) or hypermetropic (far-sighted)?

We have the observations of Von Jäger (1861) and of Ely concerning the eyes of the newly-born and of infants, but these observations are in part contradictory. The first observer is of opinion that the configuration of the eye in the earliest days is myopic, there being an inborn prolongation of the axis of the eye, which lasts, however, but a few weeks. Evidence of this he found also in measurements made in post-mortem examinations. He maintains, on the evidence of his ophthalmoscopic and anatomical investigations, that at the beginning the adjustment for shorter distances prevails, but in the more matured child the adjustment for greater distances (in the early years). Ely, on the contrary, who (1880) tested newly-born children and infants of a few weeks (living children only) with the ophthalmoscope, making use of belladonna (whereby a higher per cent can be obtained for inborn hypermetropia, as he himself remarks), found that emmetropia, myopia, and hypermetropia are all innate, with a preponderance of the last condition. König-stein, who examined nearly three hundred children, states that the eye of the child is probably hypermetropic ex-

clusively (1881). Renewed observations, without the
use of belladonna, are desirable, though they are, of
course, attended with great difficulties.

I saw the eyes of my child, on the twelfth day of
his life, shine very brightly (both pupils dark-red) when
the flame of a candle was behind my head at one side.
This glow of the eye indicates hypermetropia at that
time. Later, this child's eyes became emmetropic.

It can not be without influence on the whole mental
development of the child whether he distinctly sees near
objects only, or distant ones also, in the first years of his
life, but there is as yet a lack of data for estimating this
influence.

One thing only I would lay down as settled, viz.,
that the protracted occupation of little children with
fine work, such as the pricking of paper, the placing and
drawing through of threads, etc.—notwithstanding the
fact that these exercises are warmly recommended in
the so-called Kindergartens of Germany, and are practiced daily for a long time—must be injurious to the
eyes. The prolonged strain of looking at near objects
is for children from three to six years old, even in the
best light, unqualifiedly harmful. All strain of attention to near objects in the evening, when lamp-light must
be used, should especially be forbidden, otherwise the
apparatus of accommodation will get a one-sided use too
early, and near-sightedness will be invited.

7. The Interpretation of what is Seen.

Many suppose that the infant, if he distinguishes
at all any individual visible thing, sees "all objects as
if painted upon a flat surface"—that he has as yet no

conception of anything external, existing outside of his
eye; at any rate, no suspicion that anything moves toward him; that his seeing seems to be at this time
merely a dim sense of light and of darkness; the finger
appears to him only as a dark patch in a bright field of
vision, and does not project in relief from the surface
of the picture.*

In opposition to this I must contend—while I agree
with the view in relation to the newly-born and the first
days of life—that in the second quarter of the first year,
when this is also said to hold good, there must be already something more than a mere "dim sense of light
and dark." For, in the first place, the convergence of
the lines of vision exists much earlier; so that the attention is directed to individual points in the field of
vision. Secondly, the glance of both eyes follows moving objects much earlier, though not voluntarily. Thirdly, it is early announced, by exclamations of pleasure
and displeasure over single objects held before the face,
that the discovery has been made of the demarcation in
space of the changing fields, colored, or dark and light,
in the visual plane.

Withal a considerable time elapses before the child
is capable of *interpreting* the colored, light and dark,
large and small, disappearing and reappearing mosaics
—before he can understand and appreciate, before he
ceases to wonder at transparency and luster, reflection
and shadow. In this the normal babe is inferior, in
learning to see, to the person born blind but gaining

---

* Sigismund's work on "The Child and the World" ("Kind und
Welt"), 1856.

sight through a surgical operation; the latter learns much more rapidly to interpret the field of vision, by reason of his more abundant experiences of touch.

Some of my observations concerning the interpretation of the more common retinal impressions of the child, made at various times, may be brought together here for illustration.

6th month.—When I nod with a pleasant look to my child, he laughs with unmistakable signs of pleasure, moving his arms up and down. (When strangers accost him, however, he does not do this.) Once he observed my image in the mirror, became very attentive, and suddenly turned around toward me as if he were about to compare the image in the glass with the original, or wished to convince himself of the doubling of the face.

7th month.—The infant stares at a strange face near him fully a minute, and longer, with eyes fixed and with an expression of the greatest astonishment: he therefore interprets it at once as something strange.

8th month.—The greatest interest is aroused by bottles—nursing-bottles, wine-bottles, and bottles for water. They are "fixated" with a protracted gaze; the child wants them, and they are recognized even at a distance of two or three metres. The interest is to be explained by the circumstance that the child now gets his nourishment from the bottle, which he takes hold of several times a day and sees near by. For this reason he recognizes objects like it in the field of vision more easily than other objects (except human faces).

9th month.—Just as it is with bottles that resemble nursing-bottles, so it is now with boxes that resemble an infant's powder-box; these are gazed at fixedly, and are desired, with outstretched arms and wide-open eyes. More and more, however, the child shows his interest in other things and occurrences in his neighborhood; in particular, he turns his head quickly toward the door when it is opened or shut, and observes attentively new objects that he holds, or that are moving, for a longer time than formerly.

10th month.—Visual impressions that are connected with food are, however, most quickly and surely interpreted correctly. The child follows the preparation of his food with lips protruded and with wide-open, glistening, eager eyes.

11th month.—When the child is awake he hardly remains quiet a moment; is always moving the eyes hither and thither, and in like manner the head, while he tries to fixate with his gaze every one who comes in or goes by.

If these facts in regard to isolated sight-impressions show an early faculty of perception by the eye, since faces, bright and large moving objects, are soon distinguished from other parts of the field of vision and are easily recognized again, yet the following facts, although they come from a still later period, prove how far from correctly new impressions are interpreted.

15th month.—The child grasped repeatedly at the lighted candle, but not far enough to reach it, and when he was near enough put his hand into the flame; but never again afterward.

16th month.—In the bath the child grasps at the jets of water that flow from his head when the sponge is squeezed upon it, as if these were strings. He tries to catch them in his fingers in a pretty way, and seems surprised at his failure.

17th month.—The child grasped, at various times, generally with a laugh, at some tobacco-smoke a few feet away from him, bent his fingers and exerted himself to seize the smoke, which floated between him and a lamp. Only imperfect conceptions are formed, then, even yet, of the distance and the substantiality of objects.

18th month.—At the unexpected sight of a tall man dressed in black, the child becomes suddenly still, stares at the man about a minute, flees to his father and gazes, motionless, at the tall figure. Immediately after the man had withdrawn, the child said *atta,* and was unrestrainedly merry and loud as before.

Here an unexpected visual impression had evidently caused anxiety, without any assignable reason, for the man whose appearance the child did not know how to interpret was friendly toward him. It was not till the end of his second year that the child ceased to be so easily embarrassed by strangers in black dress.

22d month.—New impressions seem to enchain his attention in increased degree; the mysterious grows more and more attractive.

24th month.—The child observes very attentively animals that are moving, even the slowly-creeping snail and the beetle. These objects, easily followed with the eye, appear not to be at all understood, to judge from the inquiring expression of countenance. The child is surprisingly tender with them, almost timid.

At this period the understanding of actions, and of

the use of all sorts of utensils, is further developed than the ability to interpret representations of them, although an inexhaustible fancy in play has been manifested a long time already in various ways. Sigismund's child, at the end of the second year, understood a circle as representing a plate, a square as a *bonbon*, and had in his twenty-first month recognized the shadow of his father, of which he was at first afraid, as a picture, for he pointed at it joyously, crying "Papa!" Much later than this my boy called a square, *window;* a triangle, *roof;* a circle, *ring;* four points, *little birds.*

Not till after the third year is the ability to represent known objects, even by lines on paper or by cutting out, manifested. Before this the child wants to "write," *raice* (schreiben), i. e., to draw; and thinks that by all sorts of marks he is representing a locomotive, a horse, a spoon, a plate, a bottle; but does not succeed without help. I have had information of one child only that, in its fourth year, without instruction, could cut animals out of paper with the scissors (giraffes, greyhounds, horses, lions, camels, fishes) in such a fashion, and draw them so on the slate with a pencil, that everybody knew at once what the lines inclosed (even in the case where he had sketched a man sitting). Such a talent is very rare, and indicates an inherited sense of form. An average child can not, before the end of the third year, draw an approximately circular line returning upon itself. This boy of three and a half years, however, bites animals out of bread, draws them with a stick in the sand, models them in clay, sees animal forms in the clouds, and devotes himself to his art with the greatest perseverance for months, without direction, without the least stimulus from parents or brothers and sisters.*

The surprisingly persistent desire of my boy (in his thirtieth month), repeated daily (often several times in the day), to "write" locomotives, *Locopotive raiben* (he meant "draw"), sprang from his seeing locomotives frequently. These objects interested him in a remarkable degree in his third and fourth years, evidently because greater changes in the field of vision excite the special attention of the infant very early, on account of the great number of optical nerve-fibers excited by the change of light and dark. In the country the locomotive is one of the largest moving objects. It also moves swifter than horses. That this, the largest moving mass perceived, became the most interesting of all, as was the case with the steamer on the sea, seems therefore natural.

As to the rest I have not been able to determine in what way little children represent to themselves such movements. Many regarded the locomotive as tired when it stood still, as thirsty when its tank was filling with water, as a stove when it was heated; or they were afraid of every steam-engine near them, so long as it was in operation.

8. Sight in Newly-born Animals.

The perfection of sight in quite young fowls, without experience, is astonishing as compared with the incomplete development of this sense in new-born human beings. Let their eyes be kept shut, without injuring

---

* Frau Dr. Friedemann.

them, from one to three days, and, in many cases, within two minutes after the removal of the bandage, they will follow the movements of creeping insects with all the accuracy of old fowls. Within from two to fifteen minutes they peck at any object, estimating the distance with almost infallible accuracy. If the object is out of reach, they will run to it and hit it every time, so to speak, for they never miss by more than a hair's breadth, even when the kernel of grain at which they pecked is no larger than the smallest dot of the letter *i ; seizing* at the moment of pecking is a more difficult operation. Although an insect is sometimes caught with the bill and swallowed at the first attempt, they generally peck five or six times, and pick up crumbs once or twice, before they succeed in swallowing food for the first time. So Spalding reports.

His statements hold good, also, according to my observations, for fowls one day old, not bandaged but kept in the dark one day ; these, without mother or companions, at once find their way of themselves wherever they are, in the incubator or on the table in the laboratory. But I can not admit the supposed infallibility to within a hair's breadth. They miss in pecking by as much as two millimetres, though seldom. On the other hand, the attempts at swallowing frequently fail. Here it should be considered that even grown fowls are not sure in their pecking, seizing, or swallowing, as any one that observes closely may easily perceive. The accuracy is, however, marvelous at the very beginning. A duckling of a day old snapped at a fly that was just flying by, and caught it ; a turkey of only a day and a half directed its bill, after the manner of the elders of its race, attentively and deliberately, at flies and other small insects. (Spalding.)

Many new-born mammals have likewise in the very first hours of life the ability to move not only the head but the whole body toward a visual impression—e. g., young pigs. Spalding bandaged the eyes of two pigs just born. One of these was brought immediately to the mother; it soon found the teats and began to suck. Six hours afterward the other was placed at a short distance from the mother. It found her in half a minute, after going about in a rather unsteady manner. After a half-minute more it found the teats. In both cases smell and taste must, therefore, have determined the direction of the movement; in the last case probably hearing also. But it is not expressly stated whether the mother made her voice heard. On the following day it appeared that the one of the young ones that had been left with the mother no longer had on the bandage. The other was wholly unable to see, but walked about, bumping against things. In the afternoon the bandage was taken off. Then the creature ran about as if it had already been able to see before it was bandaged. Ten minutes later it was hardly to be distinguished from another young one that had enjoyed the use of its eyes without interruption. " Placed on a chair, it saw that the height required considering," knelt down and jumped off. After ten minutes more this animal was placed, together with another, twenty feet from the sty. Both got to their mother in five minutes, at the same instant.

If, in the last-mentioned experiment, smell and hearing not being excluded, imitation of the animal whose sight has not been interrupted is possible to the one that has been for only twenty minutes able to see, yet the very remarkable fact of the jumping down from the chair after the previous kneeling must be based on an act of sight. The operation of estimating distance, however imperfect it be in the brain of an animal not yet two days old, and not able to see till within ten minutes before jumping down, proves that even thus early the third dimension of space comes to consciousness through the eye, as the result of retinal impressions, otherwise the animal would not have knelt before jumping. Now, since it had hitherto had no sight-perceptions, and in those ten minutes none that gave occasion for jumping, the association of retinal excitement, estimate of distance, muscular movement for kneeling and for the jumping that followed, must be inherited. For no one would attribute to a pig so young, blind ten minutes before, such a gift of invention, as to initiate, out of independent deliberation, a proceeding so rational and so well adapted to its purpose. The animal jumps because its ancestors have jumped countless times without waiting long or estimating carefully the distance. A human infant does not possess this association of retinal excitement and coordinated muscular movement. It moves without purpose and falls from the chair. The young Guinea-pig, on the other hand, does not jump and does not fall by accident, but lets itself drop, as I have often proved.

Kids kneel and see on the first day of life, without any example for imitation and without guidance, yet quickly and efficiently. I have seen them suck in this manner before they were twenty-two hours old. They

7

stride rather awkwardly up to the mother, snuff at her teats, kneel down and suck, wagging their tails continually and pushing with their heads.

In the human being so many more associations of sight with co-ordinated muscular movements are possible than in the brute at the moment of birth, that it takes a longer growth after birth for these all to be developed.

Not before the sixth week, as O. Binswanger has discovered, are fully-formed ganglionic cells present in the human cerebrum, and at the same period are first developed the cerebral convolutions, according to the investigations of Sernoff. Therefore, not only does the human brain continue to grow after birth, but it differentiates itself after birth, not before; since not until the second month does it receive its characteristic morphological marks.

Such complicated mechanisms of associations as those mentioned can not be developed before birth, because too many other established inherited mechanisms go along with them. They are all present potentially, but which of them finally become most easily operative depends on experience—i. e., on provocation from without, the more or less often repeated treading of the separate paths of association in the cerebro-spinal system. In other words, the child learns much more than the animal.

The philosopher, Eduard von Hartmann, as early as 1872, used the following striking language with reference to this difference: "The human child seems to bring nothing at all with him, but to learn everything; in reality, however, he brings everything, or at any rate far more than does the lower animal that creeps all complete out of the egg; but he brings everything in an immature condition, because there is in him so much to be developed that in the nine months of embryonic life it can only be prefigured in the germ. So, then, in the progressive development of the infant brain the maturing of tendencies goes hand in hand with learning—i. e., with the modification of these tendencies by exercise; and the result is far richer and finer than can be attained in the brutes by mere inheritance."

The superiority of the animal, which utilizes at once its retinal excitations for its own advantage in jumping, is thus merely an apparent one, for it lacks the aptitude to learn other ways of utilizing experiences. This utilization may be conceived of as an inherited logical process—i. e., as *instinctive;* since the animal is born more mature than the human being, it is, unconsciously, earlier capable of performance such as the human being learns later through individual experience and accomplishes only with consciousness.

The same holds true of the association of seeing and touching, seeing and seizing, and other associations of which we have yet to speak.

Still, it is not to be denied that in man also the attainment of complicated combinations of this sort—of movements of the muscles of the eye and the arm upon receiving certain sense-impressions—is essentially assisted by inherited endowment. The muscular movements fall into the required groove without imitation the more quickly, in proportion as these have been the habitual combinations in the life of the race.

CHAPTER II.

HEARING.

The observations concerning the gradual development of the faculty of hearing in early childhood relate to the deafness of newly-born children—which is normally of only short duration—and to the babe's first sensations and perceptions of sound. Then follow some statements concerning the hearing of new-born animals.

1. The Deafness of the Newly-born.

All children immediately after birth are deaf. It was formerly conjectured merely that the reason why the new-born child can not hear is the filling of the cavity of the tympanum with mucus, and that this physiological deafness lasts until the cavity is emptied. It is now settled that the temporary deafness is occasioned, also, and chiefly, by the lack of air in the cavity before respiration.

Several investigators have found in the middle ear of the fœtus a yellowish liquid, others a peculiar gelatinous substance. Gellé thinks that the latter comes from a strong œdematous infiltration of the mucous membrane of that part, and has its place supplied soon after birth with air, by means of the respiratory movements, after it has become liquid—as he proved that it does become, shortly before birth. He found in a cat, half an hour after birth, both tympanic cavities filled with air, and no remaining trace of the gelatinous magma.

The animal had cried out, and its lungs contained a good deal of air.

The question how far this gelatinous tissue, hyperæmia and swelling of the mucous membrane of the tympanic cavity, a sub-epithelial layer of the membrane, fill up the tympanic cavity before the first respiration, is not yet decisively answered. Neither has the point of time been ascertained, after how many respirations the Eustachian tube, in the human being, is permeable.

Probably the advent of respiration is not alone sufficient to accomplish the emptying of the tympanic cavities after birth and the filling of them with air; rather are repeated swallowing and breathing essential to it, and a few respirations are not sufficient, as Lesser proved, to replace with air the liquid contents of the tympanic cavity of the fœtus, or to change their character. Only after several hours' respiration can air be proved to exist in the middle ear along with the liquid; but Lesser found that the rapidity with which the liquid gave place to air did not sustain a constant relation to the duration of the extra-uterine existence. As Lesser examined forty-two new-born human beings, of whom thirteen were still-born, sixteen had lived a few minutes after birth, and thirteen had lived several hours or days, greater value is to be attributed to his results than to the isolated experiences of others. His results are of practical importance, and are especially remarkable in that they show that the fœtal condition of the middle ear in children prematurely born may persist more than twenty hours after birth. Such children, according to this, must be deaf somewhat longer than those born at the full time.

As to the rest, the old view of Scheel (1798), according to which the amniotic fluid comes directly into the middle ear before birth through the Eustachian tube, as the air does after birth, namely, through swallowing, is not improbable. And we can not help agreeing with him when he observes that because some of the amniotic fluid remains in the tympanic cavity during the first days after birth, a loud sound is less injurious to the organ of hearing than if the cavity were at once filled with air. The collection of fluid in the middle ear makes adults also hard of hearing. It was well said by Herholdt (1797): "Experiments made on animals have convinced me that in the fœtus the tympanic cavity is completely filled with mucus and amniotic fluid, which enters and is renewed through the Eustachian tube. So the remainder of the amniotic fluid and that in the tympanic cavity are in equilibrium and the tympanum is pressed equally from all sides. By this the tympanic cavity is relieved during the growth of the fœtus from the obstacles that might stand in the way of its proper development, and the tender tympanic membrane is protected from harm. After birth the liquor flows out slowly through the same channel, and the atmospheric air takes its place. Then first can the organs of hearing perform their functions, though not perfectly until their development has become complete and the bones of the head are firm and in reciprocal connection. The older physicians, who did not know this, dreamed of an hereditary or inborn atmosphere."

In accord with this are the investigations of Moldenhauer and Von Tröltsch (1880). The latter is of opinion that the hyperplastic mucous membrane, which in the fœtus almost fills up, like a cushion, the aperture of the tympanic cavity, often shrinks together before birth; the mucous cushion may even disappear within the uterus, in which case something else must occupy its place, and this can only be the amniotic fluid.

Besides the lack of air in the tympanic cavity, there is also to be taken into account, as a cause of the deafness of the human being at birth, the temporary closing of the external auditory canal, which is due, according to Urbantschitsch, not to epithelial agglutination, but to absolute contact of the coatings of the auditory canal. Many animals, also, but probably no birds, are for this reason deaf, or hard of hearing, directly after birth. So much the more surprising is the sensitiveness of others, e. g., of the Guinea-pig, of which something will be said by-and-by.

If the tympanic cavity in the new-born child is already filled with air, a deafness of half an hour, or of several hours, or even of several days, may be caused by the closing of the external auditory canal (the obstruction does not very quickly disappear), or by the narrowness of the canal. The difference in the results of observations according to which infants from one to three days sometimes react distinctly upon the stimulus of sound, sometimes ignore it completely, seems intelligible, however, if we only take into account the varying rapidity with which the Eustachian tube and the auditory canal are pervious to air, apart from all other obstacles, even possible cerebral ones. On the other hand, I must positively pronounce false the statements according to which children from three to four months old possess normally very slight capacity of hearing, and according to which it is hard to give a decided opinion as to whether such children hear at all or not. My observations upon many infants and my information from trustworthy mothers leave no doubt that, long before the third month, in the normal condition, the human voice is heard; and in fact mature and sound children before the close of the first week of life react, in unmistakable fashion, upon the stimulus of loud sound, as Dr. Kroner, of Breslau, also found.

The longer continuance of difficulty of hearing is certainly of great advantage to the infant, as it stands in the way of the multiplication of reflex movements, and so of the tendency to convulsions.

But if children born at the right time make no movement in the fourth week when a loud sound is made behind them, then there is reason to suspect that such children will remain deaf and dumb.

2. The First Sensations and Perceptions of Sound.

How many hours, days, or weeks after birth the very earliest sensations of sound are experienced it is not easy to determine very accurately, for the reason that an unmistakable sign that a sensation of sound has been experienced is lacking. Movements of the eyelids, starting, throwing up the arms, and screaming, which appear in the child at the stimulus of sudden loud sound, appear readily at fright caused by any strong impression, while slight noises and soft tones remain unnoticed. The turning of the head toward the invisible source of sound does not take place till later.

Frequently-repeated attempts to test the ability of the newly-born to hear, leave no doubt that it is increased by exercise, and that an occasional temporary dullness occurs. But the experiments made thus far are too scanty and uncertain.

Kussmaul could make the loudest discordant noises near the ears of new-born children during the first days, while they were awake, without any reaction on their part. Numerous experiments made by him in this direction had only a negative result. But he adds that another cautious observer, Feldbausch, has seen sleeping children more than three days old start when he broke the silence by clapping his hands hard. Champney's child, on the contrary, did not react before the fourth week upon any noise, however loud, not even clapping of the hands, if there was no vibration of the room or of the bed. If a door was slammed-to, the child started, just as it did directly after birth when the scales of the balance in which it lay suddenly sprang up. When fourteen days old, this child turned its eyes toward its mother when she spoke to it, but as it did not at that time stir at any noise, however loud, if there was no shaking, this turning may be attributed to the feeling of warmth at being breathed upon; for the movement took place only when the mother's face was turned toward the babe, and it was presumably a movement of the head rather than of the eyes.

Genzmer was the first to make experiments by measuring. He ascertained the greatest distances at which infants' eyelids quivered at the striking of a little bell, which was done in just the same way always, with a small iron rod. It appeared that almost all children of one day, or certainly of two days, react upon impressions of sound, but their sense of hearing is, without much reference to the degree of their maturity, at first unequal, and grows more acute within the first weeks. The average distance at which the striking of the bell was heard was found to be eight to ten inches, but the figures varied from one to twenty. In one case, that of a very active child, the distance on the first day was eight, on the sixth eighteen, on the twenty-fourth twenty-four inches; with a phlegmatic child, the auditory reflexes were on the first day irregular, on the eighth they occurred at five, on the twenty-fourth at eleven inches distance from the bell. It may be seen from these figures how unequal the progress is. But as the sound could hardly be of exactly the same force in all the experiments, and as the quivering of the eyelids is not caused by the stimulus of sound exclusively, and as not every sound-stimulus is responded to by a quiver of the eyelids, this whole series of experiments, limited to about thirty observations, on fifteen children, is uncertain.

The observations of Dr. Moldenhauer likewise leave much that is doubtful, although his mode of proceeding is better. He made use, as a test of the hearing, of the French toy, *cri-cri*, which gives a loud, brief, disagreeable sound, with discordant high overtones. This sound continues almost exactly identical after many experiments, and can be made quite close to the ear without involving other stimulus. The most important result of this experiment was that, with very few exceptions, children distinctly reacted at once upon the sound-stimulus at the first trial. Yet the degree of the reaction was extraordinarily unequal in different individuals, and in the same individuals on different days. Fifty children were tested. Of these only ten were less than twelve hours old (these all reacted), and only seven from twelve to twenty-four hours old, all the rest older. The least degree of reaction was indicated by a distinct quiver of the eyelids, even without interruption of sleep; a stronger degree by wrinkling of the forehead. Then came head-movements, mostly single short twistings of the head; finally, starting, accompanied by violent quivering of the head, the arms, and the upper part of the body; sleeping children awoke and screamed. The reflexes occurred more plainly and more quickly after the end of the second day than on the first two days. In experiments that followed one another in quick succession, there was very often manifested a dullness, going as far as entire absence of reaction.

Children sleeping soundly, and babes nursing, reacted less distinctly than those awake or half asleep.

Most children, then, even those born three or four weeks too early, respond in the first days to strong impressions of sound by reflex movements in the region of the facialis. The action of those just born, in the first five hours, was not investigated. The four youngest were six hours old, as the author tells me. Deafness was in some few cases (four out of fifty) well established, even after more than twenty-four hours; thus my observation that no reaction follows upon sound-impressions immediately after birth is not modified by this discovery. In fact, I saw a strong child, of ten hours, that did not react in the least upon the *cri-cri*, and I saw one of six days react very slightly.

Moldenhauer found further that, of four children who were tested for the first time after more than

twenty-four hours and did not react, three did distinctly react in later repeated experiments in the same hour
or on the following day. A child of three days did not
react even at the second trial.

When the bell that has been mentioned was struck
by Genzmer softly, very near the ear of children that
heard well (probably more than two days old), they
sometimes turned the head to that side; if occupied
with nursing, they broke off from their occupation.
Very violent striking of the bell made them restless. I
have likewise observed that infants are greatly disturbed by strong sound-stimulus, just as new-born animals are; e. g., the shrill whistle of a locomotive near by
easily produces persistent lively movements and violent
screaming in a child previously perfectly quiet. Not
every infant, indeed, shows so strong a reaction, nor
does any in the first hour of life. But on the ninth
day the turning of the head (in my judgment accidental) toward the source of sound was observed by Moldenhauer.

Too great a range is, however, commonly allowed
for individual differences. When some children are reported as starting at loud sounds, even on the first day,
others after three days, others again not till after eight
weeks, there is reason to attribute the last statements to
inaccurate observation, unless they apply only to those
hard of hearing or prematurely born; or, unless too
deep sounds and unsuitable noises were employed.

If a small tuning-fork, in vibration, warmed and
carefully placed on the head, produces no other reaction
than that produced by a fork not in vibration, similarly
placed, we may infer that the inner ear has some share

in the deafness of the newly-born. But such experiments must be made on many individuals. Moldenhauer got no definite result with tuning-forks on account of the sensitiveness of the skin of the head.

A very vigorous male child, born after his time, was seen by Dr. Deneke, in the lying-in asylum at Jena, six hours after birth, to close his eyes tighter every time the doctor struck two metallic covers together close to his ear. In this case, however, the reflex may have been started by the current of air arising from the sudden motion. A very strong new-born child, weighing nearly four and a quarter kilogrammes, did not react upon any noise, when I tested it half an hour after birth. That is the way all ordinary children behave just after birth. By ever so loud a noise, clapping of hands close to the ear, whistling, very loud screaming, they are not within the first half hour, according to my experiments, brought to screaming from a state of quiet, nor quieted if they are screaming. But they cry out if you blow on them, if you press softly on their temples, or strike them upon the thigh, after they have begun to breathe. Only there is a noticeably longer interval between the contact and the outcry than at a later period.

I saw my child, in the twenty-first hour of life, move both arms symmetrically, at a loud call, but this is perhaps to be attributed to being breathed on; for clapping of hands, whistling, speaking, produced no result, and on the second and third days no reaction upon sound-stimulus could be induced. It was not until the first half of the fourth day that I was convinced that my child was no longer deaf. For hand-clapping, or whistling, close to him then produced sudden opening of the half-shut eyes, as the child lay warm and satisfied with food, and to all appearance comfortable. As this result followed every time on repeated trials the fourth day, but not once on the third day, there can be no doubt that in this case the sound was heard by means of the tympanum on the fourth day, but not before. It also happened for the first time on the fourth day, and indeed several times, that the child when crying stopped as soon as I began to whistle close to him. This observation was made also upon babes of two and three days old. On the eleventh and twelfth days I noticed that my child became quiet always at the sound of my voice, which seemed also to call forth a sort of intense expression of countenance that, however, can not be described.

On the twenty-fifth day pulsation of the lids often followed when I spoke to the child in a low voice, standing before and near him. On the following day he started suddenly when a dish that he could not see was noisily covered near him. He is frightened, then, already, at unexpected loud sounds, as adults are. On the thirtieth day this fright was still more strongly manifested. I was standing before the child as he lay quiet, and being called, I said aloud, without changing my position, " Ja!" (yes). Directly the child threw both arms high up quickly, and made a convulsive start with the upper part of his body, while at the same time his expression, which had been one of contentment, became very serious. The same scene was enacted at another time on the slamming of a door.

In the fifth week the sensibility to sound has increased to such a degree that the child seldom sleeps in the daytime if any one walks about or speaks in the room; whereas, so late as the seventh day, a loud call did not wake the sleeping child. The increased sensibility is also proved by the quick turnings of the head when any one sits on the child's bed without being seen by him, and also by the starting at moderately loud noises.

In the sixth week I noticed this starting at quite insignificant noises, even when the child was asleep and did not wake. About this time he could already be quieted at once, when he was screaming, by his mother's singing. The first time this happened the child opened his eyes wide, evidently a symptom of astonishment at the new sensations of sound. On the following day, when his mother again quieted him by singing, he gazed at her with wide-open eyes (cf. p. 46), so that I already suspected he had associated the tones he heard with the oval of the face he saw, as is unquestionably the case with older children (e. g., of four months) when they laugh and utter joyous cries as soon as the mother sings anything to them.

In the seventh week the fright at a loud sound was still greater than before. Dishes fell to the floor several times while the child was asleep. Instantly both arms went up swiftly, and remained for more than *two minutes* upright in that strange position with fingers outstretched and parallel, without the child's waking. The attitude reminded one of the spreading of the wings of a frightened bird. There appears to be already a greater sensibility to tones, possibly to melodies, for an expression of the greatest satisfaction is perceived on the child's face when his mother hushes him with cradle-songs softly sung. It is worth noticing, also, that even when he is crying from hunger a low sing-song causes a pause in the crying and attracts attention. Speaking does not effect this invariably, by any means.

In the eighth week the infant heard, for the first time, the music of an instrument—the piano. He made known his satisfaction at the new sensation by an unusual straining of the eyes and by lively movements of arms and legs at every *forte*, as well as by smiles and laughter. The higher and softer tones made no such impression. This delight in music manifested itself in like manner in the following months, from which we may conclude that more than a year before the first imperfect attempt at speech there is discrimination between (musical) sounds and noises. The child of two or of three months often utters sounds of satisfaction when it hears music.

In the ninth week the sound of a repeating watch, which had earlier produced not the least impression on the child, now aroused his attention to the highest pitch. But his head was not turned with certainty toward the source of sound, whereas he would follow a moving hand accurately. At every sudden noise, scream, call, tones, clapping of hands, there is a quick shutting and opening of the eyes, and very often the arms are at the same time lifted quickly, no matter in what position the body is held. The same in the fourth month. In the seventh and eighth the closing of the lids predominates. The raising of the arms has already become rare.

In the eleventh week I noticed for the first time, what some others have not perceived before the second quarter of the year, though some have done so earlier, that the child, beyond doubt, moved his head in the direction of the sound heard. I knocked on a mirror, being behind him. Immediately he turned his head round toward the source of the sound. At this period it is in general surprising with what ease single tones, scales, and chords attract the attention of the babe, to such a degree that the greatest restlessness subsides at once when these are sounded, and he hearkens with an intense gaze.

In the twelfth week the turning of the head toward the sounding body was sudden, even when the look did not take at once the right direction. When the direction was found, the child would hearken evidently with close attention (cf. p. 87.)

In the sixteenth week the turning round of the head toward a sound takes place with the certainty of a reflex movement. Before this time no notice at all was taken of more distant sound-stimulus—a hand-organ below in the garden, the voice of a person speaking aloud at the other end of the room; now both these sounds cause lively motions of the head, and an altered, not dissatisfied, expression of countenance.

The first noise artificially produced by the child himself, one that gave him apparent pleasure and was accordingly frequently repeated, was the crumpling of paper (especially in the nineteenth week). In the twenty-first week, at the beating of a gong, sounded for the purpose of taking his photograph, he became motionless—his attention was so enchained by the new noise—and stared with fixed gaze at the metallic plate. In general, his hearing became so much more acute in the fifth month that, when taking his milk, he almost

8

invariably broke off from his occupation and turned about whenever a noise, not altogether too slight, was made near him.

After a half-year the babe often kept his gaze steadily directed for minutes at a time on my face, and with an expression of wonder, with eyes and mouth open, when I sang single notes to him. He utters a joyous cry at military music.

In the eighth month there is a quick closing of the lids, a single wink of the eyes for the most part, not only at every loud, sudden sound-impression, but even at every new one—e. g., when the voices of animals are imitated. This is no longer the expression of fright merely, but of astonishment also. In fright there has come, in place of the raising of the arms, a starting of the whole body and a convulsive movement of arms and legs together, which was also observed as early as the second month. The rapid shutting and opening of the eyes continued unchanged.

In the ninth month, when the child more than twelve times in succession shut down the cover of a large "caraffe," so that a loud slam was heard every time, this winking of the eyes and starting of the whole body took place every time, the countenance meanwhile expressing great attention. The reflex movements in this case were not, then, the expression of fright, for the child himself eagerly repeated the shutting down of the cover after I had raised it. The combined tactual and visual impression surpassed in interest the accompanying phenomenon of sound; the intensity of the latter, however, was so great as to involve the reflex movements. At this period I often saw, during the sleep of the child, lively movements of the hands after sound-impressions that did not waken the sleeper, the remains of an earlier reflex raising of the arm. Not only does the child turn his head round when he hears my voice without seeing me, but (as also in the tenth month) at every new loud noise—e. g., thunder. So, too, the turning of the head in the first and second weeks, when a loud sound is heard, is not a directing of the head toward the source of sound (p. 80); this does not take place till later (p. 85).

During teething, the sensibility to acoustic stimulus is, moreover, noticeably increased. A loud word then produces winking, fright, quicker breathing, screaming, and tears.

In the eleventh and twelfth months, the screaming child generally allows itself to be quieted in a few moments by a decided "Sh!" just as it did in the first month. No other spoken utterance has this effect, not even the sharp "ss" or "pst," but any singing, even false notes, will do it.

At this time—the three hundred nineteenth day—occurred a remarkable acoustic experience, which gives evidence of great intellectual advance. The child struck several times with a spoon upon a plate. It happened accidentally, while he was doing this, that he touched the plate with the hand that was free; the sound was dulled, and the child noticed the difference. He now took the spoon in the other hand, struck with it on the plate, dulled the sound again, and so on. In the evening this experiment was renewed, with a like result. Evidently the function of causality had emerged in some strength, for it prompted the experiment. The cause of the dulling of the sound by the hand—was it in the hand or in the plate? The other hand had the same dulling effect; so the cause was not lodged with the one hand. Pretty nearly in this fashion the child must have interpreted his sound-impression, and this at a time when he did not know a single word of his later language.

In the twelfth month the child was accustomed, almost every morning, to observe the noisy putting of coals into the stove, A. On the three hundred sixty-third day it took place in the next room, in the stove, B. The child at once looked in the direction of the sound, but as he discovered nothing he turned his head around nearly one hundred and eighty degrees, and regarded the stove, A, with an inquiring gaze: that stove had already been filled. This likewise shows logical activity applied to perceptions of sound, and this before the ability to speak.

Such experiments were from time to time carried on after this, entirely of the child's own accord; e. g., in the thirtieth month the child, while eating, held his hand by chance to his ear while a kettle of boiling water stood before him. At once he becomes attentive, notices the diminution in the force of the sound, takes his hand away, listens in silence, open-mouthed and with an expression of surprise, to the modification of the sound, holds his hand to his ear five or six times, and establishes the fact anew each time, like an experimenter, until the connection between the alteration in the sound and the movement of the hand no longer seems wonderful, because he has perceived it several times.

I note here that one of the earliest sound-perceptions in which causality operated without language, is the one mentioned (p. 87), occurring on the eighty-first day.

I have not been able, notwithstanding the greatest attention and very much outlay of time, to record any more observations of this sort concerning the activity of reasoning without speech, in the domain of sound.

After the end of the first year the child strikes with his hands on the keys of the piano, and looks around occasionally while doing it, as if to assure himself that somebody is listening to him. He takes pleasure in a canary-bird, laughing when it moves and listening in silence when it sings, and then laughing again. In general, laughing is frequent in the following months at new noises, like gurgling or clearing the throat (fifteenth month). Even thunder made the child laugh.

A favorite acoustic occupation consisted in holding a watch to his ear and listening to the ticking (sixteenth, seventeenth, and twenty-fourth months). But sometimes the watch was held behind the auricle and sometimes against his cheek. If I held it above, on his head, the ticking was heard (nineteenth month), as could be told by the look of attention. The conduction of sound by the bones must have been already established for some time past.

The pleasure in music, that showed itself even in the first three months, increased manifestly in the six following months. But it was nearly the end of the second year before the child, who was roused to the liveliest movements by hearing the most varied kinds of music, performed these movements in time. He did indeed dance, but in his own fashion, not rhythmically (twenty-first month). Somewhat later, he would him-self beat time with tolerable correctness with the arms, or with one arm, trying meanwhile to sing over a song that had been sung to him (twenty-fourth month), but he did not succeed in this till later, and then imper-fectly. Playing with fife and drum at that period gave hardly more pleasure than striking some keys of the piano, and that with both hands at once. But I must add that it was absolutely impossible, notwithstanding much pains, to teach the child to name rightly even the three notes C D E (end of third year), though his hearing for noises and vocal sounds was in general acute.

Another child, on the contrary, a girl, could, in her ninth month, sing correctly every note given her from the piano, and seemed to find discords unpleasant; at least she always wept bitterly at that age whenever any one blew on a small tin trumpet. This child, and two others of the same family, could sing before they could talk, and sing correctly airs that had been sung to them. Not only the *pitch*, but the stress and the shade of tone are given by such musical children (in the eighth month), who listen to all music with the greatest strain of atten-tion. Such a child even sang itself to sleep (in the eighth month), and later (in the nineteenth month), ac-companied songs and pieces sung and played by others, clapping its hands in correct time. (Frau Dr. Friede-mann.)

Another little girl takes pleasure in hearing music (in the eleventh month), likes to strike on the keys of the piano, and when any one begins to sing airs that have often been sung to her, she springs and accompanies the singing with the movement of her body, and turns her hands this way and that. (Fr. v. Strümpell.)

Through the whole of the third year it was not easy to waken my child by sound-impressions alone. He often fell asleep even when there was a racket near him, and yet his hearing was acute enough when he was awake, as appears from the observations reported.

Even the knowledge of the direction of sound, though imperfect, still appeared earlier than in other cases. Darwin reports—e. g., that one of his acutely-hearing children, when more than seventeen weeks old, did not easily recognize the direction from which a sound came, so as to turn its gaze thither; with which should be compared the above statements (page 85); also that of Vierordt, that sometimes in the fourth month the child begins to turn his head in the direction of the sound; and that of R. Demme, who found that of about one hundred children only two, at the age of three and three and a half months, distinguished the voices of their parents from those of other persons calling to them; these children made animated movements and joyous utterances; all the other children were much later in making this distinction.

Individual differences, partly hereditary, partly acquired, are in this department very great.

3. The Hearing of New-born Animals.

Guinea-pigs not yet twelve hours old show unmistakably, by movements of the ears, as I found, that they hear all high tones of from one thousand to forty-one thousand double vibrations a second. For when, unseen by the animals, everything around being still,

I struck one of my forty small tuning-forks that ranged through that interval (from the C of the third octave to the E of the eighth) the ears of the animals were always immediately moved in time, either lowered or folded; and at loud tones the creatures invariably started. This reflex movement, nowhere mentioned hitherto, viz., the contraction of the auricles, took place with such machine-like regularity that I can compare no other movement with it in regard to precision, with the exception of the contraction of the pupil to light. In grown Guinea-pigs the auditory reflex for all these tones of the tuning-forks is likewise easy to prove; but it is sometimes very slight, especially after frequent repetition of the experiment. In the first half-hour after birth it is utterly wanting. New-born animals are accordingly deaf at the beginning.

On the other hand, it was at once demonstrable that all healthy Guinea-pigs an hour after birth, even those born some days before their time, respond to the most varied noises, both loud and soft—e. g., clapping of hands, by a quiver of the whole body; at first often by a spring and by movements that seem like attempts to flee. This behavior can have its origin only in heredity.

The reflex arc from the auditory nerve to the motor nerves has been so frequently used by their ancestors, when in moments of danger a noise made flight advisable, that the representatives of the present generation, without as yet any knowledge of danger, quiver at the first noise that comes. Even in the human babe of a few days old the starting at a sudden sound is a relic of this fright, and the same is true of adult human beings and horses. The first movement of the eyelid upon sudden noiseless sight-impressions is, on the contrary, to be explained differently, as I showed above (page 28); because the movements of flight, the starting and the drawing back of the head, are wanting in the beginning.

New-born Guinea-pigs are especially sensitive to sounds of slight intensity. They recognize their mother by hearing on the first day of their life, even when she grunts quite softly and interruptedly, whereas they do not recognize her by sight after four or five days, as I found (1878) by a series of laborious experiments. As, moreover, the voice of the mother and that of the other little ones of the same litter produces a direct movement toward the source of the sound, when the members of the family have been separated, the direction from which the sound comes must be perceived on the first day.

The same is true of new-born swine. For Spalding observed that, at the age of only a few minutes, if they are removed several feet from their mother, they soon find their way back to her, guided apparently by the grunting she makes in answer to their squealing. The mother, in one case that was observed, got up in less than an hour and a half after giving birth to the young, and went off to feed; the young ones went around and tried in every way to get nourishment, followed the mother and sucked while she ate standing. One of the young ones was put in a bag the moment it was born and kept in the dark till it was seven hours old. Then it was placed outside the sty, a distance of ten feet from where the sow lay concealed inside the house. The pig soon 'recog-

nized' the low grunting of its mother, went along outside the sty, struggling to get under or over the lower bar.
At the end of five minutes it succeeded in forcing itself
through under the bar, at one of the few places where
that was possible. No sooner in than it went without a
pause into the pig-house to its mother, and was at once
like the others in its behavior. There can be no doubt
that in this search the sensation of sound caused by the
grunting was (for the creature that had not until five
minutes before been exposed to the light) decisive of the
direction to be pursued. Still, smell does not seem to
have been excluded.

Among the animals that hear well at the very beginning must be counted the chicken just from the egg.
For soon after leaving the shell, as soon as it can run, it
follows the cluck of the hen; and even beforehand, in
the egg after the shell has begun to burst, it responds
by peeping to sounds of that kind. If it remains for a
day or two in the dark after it has been hatched in the
incubator, and is then exposed to the light at a distance
of nine or ten feet from a box in which a brooding-hen
is concealed, it will, after chirping one or two minutes,
betake itself straight to the box, following the call of the
hen, though it has never seen and never before heard
her. This takes place, too, when it involves the overcoming of obstacles in the grass, the passage over uneven ground, when the little creatures are not in condition to stand on their feet. Even chickens deprived of
sight from the first follow blindly the call of the clucking hen when they come within five or six feet of her.
Mr. Spalding, who conducted both these experiments,
also made chickens deaf before they left the shell by

sealing their ears with several folds of gummed paper, uncovered their ears again after two or three days, set them free within call of the hen which was separated from them by a board, and then saw that, after turning around a few times, they ran straight to the spot whence came the first sound they had ever heard. To them, therefore, the first sound-sensation could not be empty or meaningless. It became at once perception, and inherited memory asserted itself in a psycho-motor way. So thinks Spalding. But I have been able to prove in the case of thirty chickens hatched in an incubator, from one to three days out of the shell, that when food had been placed before them several times and a knocking upon wood made at the same time, they generally ran, every time I knocked in their neighborhood, to the spot whence the noise issued, although there was no food there. They had, therefore, recognized the direction of the sound already, and had learned something, or at least they had associated that special sound with the food. For they did not leave their place for other noises—e. g., whistling or the clucking of the hen, which they had never before heard; but they listened instantly to the clucking when I brought several clucking-hens successively into the neighborhood unseen by them, and they started at a loud report without moving from the spot. Besides, it is questionable whether the chickens with ears sealed were actually deaf, and whether they had not heard the voice of the hen before the stopping of the ears. The chick peeps before the shell has a crack in it, as I often perceived; has, therefore, heard its own voice, certainly, before emerging from the shell, and possibly the voices of others likewise.

At all events, the hearing of chickens just out of the
shell, and of many new-born mammals, is vastly superior
to that of the just-born human babe, both in regard to
the discrimination of pitch and loudness of sound, and
in respect to the perception of kinds of sound, the direction and perhaps the duration. It must be the case that
the normal human being at birth hears nothing, then
hears individual sounds indistinctly, then hears much
indistinctly, and very gradually hears distinctly an individual sound out of the number of those indistinctly
heard, finally hears much distinctly, and distinguishes
strong, high tones earlier than deep ones. Every mother
loses many thousands of words that she speaks, whis-
pers, or sings to her child, without the child's hearing a
single one of them, and she says many thousand words
to him before he understands one. But if she did not
do it, the child would learn to speak much later and with
much more difficulty.

CHAPTER III.

FEELING.

THE observations concerning feeling in the newly-
born and the infant relate chiefly to sensibility to contact, to the first perceptions of touch, and to sensibility
to temperature.

1. Sensibility of the Newly-born to Contact.

The mature new-born child is known to be less sensitive to painful impressions than are adults. But it
would be a mistake to infer from this a condition of

anæsthesia or analgesia. For apart from anomalous cases, as of new-born children apparently dead, screaming and movements can be elicited from children and animals just born, when they are for the first time quiet and motionless, by pinching the skin; or, in the case of a child, by slapping the upper part of the thigh. I have convinced myself most fully of this in regard to children born at the right time, and prematurely born animals some minutes after birth, but at the same time I was convinced that the expressions of pain lack by a great deal the intensity and duration they have in older children. In this respect the newly-born resembles the fœtus, differing from it, however, to this extent, that immediately after pulmonic respiration begins, every sort of irritation of the skin produces stronger reflexes. Often the reflex mechanism starts into activity at once, the first time air is breathed. The clock was already wound up, as it were, but the pendulum gets its regular swing only through respiration. Before this it oscillated temporarily and with breaks, urged only by weak impulsions. By the act of birth the central nervous system is first literally awakened. And there is nothing against the assumption that the first contact, pressure in the act of birth, causes pain. I have twice heard a child scream whose head only was as yet born, and the expression of countenance in this half-born condition was one of extreme discomfort. The compression of the body, and the compression of the skull that had just preceded, probably awakened the child out of its intra-uterine sleep.

That rude contact in the act of birth may cause pain, in the strict sense of the word, to the mature fœtus, is probable, because the fœtus may in the same circumstances experience pleasure; for when I put into the mouth of the screaming child, whose head alone was as yet born, an ivory pencil or a finger, the child began to suck, opened its eyes, and seemed, to judge from its countenance, to be " most agreeably affected " (cf. p. 32).

Since in adults the sensibility of the skin and of the mucous membrane varies greatly according to the number of nerve-extremities of the part of the skin that is tested, we are especially interested to know whether such differences in sensibility to contact are already manifest in the newly-born. Kussmaul, whose experiments of the year 1859 were repeated and supplemented by Genzmer, 1873, was the first to investigate this question experimentally. He found several facts that indicate the hereditary character of certain differences. I will give the results of these observers on this point along with my own.

Tongue.—Tickling the tip of the tongue on the upper surface with a smooth glass rod occasions sucking movements; meantime the edges of the tongue curve upward on both sides of the rod and the lips protrude like a snout. At the same time appears the pantomime that indicates the sensation "sweet." When the middle of the tongue is touched on the upper surface, the eyes are shut tight, the nostrils and the corners of the mouth are raised; there is no sucking. Tickle the root of the tongue and of the palate, and the results are choking, opening the mouth wide, sticking out the tongue, lifting of the larynx, increased secretion of saliva, pantomime for "bitter" corresponding to the expression of nausea in adults.

These differences in the reflex movements and the sensations, according to the part of the tongue tickled by the rod, whether the tip of the tongue, the middle, or the root, may be regarded as established in general, but can not be proved in every individual case. Thus movements do not invariably follow the touching of the middle of the tongue. I have often been unable to elicit any movements at all from new-born children by using the glass rod. Yet in most cases children act exactly like just-born rabbits and Guinea-pigs in this respect, sucking at the rod when it presses in front, and pushing it out when it presses in the back part of the cavity of the mouth. When an infant has eaten enough, it does not suck at all, and when tired it sucks irregularly and feebly. But the results obtained in regard to new-born children whose stomachs are empty leave no doubt that even before birth the two paths from the sensory nerves of the tongue to the beginning of the motor nerves of the tongue, the nervus hypoglossus, and from there to its extremities in the tongue, are developed and passable, and that the sensibility of the upper surface of the tongue— from the tip to the root—to contact is, like that of the palate, inborn and already considerable, entirely apart from sensibility to taste. That along with the sucking at the rod there should be movements of swallowing is a further consequence of that practicability of the reflex path established before birth in the swallowing of the amniotic fluid. But none will assume the existence of the sensations " bitter " and " sweet " at the mere touching of the tongue, for they do not appear in such conditions even in adults. The mimetic movement for " sweet " is rather that of satisfaction associated with the agreeable feeling that comes with sucking, and the mimetic movement for "bitter" is that of discomfort associated with the disagreeable feeling manifested by choking.

Lips.—The sensibility of the lips to contact is great immediately after birth, for even very faint touches of them with a feather produce (on the sixth day) starting or movements of sucking, provided the newly-born are awake and hungry. Especially stroking of the lips with the finger easily produces sucking.

But I have not seen these sucking movements appear invariably in mature children just born or in animals. A machine-like certainty in their appearance is wanting, probably because those just born are not in every case hungry. The situation of the human fœtus makes it easy for the lips to be touched by the hands long before birth, and the swallowing of the amniotic fluid presupposes a streaming of it over the edges of the lips and so a frequent excitation of the nerve-extremities.

The reflex sensibility of the upper lip even outside the red border, which is surprising on the first day, I found also in the seventh week, when the touching of the lip produced an animated play of feature perceptibly greater than in adults.

Mucous Membrane of the Nose.—Irritation of the mucous membrane of the nose causes, in the mature newly-born, strong reflexes. The vapor of acetic acid and of ammonia occasions violent sneezing, or corrugation of the forehead, or at least blinking, sometimes rubbing of the face with the hands. Tickling the inner surface of the wing of the nose produces movements of the eyelids, stronger and appearing sooner on the side tickled than on the other. If the irritation is increased, the child moves its head and puts its hands toward its face. Sometimes, too, there is a secretion of tears, which is the more remarkable as children generally shed no tears in the first days of life.

The reflex excitement of the lachrymal nerves (ramus lacrymalis nervi trigemini) and the reflex secretion from the nerve-extremities in the mucous membrane of the nose outward, are accordingly possible at a surprisingly early period. Here we have, besides, a case of inborn reflex activity of a gland within the domain of one and the same nerve; for the centripetal and the centrifugal (secretory) fibers, which go to the tear-gland, belong to the fifth cranial nerve (trigeminus).

The great sensibility of the nasal mucous membrane to contact is, I must add, not present until the last weeks before birth, as children born at seven months make only doubtful responsive movements. Yet this sensibility has been found to be just as great in a child born at eight months as in those born at the right time. It is a purely hereditary peculiarity. Since there is hardly any occasion within the womb for an excitement of the inner surface of the nostril, this reflex arc from the nasal branches of the fifth cranial nerve to the face-nerve (facialis) must be a very firmly established one.

The same is true of the reflex paths that go from the extremities of the trigeminus in the nasal mucous membrane to the spinal motor nerves, inasmuch as a regular shaking has been observed by me to follow upon a gentle touch of the nasal mucous membrane. In the first three months of the second year, my

9

boy one day accidentally touched the septum of his
nose with a raveled string. He at once made a wry
face (excitement of the facialis), did not cry out,
but shook, throwing his body violently this way and
that, as if the certainly very disagreeable sensation of
tickling in that spot were to be *shaken off*.

*Conjunctiva and Cornea of the Eye and the Eye-
lid.*—If the conjunctiva, the edge of the cornea, or an
eyelash be touched in the newly-born, a closure of the
lid follows. Which of these parts are the most sensitive is matter of dispute. Kussmaul thinks the lashes,
but Genzmer could touch these three or four times in
some children without causing closing of the lid, whereas the closure never failed when the cornea was touched,
and generally touching of the conjunctiva was followed
by a bilateral closing of the lids. If we consider the
fact that in adults the lashes can be touched without
even an inclination to close the lid, but not so the conjunctiva or the edge of the cornea, we can not agree with
Kussmaul in this case. I find also in new-born Guinea-
pigs and in chickens just out of the shell the periphery
of the cornea more sensitive to contact than the lashes
or the lids and their edges. In all three cases, however,
closing of the lid appears soon after birth, most quickly
of all upon the touching of the cornea.

Blowing in the face of new-born children through a
tube also causes closing of the lid, but only when the
cornea or the conjunctiva or the lashes are reached by
the air, and the eye of the side that is blown upon is
shut tighter and more quickly than the other.

From my experiments upon new-born, normal
chickens and Guinea-pigs, it appears that the closing of

the lid does not follow quite so promptly immediately after birth as it does later. Still, the interval during which the inactivity of the reflex can be recognized, without arrangements for measuring the time, is very short, since with chickens, e. g., only a few hours after leaving the shell, the nictitating membrane is pushed forward when I touch the corner of the eye.

In a babe of eight days the eye shuts, when I touch the upper lid without touching the lashes; but in one of eleven days the closing of the lid upon the touching of the conjunctiva is considerably slower than in adults (p. 26).

On the fiftieth and fifty-fifth days the lightest touch of an eyelash produces an instant closing of the lid. In contrast with this sensitiveness stands the fact already mentioned (p. 27), that the child in the bath, during the first weeks of life, keeps its eyes open even when luke-warm water touches the cornea. In the seventeenth week the eyes were closed if even a drop of water touched the lashes. The persistent keeping of the eyes open in spite of wetting, at a considerably earlier period, which always surprised me afresh, considering the great sensitiveness of the cornea to the touch of the finger, suggests the surmise that even before birth the eyes have been accustomed to contact with liquid, through being sprinkled with the amniotic fluid, and so have sometimes been opened. The embryo chick occasion-ally opens its eyes many days before leaving the shell, as I perceived.

On the whole, it appears that this reflex arc from the trigeminus to the facialis is capable of performing its function before birth, inasmuch as the reflex closing

of the eye upon being touched takes place immediately
at birth even in animals born prematurely, and is thus
an ancient inheritance; but sprinkling with water, as
in the case of the adult, is not equal, as a reflex stimulus,
to a dry touch; on the other hand, blowing induces a
vigorous closing of the lid, and even sneezing, in the
very young infant as well as in the one of six
months.

Nose.—When the tip of the nose is touched, the
new-born child shuts both eyes tight; if one wing of
the nose is touched he closes, generally, only the eye on
the side touched; at a stronger irritation both eyes are
shut, the head being meanwhile somewhat drawn back:
these being inborn reflexes of the nature of defense.

Palm of the Hand.—Put a finger into the hand of
a new-born babe, and his hand closes around it. A fillip
of the finger against the hand produces a withdrawal of
the latter, and very likely a movement of the other arm.
But I find the sensibility of the palm of the hand to be
less than that of the skin of the face, for rude touches
of the hand may often fail to call forth reflex movements.

Sole of the Foot.—Touching the sole of the foot of
a new-born child causes spreading of the toes; slapping
the sole causes a backward bending of the foot, a bending of the knee and of the hip joint. If the stimulus
be greater, the same movements are generally made in
addition, in the same order, with the other leg. The
prick of a needle most easily causes, in the newly-born,
reflex movements of pain, from the sole of the foot outward, viz., restlessness and screaming, but the time
that elapses between the first touch and the beginning

of the movement—the reflex period—is longer than in
adults, and extends to two seconds.

The skin of the forearm and of the leg, in the newly-born, has an inferior sensibility to contact; that of the
shoulders, the breast, the abdomen, the back, the upper
part of the thigh, is less sensitive still. If the new-born
child is not merely touched, but slapped with the hand,
then general movements take place, often screaming and
persistent restlessness, which indicate that the stronger
sensation of touch has become painful. Yet, according
to Genzmer, the prematurely born do not react at all
upon moderate pricks of a needle, during the first days;
the mature newly-born, immediately after birth, do so
indeed only faintly or not at all, but after one or two
days they do so plainly. This shows the dependence
of the force of the stimulus upon the number of the
nerve-extremities that are affected. The slap reaches
many, the prick few extremities of the cutaneous nerves.
But the sensibility to pricks of the needle, which is
greater from the beginning in those born too late, increases noticeably during the first week.

I found in the case of my boy that the sensibility of
the skin in different places was not so unequal in the
first twenty-two hours as it was later, but it was surprisingly great; for the child reacted by movements upon
the slightest touches of his face. On the second and
third days, for instance, he started with a movement of
the arms at gentle touches. On the seventh day the
child is not waked by loud sound-stimulus, but is waked
by a touch on the face. On the forty-first day, when
the child had gone to sleep in my arms, I laid him on
a sheet and then drew the sheet slowly away. At the

first pull, both arms were moved quickly and simultaneously toward the head and back again, without the child's waking. Here we have not a localized touch, but a general slight agitation, calling forth the same reflex movement as a touch or a sound would do. In the fourteenth week, too, a sudden touch of the sleeping child occasioned a quick throwing up of both arms.

According to this, the reflex excitability for local tactile stimulus is undoubtedly greater in the first weeks than it is later. In the second year of life I found it a good deal dulled.

I may mention here also two remarkably sensitive regions in the skin of the infant. In the second quarter of the first year it appeared that the greatest disquiet, the loudest crying, the most distressed expression of countenance, as the child was turning and tossing hither and thither, at once vanished when a person put his little finger into the auditory canal. The child's eye assumed a peculiar expression of strained attention. If this sudden alteration had not invariably taken place even when the child was screaming, one might think rather of an acoustic than of a tactile excitation. Or, could the diminution of the loudness of his cries through the stopping of the ear attract his attention? In that case we can not understand why the child that is not crying but is quivering in the bath becomes quiet. For the rest, the experiment failed almost invariably after the end of the first six months; from that time on it always failed, and Kroner found that not all newborn children were quiet when the external auditory canal was tickled, but that some put their hands to the face and not to the ear.

How sensitive the dry skin of the forehead is to wet, is often shown by the reflex movements of babes at church-baptism. I once saw an infant of thirty-eight days, which remained tolerably quiet through the whole baptismal ceremony, make a sudden movement of both arms at once toward the head, without screaming, as soon as the lukewarm water trickled on its forehead. At the second wetting, directly afterward, there was a similar convulsive movement almost as of repulsion; and at the third, the child sneezed. According to this, the reflex excitability of the surface of the face in regard to wet is greater in the sixth week than it is in adult age. The adult can not be stirred to so vigorous reflex action by such a wetting as this of the christening with a few drops of water, although he may be by sprinkling.

Yet it seems difficult to determine the exact time when the great reflex excitability to contact manifested by the above facts, has so far subsided that a degree of excitability corresponding to the normal condition of adults is reached.

Apart from hereditary individual inequalities, and the frequent morbid development of the reflexes in early infancy into convulsions, the time when the reflexes begin to be inhibited is of the greatest account, no less than is the wearing out of the nerve-paths by frequent repetition of the excitements, in regard to the ultimate decline of the sensibility to touch. In the very earliest period, and before birth, the nerve-paths are not yet so easily passable as after repeated reflex excitation; hence the longer time occupied in the reflex. It appears from numerous experiments of mine upon unborn animals, and of Soltmann upon new-born and very young ones, that the sensibility of the nerves of the skin, estimated by the ease with which the reflexes take place upon slight stimulus, is continually on the increase, up to a certain point of time that may be designated as the beginning of inhibition of the reflex. But it is to be observed here that, while the central paths are traversed more and more easily through frequent use of them (and more rapidly, up to a certain limit), the peripheral extremities of the cutaneous nerves must be dulled through the inevitable stimulus of contact of wet and of cold, soon after the reflex activity has attained its maximum. For the permanent excitations of the skin of the infant must diminish the excitability of the nerves of the skin. What is gained, therefore, in central excitability (cranial and spinal activity and excitability) is lost in peripheral, and it is very probable that the reason of the slighter sensibility to pain in the newly-born is of a central character, because in the long repose before birth the extremities of the cutaneous nerves may have become very excitable while the brain was not yet active.

2. The First Perceptions of Touch.

From sensibility to contact it is a great step to the perception of touch. To the original consciousness belonging to sensation is added the experience of succession, and with that the consciousness of time; then the simultaneousness of the sensations of contact, and with this the consciousness of space; finally, the consciousness of the causal connection of two or more contacts that have come to consciousness in time and space, and with this the idea of the body touched.

If the new-born child is slapped, it has a sensation, for it cries out; but it knows nothing of the place where it is struck, and nothing of the cause of the blow. If it is struck again after an interval, then there is the possibility of a recollection, and so of a distinction of time. If the blow falls frequently upon different parts of the skin in like fashion, then distinctions of space will also come gradually into the child's consciousness besides the mere sensations of pain, since different extremities of the skin, different nerve-fibers, are each time excited by the blow. If the blow is renewed with intervals of freedom from pain, then the hand that strikes will gradually, only after considerable time, to be sure, be pushed away or avoided as the cause of the pain. If the sensation of contact is, on the contrary, pleasurable, then it will be desired. In both cases movements must be executed, and these lead again to new sensations of contact, which may be even more important in the genesis of mind.

Thus, the sensation of touch in the tips of the fingers, upon the first successful attempts at seizing, must assuredly be very interesting to the child, otherwise he would not, after grasping at and getting hold of an object, observe his own fingers persistently and attentively even when (in the twenty-third week) one hand accidentally gets hold of the other in moving the hands about. Here the discrimination between the mutual contact of two points of the skin of his own body and the contact of one point of the skin with a foreign object is undoubtedly a great step toward the cognition of the self (des Ich).

The earliest association, in time, of one sensation of

contact with another, is probably that which is given in the act of nursing. When the nipple comes between the lips, there follows upon this sensation of touch the sensation of wet (the milk) in the mouth (to which the new sensation of sweetness also joins itself). Herein is given the first perception of touch. The newly-born makes one of his first experiences, namely, this, that upon a certain contact of the lips follows a different, an agreeable sensation in the mouth. Hence the contact with the lips is desired. Every similar soft touch of the lips is therefore agreeable. But how far from being firm the association of the space-element with the time-element is, appears in this, that the newly-born sometimes, as I observed, after "trying" at the breast, take the skin of the breast near the nipple into the mouth and suck at it a long time. And how late in being established is the causal connection between the lip-contact with the nipple and the sensation of liquid sweetness in the mouth when nursing, is manifest from the fact that the infant keeps up for many months the habit of sucking his own fingers and foreign objects.

From this it appears, at the same time, how much more easily and more strongly the time-succession of two sensations impresses itself than does the connection in space or the causal connection. For the first act of sucking, after the first contact of the lips, brings countless other sucking movements in its train. Because it induced an agreeable sensation (of sweetness), it remains in the memory. The first causal connection of the lip-contact with the nipple, localized in space, with the sweet taste of milk, occurs not only later and so with more difficulty, but also is more easily forgotten. Else, after seeing that the desired sensation of sweetness and the flow of the milk occur only on sucking at the well-distinguished breast or the nursing-bottle, the child would not keep up so long the useless sucking at every object, capable of being sucked, that is brought to the mouth (even the fingers) when the feeling of hunger begins. However agreeable to the child the sucking at the fingers may be, his hunger is not lessened by it, and the sweet taste is not induced. Yet he sucks away obstinately, as if he thought the milk might be drawn from the fingers too. The fact that the milk in the breast is not visible may help to keep up the physiological error, and it would be worth while to investigate whether infants that take milk exclusively from the breast of the mother continue the useless sucking of all sorts of objects longer than do those who draw their milk exclusively from transparent bottles.

The habit of useless sucking seems the more strange, as the infant shows very early a sort of activity of understanding in this field ; shows it by unambiguous movements, viz., by opening wide the eyes at sight of the mother's breast.

3. Sensibility to Temperature.

Concerning sensibility to differences of temperature the observations are few.

Whether the sudden cooling of the child immediately after birth, which may amount to several degrees, occasions a *sensation* of cold, is a question with regard to mature newly-born children, as well as the prematurely born, even in the cases where they shiver. For although an unpleasant feeling is certainly associated with the with-

drawal of warmth, yet in this particular case the possibility is lacking of *comparing* temperatures. Within the
womb the constant, unfelt temperature of the fœtus is
somewhat higher than that of the mother. From the
first instant of complete birth there begins a general
and probably a pretty uniform cooling, because the air
that surrounds the just-born child has only one temperature, and the child is wet all over the surface of its body,
and so the evaporation must cool off the whole of the
skin. Now, the great difference in the temperature of
the skin, before and after birth, will be perceptible, in
part indirectly, through contraction of the vessels, and
in part directly, through peripheral excitation of the
nerves, but at first only as an unpleasant feeling. As
soon as the warm bath, into which the newly-born is
usually dipped, brings back the skin nearly to the temperature that has been kept constant for months within
the womb, the excitement (which had never before existed) of the nerves susceptible to temperature subsides,
the contraction of the capillaries of the skin ceases, the
feeling of discomfort passes away, and the first agreeable sensation of comfortable warmth is given ; in general, the first agreeable sensation since birth, for most
children. It is agreeable, through the contrast with the
refrigeration, as the altered physiognomy of the newly-
born in a bath of 36° C. shows, in comparison with that
of the still wet, shivering, screaming, just-born babe, to
whose head the vernix still adheres. Besides, I saw—
at the second bath—that the dry fingers were spread
out, a thing that could not be caused by the moisture.
As early as the seventh day the expression of pleasure
in the widely-opened eyes, immediately after the bath,

was different. No sensuous impression of any kind is capable of calling forth such an expression of satisfaction, at this period, in the infants observed by me. Still, in addition to the sensation of warmth, there is the freedom from swaddling-clothes which are often associated with a disagreeable irritation of the skin.

In any case, the feeling of warmth and the feeling of cold are plainly manifest after the first bath, neither of these having been distinguished as such before birth, or probably directly after birth.

It is likely, also, that the powerful effect of a sudden general refrigeration upon the nerves of the skin, through the dipping of the just-born babe into ice-cold water, which has been made use of with the greatest success in restoring to life children apparently still-born, is attended with discomfort, even where the danger of strangling has been obviated. If the breathing has begun, this very strong stimulus produces a remarkable effect, the low whimpering being changed to a loud outcry. This cry is the same as that which follows upon a vigorous (painful) slap. From my experiences with newly-born animals, which cry out lustily on the application of electricity to the skin, and at other kinds of strong cutaneous stimulus, I can but regard this outcry as an utterance of pain; but it does not follow that the cooling of the child just born produces a sensation of cold. This can only come, as has been said, through contrast, where the possibility of comparison exists; therefore, after the first warm bath. The first cooling produces merely an unpleasant feeling.

We have but few experiences also with regard to *local warming* and *cooling*.

About twenty children were tested by Genzmer, who touched different parts of the surface of the skin with an ice-cold iron rod, and saw lively reflex movements invariably appear. But, as the stimulus of touch was not excluded in this case, his further experiments of wetting and then blowing on the skin in special places are of rather more account. This sort of stimulus, applied to the sole of the foot, produced withdrawal of the foot; applied to the hollow of the hand, it produced closing, then withdrawal of the hand. When the cheek was cooled the head was turned to one side. Unfortunately, nothing is said of the age of the children. In such cases the age should be reckoned by hours, and when new experiments are instituted, the blowing, which of itself acts as a reflex stimulus, is to be avoided; and, above all, the previous temperature of the skin ought to be determined. Little children very often have cold hands and feet without making any complaint. Possibly this in itself causes less reflex sensibility to the stimulus of cold and greater to the stimulus of warmth.

It is known that even quite young infants become restless and cry readily when they are wet anywhere with cold water. This dislike of the local withdrawal of warmth persists, during the first years of life, until at length the knowledge that a washing with cold water is refreshing overcomes the fear of cold (in the third year).

Moreover, how sensitive individual children are, in perfectly sound health, in regard to the discrimination of cold and warmth, was evident to me in the experiment of ordering the daily bath to be made colder gradually. The water could be cooled to $32\frac{1}{2}°$ C. with-

out lessening the child's pleasure. But every time the
water was reduced to the neighborhood of $31\frac{1}{4}°$ C. or
less, the child screamed uninterruptedly until warmer
water was added. The temperature of the skin, therefore, was presumably very near $32°$ C. But when the
child was two and a half years old, he laughed and uttered joyous sounds in water of the temperature of the
room—in a cold bath, therefore, such as formerly made
him cry; and in his fourth year he objected to taking
a warm bath $36°$ C. In the seventh month he became
pale, always, at being put into water from $34°$ to $35°$ C.,
but regained his ordinary color within one or two minutes. The case here is not one of direct contraction of
the capillaries of the skin through sudden withdrawal
of warmth, but is a case of vaso-motor reflex action,
because it was precisely the skin of the face, which was
not dipped in the water, that became most pale, and
this happened as late as the age of more than two years.

The sensibility of the mucous membrane of the
mouth, of the tongue, of the lips, to cold and warmth
is also surprisingly great in many infants during the
first days. If the nursing-bottle is but a little more
than blood-warm, it is refused, often with violent screaming; and if it is some degrees colder than the milk sucked
from the breast of the mother, it is refused likewise.
Therefore, in experiments designed to test the gustatory sensibility in new-born children, the liquids employed must have the exact temperature of $37°$ C. Yet
infants learn easily to drink water and milk of the temperature of the room they live in, if their drink is given
to them, when they are hungry, only at this temperature.

The sensibility of the lips to differences of temperature in liquids is in any case determined by the constant temperature of the amniotic fluid before birth, and of the mother's milk after birth.

The difference in the neutral point of temperature between the mucous membrane of the mouth (tongue), and of the skin (e. g., the hand) which in the adult amounts to 5° or 6° C. (whereas before birth it is zero), can in general hardly establish itself in the first days of life. The tongue and the mucous membrane of the mouth maintain through life almost the same neutral point they had before birth; whereas the external skin only gradually gets its varying neutral points through unequal refrigeration.

<hr />

CHAPTER IV.

TASTE.

THE observations concerning the sense of taste relate chiefly to the question whether the newly-born have a sensibility to taste such as makes possible at once the distinction between different savors. Next comes the comparison of gustatory impressions already recognized as different. Then follow some statements as to taste in newly-born animals.

1. Sensibility to Taste in the Newly-born.

We know, from mimetic reflex movements of the same sort as those of adults, that the newly-born, and even those born a month or two before their time, react upon substances that have a taste, when these are introduced into the mouth by means of a pencil. Kussmaul tested the sense of taste in this way in more than twenty newly-born children, making use of cane-sugar, quinine, common salt, and tartaric acid. Genzmer repeated these experiments with twenty-five children, most of whom he observed immediately after birth and from three to six days after, some up to the sixth week. Kussmaul found that the salt, the quinine, and the acid occasioned grimaces as an expression of dislike, but with much variation in the manifestation in individual cases. The sugar, on the other hand, produced movements of sucking. The liquids to be tested were all warmed, so that the reaction upon them can not be ascribed to a feeling of cold in the mouth.

As the acid, however, acted on the mucous membrane, it might cause pain in addition to the sour taste; yet the children did not cry out, and after the edges of the tongue were touched with a crystal of tartaric acid, the grimaces appeared instantaneously in two new-born children, while the crystal placed in the center of the upper surface of the tongue caused no change in the countenance for a considerable time, until the acid was sufficiently dissolved to reach the edges of the tongue that were sensitive to it. So that it is the sour taste, and not an incidental painful effect of the acid, that elicits the "sour" look. The suspicion that the latter is generated only by excitation of the nerves of taste through the acid, is not pertinent; accordingly, we have here a certain ability to distinguish sensations of taste, active directly after birth, before anything has been swallowed except the amniotic fluid swallowed before birth.

10

The psychogenetic importance of this fact demands a more detailed examination of the observations on which it rests.

Kussmaul found that the newly-born sometimes respond to the taste of sugar with the mimetic expression for bitter. It might thus be thought that the sensations were not distinguished, but were responded to irregularly, now with one, now with another, reflex movement. But the circumstances under which the reflex takes place are not irregular. "Some made a wry face at the first introduction of the solution of sugar, while they took in the rest of it with satisfaction. It was not the sensation of taste in itself apparently that was in fault, but another psychical experience, the surprise caused by the sudden effect on the sensitive nerves. One of the children even started directly with fright, when it came so suddenly to taste the unfamiliar liquid (which was warmed). Children that had reacted strongly upon quinine, commonly made a grimace again, or several times in succession, when a solution of sugar was introduced, but with decreasing animation, until finally a comfortable sucking and swallowing were substituted. This accords with the experiences that every adult has in his own case, viz., that a very bitter or nauseous taste does not allow itself to be at once supplanted by a sweet one, but at every fresh stimulus of the gustatory sense by substances of different savors, it recurs with decreasing force."

These deductions I must agree with, in every respect. I saw my child, the first day of his life, lick off the powdered cane-sugar that was put on the nipple, whereas he licked nothing else; so the sweet alone seemed desirable. On the second day, however, he licked at the mother's milk just as he had done at the sugar, with a calm, satisfied expression of countenance. When this child later received salted food and food of different kinds, the first thing that was remarkable at every new sensation of taste was the expression of surprise; and, as late as the second quarter of his second year (nay, occasionally in his fourth year), he would shudder, shut his eyes and distort his face in the strangest fashion, when he tasted a new food that was agreeable to him in spite of his grimaces; for he often wanted it directly afterward, and took it then soon with the expression of satisfaction. On the other hand, it was often easy to persuade the child, after he had learned to speak (as a hypnotized adult may be persuaded), that a sourish or generally unattractive food, which he at first refused, was very pleasant to the taste, so that he would then want more of it. It is necessary to distinguish sharply from the very first, on the one hand, the expression for the disagreeable manifested at the sudden new sensation, and the expression, not appearing till after this, of the agreeable that is excited by the pleasant taste; and on the other hand, the expression for the disagreeable at the bitter, the salt, or the sour taste, and that for the agreeable at the sweet taste.

It is certain, from all observations, that the newly-born distinguish the sensations of taste that are decidedly different from one another, the sweet, sour, and bitter.

But then Genzmer found in his experiments that individuals newly-born responded to an attenuated solution (one quarter to one per cent) of quinine, and one

of vinegar, by sucking movements, just as they did to
a solution of sugar. In one case, indeed, a child on the
first day, as also in the sixth week, sucked at a five-per-
cent solution of quinine without any sign of dislike (Kussmaul's solution was of four per cent). If the solution was
more concentrated, the child made a wry face of complaint, as the others were wont to do at a weaker solution (beyond one degree), then began to cry, and made
it manifest that the disagreeable nature of the taste had
become perceptible to him.

Inasmuch as it has been established that there are
great individual differences among the newly-born in
their gustatory sensibility, and that, allowing for a considerable blunting of this through experimenting, there was
only in the case of individuals in the first week a refine-
ment of taste for differences in intensity, the hypothesis
is forced upon us that, in the case of the attenuated solutions the gustatory sensations of many children were too
weak to be found either agreeable or disagreeable ; that
new-born children especially are not yet in condition to
press the substance to be tasted against the hard palate
with the upper surface of the tongue, whereby the distribution to the end-organs of the nerves (these, moreover, being probably less numerous in the little tongue)
is favored and hastened. In the case of these attenuated solutions there remains, then, only the effect upon
the sucking-mechanism, as in the case of touching the
tongue with the finger. There is no need of the addi-
tional hypothesis that a weak bitter or sour taste is
agreeable to individuals among the newly-born, in order
to understand that the reaction upon a weak bitter or
sour is not accompanied with the same animated reflex

movements as a strong stimulus induces, but is accompanied with sucking. In general, the newly-born make a wry face after the introduction of a three to five per cent quinine solution; they shut the eyes tight, the throat is convulsively contracted, the mouth is opened wide, and the liquid is ejected along with the mucus of the mouth, which is generally secreted very scantily, but in this case abundantly. The "bitter" expression of countenance is thus quite a different one from the "sweet," even on the first day of life. But it is different also from the "sour," as in the case of adults, since in the movements of choking the corners of the mouth are drawn sharply up and sidewise; so they are, according to Genzmer, at the introduction of pretty strong acetic acid (which any way is unsuited to such experiments on account of its smell). The strongest solutions caused, besides, in his experiments, agitation and screaming for the most part; sugar, on the contrary, is tasted with satisfaction by all newly-born children, when it acts in sufficient quantity, after the first surprise is over. About this there is no doubt.

Since very sour and very bitter substances call forth in the newly-born different reflex movements under circumstances otherwise similar, and very sweet substances call forth quite different movements still, therefore these various gustatory qualities are distinguished.

The fact that weak solutions of bitter and of sour are by some taken in much the same way as weak solutions of sweet, with sucking movements, with no sign of discomfort, is explained by the slight sensibility of the tongue for degrees of intensity. The sensations of contact caused by the substances to be tasted, sensations which of themselves start sucking movements, overpower at that time the weak sensations of taste. But what to one child tastes strong, to another tastes weak. For many children one per cent of acetic acid was too sour, while they would suck away at a two-per-cent solution of quinine; with others it was the reverse. This fact, too, is in accord with the above statement.

The association of certain mimetic contractions of muscles with certain sensations of taste is a surprisingly strong one—it is inborn. Children born about two months or more too early are no less sensitive to the gustatory stimuli spoken of than are those born at the right time.

Accordingly, the opinion, often expressed, that the new-born infant possesses only a general sensation of taste, and that the qualitative differences of taste become perceptible to him only through his becoming accustomed to them—this opinion falls to the ground. Were it correct—did every moderate stimulus whatever of the nerves of taste cause sucking movements as a simple reflex, and did any strong stimulus whatever, on the other hand, cause choking, likewise as a simple reflex—then the most intensely sweet taste must be regarded as only a moderate stimulus, and the fact before recognized as established would be inexplicable, that under circumstances alike in other respects the mimetic expression for bitter is different from that for sweet and from that for sour, when the corresponding gustatory stimuli are strong enough.

Kussmaul's inference from his experiments is therefore correct, that the sense of taste in the newly-born is already capable of acting in its characteristic forms of sensation; the sensation received by it is not one altogether undefined and vague.

2. Comparison of the Gustatory Impressions.

The sense of taste seems to be the first of all the senses to yield clear perceptions, to which memory directly attaches itself, as Sigismund rightly pointed out. The gustatory impression of the milk to which the child is accustomed abides, so that a comparison may be made with strange milk. Of this ability to compare the child soon makes use, for, during the whole nursing period and even longer, the taste of sweet is preferred by far to all other tastes, and these others are experienced with signs of disgust when they are strong, and this from the first day on.

Burdach is wrong in affirming that not till the end of the first month does the babe begin to object to medicines, on the ground that then first is the child disagreeably affected by astringent, bitter, salt, sour tastes, whereas at the beginning he takes every liquid— e. g., camomile-tea and tincture of rhubarb, just as willingly as milk, and does not yet manifest choice. If the camomile-tea and the tincture of rhubarb are sweetened, and are not cold or hot, he takes them; but liquids that are not sweet, or that have a strong taste, or that are cold or hot, he does not take so readily as he does milk. The cavity of the mouth is, even for the newly-born, something more than a mere "sucking-organ." Although the food is not so mixed with saliva, by muscular movement, and so brought into contact with the mucous membrane of the mouth as it is later, still it is tasted and especially its temperature is noticed.

In fact, I have found the gustatory sensitiveness toward different degrees of intensity considerably increased very early. Thus, my child on the second day
took, without hesitation, cow's milk diluted with water,
which on the fourth day he stoutly refused. He must
have compared the less degree of sweetness with that of
his mother's milk. But an extremely small quantity of
cane-sugar sufficed to make the bottle acceptable. It
only needed a few grains applied to the mouth of the
bottle.

Now, as bad-tasting medicines generally have some
corrective, especially sugar, added to them, it is not surprising that infants often take them at once without
discrimination. I have repeatedly convinced myself
that this is the case, and at the same time that those
medicines tasted sweet. If they are very sweet—e. g.,
one hundred parts sugar to one part calomel—they are
taken willingly, even by the child of six months and
more; the younger child does not need so great an addition, precisely because it does not discriminate so
nicely, but it rejects strong-tasting substances that are
offered to it without any corrective.

Every new taste occasions in the babe of more than
six months old a play of countenance which at first suggests surprise, then either a desire for more, or disgust.
But very often the food that was at first desired is
ejected after a second trial, with turning away of the
head; and, as has been mentioned (p. 119), that which
at first caused expressions of displeasure is directly afterward desired. Here are at least four different points
to be noticed: 1, the stimulus of the new; 2, the sensation of taste; 3, the sensation of touch and of tempera-

ture in the mouth ; 4, the sense of smell. All four may
act in harmony, but they may also counteract one another so that the child does not know whether the new
thing tastes good to him or not, etc. Where the taste
alone varies in two impressions of like sort, as with sweet
and salt, the child of six months can discriminate accurately at once.

How far the comparison of the gustatory sensations
discriminated may be carried after the weaning of a
child has taken place, is shown, in the case of my child
and some others, by the following observations:

From the one hundred fiftieth day on, the breast was
to be given him only in the night. But after five nights
the child refused to take the breast as hitherto, probably because in the days preceding so much cane-sugar
had been added to the boiled and diluted cow's milk, that
it tasted somewhat sweeter than milk from the breast.

At the end of the twenty-third week the child had a
new nurse, whose milk it took eagerly. Then were
taken, apparently with equal willingness, this milk and
diluted, sweetened cow's milk, as well as meat-broth
with yolk of egg, and yolk of egg beaten up in cow's
milk.

From the one hundred and eighty-fifth day on, no
more nurse's milk. Cow's milk boiled (one part water
out of four parts), with a little egg, seems to relish.
Water-gruel with yolk of egg was taken once, but not
again; leguminous food of that sort is refused after a
single trial.

From the eighth month on, the child was fed almost
exclusively for months on Nestle's "prepared food"
(Kindermehl), which was most agreeable to him. He

utters a cry of joy, as if to make known his pleasure at the good taste, and this more loudly and persistently than over any food thus far tried. It would hardly be possible for an adult, owing to the sameness of the taste, to take for so long a time uninterruptedly, several times a day, nothing but this prepared food.

9th month.—With great surprise—at the new taste—the child took yolk of egg mixed with cane-sugar. He drinks water with liking, and sucks with pleasure at a piece of white bread. But in this the sucking doubtless yields more pleasure than the taste.

11th month.—The child takes, without pleasure, meat-broth with egg that has a slightly salt taste. He rejects obstinately scalded skimmed milk without sugar, but likes dry biscuit.

12th month.—The child is very fastidious (wählerisch) in regard to the taste of his food; refuses farinaceous food except "prepared food" and biscuit. Everything bitter was now, and for the two years following, detested, slightly salt food no longer so.

The idiosyncrasy of antipathy to many articles of food (even in the fourth and fifth years) went so far that even the sight of such food (e. g., peas) called forth lively demonstrations of disgust, even choking movements, a phenomenon exhibited by many children, and one that leads us to infer a largely developed capacity of discrimination in taste and smell.

As to the practical bearing of this, I hold, as a fixed rule—however much it may be at variance with the prejudices of a traditional method of training—that a young child should in no case be constrained to eat food that is distasteful to him. I can see no advantage whatever to the child from such severity, but it may very likely have an injurious effect upon the nutrition and the development of character, even if vomiting does not follow soon after the meal.

The refusal of the little child to eat certain kinds of food is by no means—as Heyfelder thinks it is—naughtiness. The babe is right in refusing to drink sour milk in the first place; and at the critical period of weaning it is not the child that deserves punishment when he rejects the salted food or food hard for him to digest, but the nurse that forces it on him who deserves it. Such constraint first develops often enough an antagonism to some dishes, and general willfulness. This is afterward vainly contended against as idiosyncrasy or naughtiness. But let the child's taste in the beginning have free course—guarding him always against excess—and he will of himself become accustomed to the food of the family. In this matter it should not escape notice that this last presupposes a certain blunting of smell as well as of taste, which the child gains only in the course of years.

3. Taste in Newly-born Animals.

In newly-born animals, also, whose sense of taste I tested, there is certainly a decided preference for substances of certain particular tastes, along with indifference to solutions that are qualitatively unlike and weak to the taste, and the memory of tastes is developed on the first day.

Experiments on little Guinea-pigs, only eight to sixteen hours old, and separated from the mother after two hours, proved to me absolutely that concentrated water-solutions of tartaric acid, soda, glycerine, introduced

into the mouth through glass tubes, are swallowed just
as greedily or eagerly as cow's milk and water, with
vigorous sucking. But then the empty tube, placed
with the end upon the tongue, occasioned just such
sucking. The experiments conducted in this manner
can not, therefore, yield much that can be depended
upon. Touch, as a reflex stimulus to sucking in hungry
new-born creatures, overpowers any taste-stimuli acting
at the same time. Newly-born animals that have eaten
enough do not, however, suck regularly in general.

For this reason another criterion, at least for the
recognition of an agreeable sensation of taste, is of especial value, viz., licking. This must be regarded as a
sure sign of enjoyment of the sweet in the case of new-
born human beings also—they lick persistently sugar,
but not crystals of tartaric acid, or the nipple-shell that
is not sugared.

A Guinea-pig, not yet seventeen hours old, was placed
by me in a glass box along with a bit of oil of thyme,
a bit of camphor, and a piece of sugar-candy. The
creature ran about, stayed longest by the sugar, gnawed
at a corner of that, and thereupon began to lick the
sugar very eagerly. One could see plainly how it
stretched forth the tongue and drew it along the smooth
surface of the crystal. After it had kept up this operation for some minutes, apparently with great satisfaction, I removed it, bandaged both its eyes, and repeated
the experiment after twenty-four hours. To my surprise the animal now again distinguished the sugar, although it had not touched the oil of thyme and the camphor, and although it could not see. This was probably
owing to the smell. The glass and the wood were not

licked, but the sugar was licked just as before, and just as it was after the animal was again allowed the use of its eyes. I have not seen other Guinea-pigs manifest on the first day such decision in taste. But the one instance proves that the sensation of sweet can be discriminated on the first day, can be desired and be found agreeable.

The chick just out of the shell also distinguishes different kinds of food by the taste. For when I placed before a chick boiled white-of-egg, boiled yolk, and millet, it pecked at all three, one after another, as it did at bits of egg-shell, grains of sand, spots and cracks in the wood floor; but only at the yolk-of-egg did it peck often and eagerly. When I took the last away, and then, an hour later than the first trial, placed it again before the chick, the creature ran directly to it and took some of it, whereas at the first trial it had tasted the white-of-egg only once, and had swallowed only one grain of millet, rejecting the rest obstinately afterward as before. This preference of the yolk-of-egg rests accordingly upon discrimination and taste-memory.

New-born animals, therefore, distinguish qualities of taste without having had any other gustatory impressions than those of the amniotic fluid swallowed in the egg.

This remarkable capacity can rest only on inherited recollection—on an *instinct* of taste.

Further experiments in this matter, especially upon newly-born human beings, are urgently to be desired, in order to ascertain in detail, better than hitherto, the gradual increase of sensibility according to the different degrees of concentration (in solution), and the charac-

teristic reflexes for agreeable and disagreeable sensations
of taste.   Only chemically pure, odorless, strong-tasting
substances should be used, in accurately graded quantities, for such experiments; preferably dissolved in lukewarm, distilled water; for sweet tastes, glycerine, cane-
sugar, and sugar-of-milk; for bitter, sulphate of quinine; for salt, cooking-salt; for sour, tartaric acid and
lactic acid ; for alkalines, soda.

CHAPTER V.

SMELL.

THE observations concerning the faculty of smell relate first to the evidence of its existence in the new-born
human being; next to the discrimination of impressions
of smell on the part of the infant.   These are followed
by some statements concerning smell in new-born animals.

1. Faculty of Smell in the Newly-born.

The child can, even in its first days, be constrained,
by strong-smelling substances, to mimetic movements.
Kussmaul has ascertained that new-born children in
sleep, when the odor of asafœtida or of the very bad-
smelling Dippel's-oil enters their nostrils, frequently shut
the eyelids tighter together, distort the face, become
restless, move the head and the arms, awake; and go
to sleep again when the cause of the smell is removed.
Genzmer observed that well developed, lively children,
are brought to screaming by strong impressions of smell.
He made use of the ill-smelling aqua fœtida anti-

hysterica, which was rubbed with a pencil upon the upper edge of the upper lip of sleeping and waking children. The infants made movements of sucking, when but little liquid was put on; of choking, when more was put on; the eyes, too, were screwed up and the countenance was distorted, as after strong gustatory impressions. How many hours old the children were, is not stated.

In these observations the sensation of wetness has been overlooked, and both investigators have failed to consider that in their experiments there was by no means an excitement of the nerves of smell exclusively. The failure of the first to obtain decisive results when he selected waking infants, and the circumstance that only strongly stimulating substances were found efficacious, as well as the appearance of strong reflex movements, points rather to an excitement of the sensitive nerve (the trigeminus) than of the nerve of smell (the olfactory). Still the tests with asafœtida are to be referred to the latter alone. Children born a month too soon likewise react on odorous substances in the above fashion (Kussmaul).

The proof of the existence of the faculty of smell in the newly-born child would be produced, if its mother or nurse would make up her mind to smear her breast with a strong-smelling substance that has no taste, or if some volatile stuff like petroleum, spirits of wine, cologne-water, asafœtida, in small quantity, were put upon a nursing-bottle or a nipple-shell. If the child then refuses to suck at the breast or the bottle that smells of the stuff, and does not refuse the source of milk that has been left in its natural state, then the child can smell. For in case of weak odors of this sort it is not to be assumed that there will be perceptible accompanying excitement of the nasal fibers of the trigeminus. Such experiments are urgently to be wished. A girl babe of eighteen hours obstinately refused the breast upon the nipple of which a little petroleum, or oil-of-amber, had been rubbed, but gladly took the other breast. This experiment of Kroner's alone corresponds to my suggestion given above (made in 1878); only it ought to be repeated with a number of very young children. For the observation that infants in the first days reject the breast of the mother, when this has by accident acquired a strange smell, was not instituted with regard to infants just born. And the fact that many new-born children after having once tasted their mother's milk, refuse for a long time, in spite of hunger and thirst, to take any other food, is not convincing, for this is not a case of sensations of smell exclusively, nor again of children just born.

On the other hand, some of Kroner's observations are decidedly in favor of the view that the normal child can smell, a quarter of an hour after birth, and a few hours or days after. For it turns up its nose and makes a wry face when Dippel's-oil or amber-oil is offered it, and "children several hours old become generally restless, screw the eyelids tight together, open the mouth, and thrust out the tongue."

In all experiments of this kind concerning the sense of smell in the newly-born, care must also be taken that the nostrils shall be perfectly open to the passage of the air. The child must breathe easily with his mouth shut. The filling of the nostrils with amniotic fluid excludes the possibility of a sensation of smell before birth. But directly after the beginning of respiration this liquid is displaced by air, and it is a question whether then the olfactory mucous membrane needs first a longer invigoration by the air before the olfactory cells can be the means of a sensation of smell, or whether a reaction follows immediately upon the inhalation of air that has an odor.

2. Discrimination of Impressions of Smell.

The sense of smell, when it has once been aroused to activity, continues to be of decisive importance to the infant in the choice of food, and this from the beginning. Sensations of smell are present, for the first time, not at the age of four weeks, or from the second month on, as many think, but even in the first days, and the pleasant and unpleasant feelings occasioned by them increase in intensity from day to day. Children of a few weeks sometimes do not take the breast of a nurse whose skin has a disagreeable smell, and they cry out as soon as the breast approaches them. There is no doubt that children born blind very early smell the spoon filled with milk or broth, and the disinclination of many infants, in the first week, to take cow's milk after they have had the breast, must be ascribed to the smell rather than to the taste, since they sometimes refuse the milk when it is brought near them without tasting it. In such a case the decisive experiment would be to hold the child's nose and bandage its eyes, to see whether it would not then take willingly the new food. At all events, the sense of smell in children born blind plays an essential part in the taking of food, and develops its own memory as early as does the sense of taste.

11

Whether the babe, however, knows its sleeping mother in the night by the smell, as animals undoubtedly do, must be left undecided. To me it is probable that the child does not recognize her when it does not see, hear, or feel her.

That the sense of smell is concerned in the seeking of the nipple, on the part of the babe that is merely laid by the nurse but not otherwise assisted (as is the case with animals), also seems to me improbable from my own observations in the lying-in hospital. For the children, indeed, push hither and thither (often with surprising quickness and violence), with the whole head against the breast (like young lambs, kids, calves, foals) with open mouth and intermittent movements of the lower jaw; but in my own child it was not till the eighth day of life that I saw this groping about; and whether the sense of smell co-operates in this is doubtful, for the child often sucked at the wrong place.

Later, long after weaning, the sense of smell is unquestionably the least turned to account for the knowledge of things. Impressions of smell are regularly confounded with impressions of taste. The following notes regarding the behavior of my child show how late in his case smell appeared distinctly:

In the fifteenth month, freshly-ground coffee and cologne-water, both of which he liked very much to smell in his third year, made no impression at all, or only a slight one. They were not desired, neither were any movements made to repel them if they were held under the nose of the child when his mouth was shut. At the end of this month, however, cologne-water held under his nose made the child laugh. He took pleasure

in the odor as in any other new, agreeable sense-impression. In the sixteenth month he was affected in just
the same way by the odor of oil-of-roses.

In the seventeenth month, however, the inability to
separate smell and taste showed itself still in unmistakable fashion. For every time that I wanted to make
the child smell something—for example, when I held a
hyacinth or an essence to his nose—he would open his
mouth, and in fact take the sweet-smelling flower into
his mouth. He thought, therefore, that as he had hitherto had agreeable sensations of smell only in connection
with taste (of milk), he must now, since he was smelling,
also taste—a very interesting proof, in relation to the
genesis of mind, that sensation is independent of the
knowledge of the organ of sensation; and that the
reasoning processes depend upon the preceding associations of sensation.

In the eighteenth month the child no longer carried
regularly to his mouth the objects he was to smell or that
he wanted to smell; he had therefore recognized the
separation of smell from taste. If I gave him a rose, saying, "Smell of it !" (" Riech einmal ! ") he would put
the flower to his nose, with his mouth shut, and inhale
the aroma through the nose, though, to be sure, only
after exhaling the breath many times against the flower.
For a long time " smell " was understood to mean exhaling, probably because the nurse, in order to indicate
smell, had always feigned a sneeze. Yet the opening
of the mouth occasionally appeared later also, when the
child was to smell anything. Genuine snuffing, taking
in the air for the purpose of smelling, did not take
place.

As no exercises in smelling are in general instituted
for children, and as the infant almost always has a sourish smell of half-digested milk, and has little opportunity
to smell anything except milk and his own perspiration
and that of his nurse or mother, the late development of
smell, as a conscious act, is not surprising. The importance of this function for testing the atmosphere and
food, and for cleanliness, is unfortunately almost universally underestimated. We find, too, as is well known,
in many, probably in most, adults, a great uncertainty
as to whether they have a sensation of smell or a sensation of taste, or both. The civilized child ordinarily
grows up without instruction in this respect, although
it would be very useful to impress upon him early the
various kinds of smell, in association with definite expressions for them, as is usually done with colors and
tones.

3. Smell in New-born Animals.

Many mammals are capable of distinguishing different impressions of smell only a few hours after birth.

Especially in the case of new-born Guinea-pigs, no
one of which was more than seventeen hours old, I was
able easily to establish this fact. For when I put ill-
smelling substances, like asafœtida, in not too small
quantities, on the bottom of a wide-mouthed glass bottle,
lying in a horizontal position, into which the animal
under observation crept, the creature repeatedly wiped
and rubbed its nose with the fore-feet. Further, the
animals turned away, with a quick sidewise movement
of the head, after concentrated propionic acid, or car-
bolic acid, or water-ammonia, had been held before them
some seconds. Often they sneezed at the same time

with a peculiar noise. The smell of camphor, on the other hand, seemed to be not disagreeable to young Guinea-pigs; for they stayed a long time in a glass half filled with pieces of camphor, when they might easily have left it, and they made none of those movements of repulsion. The same is the case with gum-benjamin. Here, to be sure, the rapid blunting of sensitiveness to odors should be taken into account.

I tested several more odorous substances in this way, especially oil-of-thyme, alcohol, ethylic ether, chloroform, prussic acid, and nicotine. Toward these last the Guinea-pigs did not act with so much decision on the first day as they did toward the first-mentioned, probably because the attenuation, in order to avoid its being poisonous, was too great. Thus much, however, is settled: new-born animals a few hours after birth discriminate between agreeable and disagreeable smells. The impressions must simply be strong enough. Any one who has seen how animals, when only half a day old, behave toward asafœtida and camphor, will not doubt that the former causes them discomfort, while the latter does not. Tobacco-smoke also is offensive to them, and when blown against the face causes, even before the close of the first day of life, shutting of the eyes and drawing back of the head—accordingly, purposive reflexes of defense.

We are not justified, indeed, in assuming that mammals just born perceive the odorous substances mentioned by means of their olfactory nerves only, for the sneezing, the rubbing of the nose with the fore-feet, the closing of the eyelids, the turning away and drawing back of the head from strong-smelling substances, the surprising indifference toward substances having a less intense but still a decided odor, indicate, in the experiments upon animals of one day old, an excitement of the nasal branch of the trigeminus. But it is demonstrated by other facts that mammals, dogs, rabbits, cats, can really smell directly after the first respirations.

Biffi bisected the olfactory lobes in very young puppies that had not yet their sight. They bore the operation well, and the mother's licking helped to heal the wound. Animals thus treated could no longer find the mother's teats, so long as they were blind. They crept about on her belly, trying to suck everywhere—*tentando quà e là col muso gli oggetti*. In most cases somebody had to open their mouths and put the teat in. On the contrary, blind puppies in the normal state find the teats at once, as if they saw them. Accordingly, it is not to be doubted that in trying to find the source of the milk, the young are guided by smell, for they could make use of touch (after being operated on) as they could before. We may conclude, then, that the olfactory nerve is excitable in other just-born mammals also, and that it was concerned in the above experiments.

This inference is confirmed by the experiments of Gudden, which show that in rabbits one or two days old, the closing of one nostril, or the removal of one hemisphere of the brain, hinders the development of the olfactory nerve, of the olfactory bulb, and of the tractus of that side. With the removal of one bulbus, the tractus almost entirely disappears. After the removal of both the olfactory bulbs, which makes a comparatively insignificant wound, the little creatures, entirely deprived of the sense of smell, soon perished in consequence of deficient nourishment, since they no longer found their way well to the old ones and their teats, notwithstanding the assistance they got from the nervi trigemini. It is then as it is in the case of simple bisection of both olfactory nerves. When, on the other hand, the organs of smell were left unharmed, and both eyes were taken from the newly-born, and both ears stopped, then the sense of smell was developed in a very high degree, the olfactory bulbs being demonstrably enlarged beyond the ordinary measure. In like manner, the external ears of a rabbit, that had been deprived of both its eyes soon after birth, had a vigorous development, and the hearing became acute beyond what is normal.

From these experiments we infer both the dependence of the organic development upon stimulation from without and the power of physiological concurrence, but in particular we infer that rabbits very soon after birth can smell and that they make abundant use of this capacity in finding the teats. Otherwise it would be incomprehensible that they can no longer find the teats after the destruction of the olfactory nerves alone, and that they perish of hunger.

Spalding has observed, further, that four kittens, three days old, and still blind, when he put near them his hand, which a dog had just licked, began to spit in a way that was amusing. He infers from this that the cat abhors her hereditary enemy even before she can see him. Here the fact ought to be brought to notice that on the third day the cat possesses a finely-developed sense of smell.

At the same time, however, by this observation and

many others, especially that of the "pointing" and
"setting" of young bird-dogs, the fact is proved that
the memory of certain impressions of smell is inherited.
In man such olfactory instincts probably no longer
appear. With him the sense of smell plays in general
a much less pronounced part in the genesis of mind
than it does in the brutes, which are well known to
surpass him greatly, at an early stage, in recognizing
and discriminating odors, and which are occupied all
their lives, much more than man is, with perceptions of
smell.

CHAPTER VI.

THE EARLIEST ORGANIC SENSATIONS AND EMOTIONS.

WITH regard to the physiological conditions of the
organic sensations and emotions of adult human beings,
so little that is of general application is established, that
an investigation of these in the child who can not yet
speak seems premature. I have, therefore, directed my
attention merely to a small number of sensations and
emotions in the child. My observations are, unfortunately, as yet very fragmentary in this direction. But
it is better to communicate them than to be silent about
them, if only to show that here many new problems are,
as it were, growing up out of the ground, close upon
one another.

The whole behavior of the child is determined essentially by his feelings of pleasure and his feelings of
discomfort. For this reason I shall speak first of these

in general. Next appear in the life of the child, among the special feelings, the feeling of hunger, and the feeling of satiety, concerning which I append some observations. I have likewise considered the feeling of fatigue, which is much less marked in children.

Of emotions, fear and surprise are prominent in importance for the mental development of the very young child.

1. Feelings of Pleasure in General.

In the first three months the feelings of pleasure are not manifold. Besides the appeasing of hunger, with the enjoyment that ever recurs along with it, of sucking and of the sweet taste, there comes in the first month, and indeed from the first day on, a pleasurable feeling through the warm bath. The less intense but constant satisfaction in moderately bright impressions of light comes next, and, somewhat later, that in objects moved slowly before the eyes. The pleasure in both steadily grows, but is not so great as the pleasurable feeling in being undressed, which likewise makes its appearance in the first weeks. The release from clothing, etc., is followed regularly by lively movements, especially by alternate stretchings of the legs and visible comfort. Great satisfaction is also afforded the infant by the process of wiping it dry.

Acoustic impressions regularly produce pleasurable feelings in the second month. Singing, piano-playing, and all sorts of musical sounds, sometimes quiet the restless child, sometimes cause lively expressions of joy in the child, as he is lying comfortably or is held in the arms. So it is when he is spoken to by members of the family. The large, bright oval of the face, that

moves close in front of the child's face, and speaks and
sings and laughs, arouses attention and produces cheerfulness early through its peculiarity, being different
from all other optical impressions, yet the human child
hardly knows its mother before the third month.

In the fourth month, the pleasure of grasping at all
possible objects comes gradually into view, becomes
plain in the fifth, and continues to increase in the
sixth.   The delight of being taken out-of-doors at this
period is probably occasioned more by the change, the
greater brightness, and the fresher air, than by the
sight of trees and houses.   The child's own image in
the mirror was in one case observed with unquestionable signs of pleasure in the seventh month; animals
and watches do not generally excite the child's pleasurable interest till later.

A new sort of pleasurable feelings, in which an intellectual element already mingles, appears when the
child begins himself to produce some change, especially of form, through his own activity, so that he
gradually acquires the knowledge of his own power.
Here belong not only the effects of the voice, especially of screaming and of the first sounds uttered by
himself, but also the first plays.   First of all, and that
in the fifth month, in the case of my child, it was the
act of crumpling a sheet of paper, that was taken up
and repeated with evident gratification.   Tearing newspapers to pieces and rolling them up into balls afforded
him great pleasure from that time to his third year.
A like enlivening effect was produced by the long-
continued pulling of a glove this way and that (practiced from the fifth month to the fourth year, from time

to time), also by pulling at the hair of one's beard (at
the same period), then by the ringing of a little bell,
continued an intolerably long time. Later it was the
movements of his own body in locomotion (in march-
ing), and purely intellectual pleasures that amused him:
putting things in and out, cutting with scissors, turning
the leaves of books, looking at pictures. Last came the
inventive, embellishing and yet moderate imagination,
that gives life to shapeless blocks of wood, transforms
the leaves of trees into savory food, and so on.

On the whole, however, it is manifest in the case
of all children in the first part of their life, that much
more happiness comes through relief from disagreeable
conditions than through the provision of positively
agreeable conditions. Hunger, thirst, wet, cold, swaddling-clothes—the getting rid of these produces pleasurable feelings, which are in part stronger, in part not
weaker, than those occasioned by mild light, moving
tassels, lukewarm baths, song, and the friendliness of
parents. It is not until the second three months that
wholly new scenes of enjoyment are entered upon with
the first successful attempts at grasping objects.

The first period of human life belongs to the least
agreeable, inasmuch as not only the number of enjoy-
ments is small, but the capacity for enjoyment is small
likewise, and the unpleasant feelings predominate until
sleep interrupts them.

The *expressions* of pleasurable feeling are at the
beginning not very various; but from the first day
signs of pleasure are open eyes, and soon after an animated gleam in them—a slight excitation of the secretory nerve of the lachrymal gland.

The voice is in the first days an altogether different one when pleasurable feelings are expressed from what it is when the child is hungry, and high, crowing tones, as a sure sign of joy, have in fact been observed by me in the fourth month. They were always employed with the same significance even in the fourth year. Toward the end of the first year there appeared in the case of my boy, as an acoustic expression of pleasure, a peculiar grunting, caused probably by oscillations of the uvula with the mouth shut. This made its appearance especially when the child had a joyous anticipation, was expecting something agreeable, and it used to be associated frequently with a movement of abdominal pressure. A genuine pressure or straining, accompanied by a strong expiration, or by that grunting with shut mouth, was for months an indubitable expression of pleasure. I have not succeeded in finding an explanation of this peculiarity.

More commonly, movements of the extremities are found in infants as signs of pleasurable feelings—stretchings and bendings, drawing up and throwing out the arms and legs (especially in the bath, and when the piano was played, were these clearly manifested, even in the second month); at a later period these are multiplied and are associated with very loud, joyous shouting, as early as the third quarter of the first year. What is called "Strampeln" (kicking), is also frequently observed after the clothes are taken off, when the infant has been fed and is comfortable in a warm, dry bed, in a moderate light, not excited by new impressions. I saw also, in the sixth month even, the quick, bilateral, symmetrical movement, up and down, of the arms (not of the legs), joined with laughing, as an expression of pleasure, when one simply nodded to the child in a friendly manner. The striking of the hands together and laughing for joy, perhaps at the lighting of a lamp, does not occur till later (ninth and tenth months). But loud laughing from this time on is not always an expression of joy ; for, from the end of the first half-year, my child very often laughed when others laughed to him, and from the end of the first year almost invariably when any one laughed near him, merely in imitation, and quite mechanically, vacantly, without knowing why. If he crowed meantime, with vigorous employment of abdominal pressure, then, indeed, he had some special reason for joy. But when (in the second month) he laughs on being tickled upon the sole of the foot, the laughing is reflexive. Intentional laughing for pleasure—e. g., at the repetition of an agreeable play, or of a musical chord (in the first quarter of the second year)—is, even for the practiced ear, difficult to distinguish from reflexive laughing, but the countenance of the child, smiling as he regards the face of his mother, is easily distinguishable, even in the third month (by the direction of the look), from that of the child smiling vacantly, upon a full stomach. In both cases the smile is a sign of pleasure ; but in the first case it is a sign of a special sensation—in the last, of nothing more than a general sensation.

With regard to the connection of all these muscular actions with the nervous processes underlying the joyous emotion, nothing is as yet known. Screaming from pain and laughing from pleasure are modified expirations, and not the least help is to be elicited from the relation of the respiratory apparatus to the sensorium for the explanation of these expressions of antagonistic emotions. The excessive inclination to movement as a symptom of joy, in little children and young animals, seems mysterious, and the hysterical leap from crying to laughing in a moment, in children three to four years old, which has nothing morbid in it, can not lessen the difficulty of the attempt at a physiological explanation. It is probably true of little children in general, that every strong feeling brings in its train a motor discharge. It is, in fact, very difficult, even for older children—nay, for many adults as well—not to betray great joy, just experienced, by some look, or by the brightness of the eyes, or an increased animation, and not to make some movement on hearing merry dance-music.

2. Unpleasant Feelings in General.

In the first half-year of life, unpleasant feelings are more frequent than afterward. Even with the most careful nursing, ventilation, regulation of the temperature of the air and of the bath, control of the milk of mother, nurse, or cow, or of the substitute for this, and with the most favorable surroundings, it is not often granted to a human child to continue in perfect health, without a day of suffering. Birth itself may be painful to the child, or may involve inevitable treatment of a painful character; and the number of children's diseases that are in part accompanied by severe pain is not small. In no period of life is the mortality anything like so great as in the first year. Through this tendency to illness, which is shown in the helpless, defenseless, inexperienced infant, many unpleasant feelings must arise. for only the healthy organism can experience unalloyed pleasure.

But I do not mean to speak here of the numerous unpleasant feelings caused by illness, and by attempts at cure, but only of such as even the perfectly healthy child can not be spared, not even under the most favorable circumstances. To these belong hunger and thirst, discomfort in consequence of inconvenient position in lying or in being held, or of cold, or wet, or ill-smelling air ; then the discomfort arising from the tight swathing that unfortunately still prevails far too widely in Germany ; the pain of teething, the disagreeable effects of driveling (" drooling," *Geifern*), and of sucking at objects not fit to be sucked ; later, the pain of being denied things eagerly craved.

It is an error to maintain that the very young child is not yet capable of having the genuine feeling of pain or even a high degree of unpleasant feeling ; for he who can enjoy must also be able to suffer, otherwise he could not enjoy. And that the new-born child experiences pleasure in sucking at a full, healthy breast, nobody doubts. The outward signs of unpleasant feeling in the infant are also unmistakable for every diligent observer.

Above all, crying is characteristic : it is piercing. and persistent in pain ; a whimpering in an uncomfortable posture ; uninterrupted and very loud in the cold bath ; interrupted by frequent pauses in hunger ; suddenly waxing to unexpected intensity, and again decreasing quickly, when something is desired and not obtained. Soon are added, as expressions of discomfort, inarticulate and articulate sounds. The infant can not yet moan and groan, he only utters cries, and in the first days does not feel pain at many kinds of treatment that would cause pain to older children—treatment confined to a small area of the skin; for example, pricks of a needle, cooling with ice, sewing up of wounds after operations (Genzmer)—for he often keeps perfectly quiet under such treatment, and even falls asleep. All new-born infants, besides, react much more slowly by crying, in response to the strongest impressions, than do older infants.

A second sign is the shutting of the eyes and holding them tightly closed, which often takes place in adults also in the same fashion. In the first year the child regularly closes his eyes when he manifests a strong feeling of discomfort by screaming. He often shuts the eyes (especially in the ninth month) without screaming, with corrugated brow, when he has to endure something disagreeable; e. g., when he is dressed, or when a finger is put in his mouth, at the period of teething, in order to feel the coming of a tooth.

A further symptom of discomfort is the turning away of the head, which I likewise perceived unaccompanied by crying, under the circumstances just mentioned (distinctly marked in the first as in the ninth month).

The most delicate index of the child's mood is, however, the form of the mouth, as even the least degree of unpleasant feeling is surely expressed at once by drawing down the angles of the mouth. But this alteration of the child's countenance, which appears more and more distinctly up to the fourth year in every single case, is not developed so early as the three previously mentioned expressions of discomfort. In my child, whom I observed carefully, this action of the muscle that depresses the angles of the mouth was not perceived at all before the eighteenth week. But during and before the twenty-third week, whenever the child was addressed in a harsh tone, the stern countenance of the speaker was stared at a moment, then both angles of the mouth were drawn down. Hereupon began for the first time the plaintive cry, accompanied by the appearance of the naso-labial corrugation; the cry, however, ceased as soon as the countenance that had been severe toward the child changed to friendliness. Very soon the previous cheerfulness returned. Darwin saw even earlier this form of the mouth, from about the sixth week to the second and third month.

Accordingly, the first appearance of this peculiar sign of discomfort is in some cases in the first three months; in others, in the first half of the second three months. From this time on, every vexation, but nothing else, is announced by this sign, which is especially pronounced from the sixth month on. Finally, from the eighth month to the end of the third year, appears also, together with violent screaming, another singular form of the mouth. The mouth becomes, viz., as I often observed, quadrangular, a parallelogram, sometimes almost a square—a form which presents itself at once (even with perfectly deaf children, to judge from the mere look) as a sure sign of the highest degree of discomfort, as Darwin rightly brings to notice.

In spite of all these signs of the existence of unpleasant feelings, it is often extraordinarily difficult,

12

especially in the first year, to find out what causes underlie them.

Why does the little girl (of four months) weep when her mother comes near her with a great hat on her head, whereas the child smiles at her when the mother appears without a hat or lays the hat aside? (Frau Dr. Friedemann). Probably fear mingles with the surprise at the strange, as is the case with brutes.

I once had a good horse, that knew me well, but was afraid and began to tremble somewhat when I dismounted and crouched down upon the ground (to get a shot at a bird without being seen). The beast was evidently afraid of the new phenomenon. His master in that hitherto unseen attitude had become to him a strange being. In like manner the very young child will often fail to understand an alteration in persons whose image is well impressed upon his mind, and will be afraid. Children may turn away with horror from hands they like to kiss, if these hands are covered with black gloves, and they may be brought to weeping just by the sight of a figure, well known to them, if it be clothed in black. It was not till the nineteenth month that my child ceased to be reserved toward strangers, and occasionally condescended to give his hand to them when asked, provided only they were not dressed entirely in black (cf. pp. 145–147).

In many children a high degree of uncomfortable feeling may exist, and in a fashion decidedly comical for adults, especially through pity. When figures of all sorts—e. g., human forms—were cut out of paper with scissors for the amusement of my child, he would often weep if a paper figure was in danger, through hasty cutting, of losing an arm or a foot (twenty-seventh month). A like account has been given me of a little girl.

When an infant, fed, warm, and dry, one that we are justified in declaring to be perfectly healthy, nevertheless screams, screws up his eyes, draws down the corners of his mouth, and does not suffer himself to be quieted—we can not easily assign an external cause of his discomfort. It must, therefore, be an internal, unknown cause. I once let my child, of three months, in such a situation, cry on. It was not quite twenty minutes before he fell asleep, and he awoke in good spirits after several hours. Often it is not mere ill-humor that expresses itself in such cases, but an unconquerable impulse to cry out, which can not be called morbid. In some children it is sleepiness, weariness, even after nursing, that manifests itself in crying, especially when anything hinders them from going to sleep. Screaming also is a substitute for the deficient movement of the limbs in the case of children in swaddling-clothes.

When no one of the symptoms mentioned of a strong feeling of discomfort is present, a state of discontent of a low grade may be announced by a lack of luster in the eyes, indolent movements, cessation of the play of countenance, or a somewhat paler complexion. But in this case the cause is usually some disturbance of the health, however slight, just as it is with orangoutangs and chimpanzees. In the babe, as in the weaned and even the older child—nay, even in adults that have not toned down the natural play of feature, or concealed it by self-control—even in this case I am

compelled to designate the drawing down of the angles
of the mouth as the most delicate form of reaction, one
which does not fail even in sleep, since it continues
after the falling asleep, in case of illness, and imparts
to the countenance an extremely doleful, piteous expression. Whether a cheerful or a sad mood prevails,
may be discerned, without seeing any other part of
the face, from the appearance of the angle of the
mouth alone.

3. The Feeling of Hunger.

Soon after birth hunger and thirst assert themselves.
They are unmistakably recognizable in this, that, after
objects capable of being sucked are put into the mouth,
sucking movements appear, whereas the babe that has
had enough does not suck, as I very often proved.

If the feeling of hunger and thirst continues, the
child cries and becomes restless. But the restlessness
always disappears temporarily during the first days of
life when something to suck is put into the mouth, be
it only the corner of a pillow or a finger, so that we are
justified in assuming that the discomfort that is joined
with hunger is displaced by the pleasure that belongs to
sucking. Yet in many children, even a week after birth,
the crying from hunger can not so surely be checked
by letting the child suck at strange objects as it could
earlier (Genzmer). So early as this, then, the child
has had a useful experience. In the first days, almost
every hungry child sucks at its own fingers. Then the
crying begins again. This is from the beginning a different thing from the crying caused by pain, and is distinguished from it especially by the fact that it does
not continue so long uninterrupted; on the contrary, I

have always found—and I am confirmed in this by experienced nurses—that very small children, when hungry, cry with short and long intervals. The voice, too, has a different ring; the cry of pain is higher than that of hunger. The cry of hunger is, likewise, easily distinguished from the cry of satisfaction, even during the first days: for, when the child cries from hunger, the eyes are generally tightly closed; when it gives a cry of joy, they are open. Moreover, my child, when crying with hunger, used to draw back the tongue and spread it out; this does not take place in other kinds of crying. (In my boy this appeared plainly as late as the twenty-ninth week.)

The reflex excitability of the infant is, as others also have observed, increased during the condition of hunger, especially in regard to touches, most of all on the lips and cheeks.

A sure sign of hunger, or of the lively desire arising from it, is, further, the opening of the eyes widely on being brought near the breast, even before being placed at it, a thing which occurs regularly in the first weeks of life, but not before the very first experience of the breast. Experience, then, is necessary for this also.

I have not seen any other than the hungry child, directly before beginning to suck at the breast, make the peculiar shaking movements of the head, which take place in the same way when an artificial nipple is put to the lips of the babe (in the first and second months); these movements, however, become fainter and cease if the rubber is often removed from the mouth and again put in, as if the uselessness of those movements were perceived. Although these move-

ments soon cease entirely, the animal eagerness for
food manifestly increases in the first year. While
draining the bottle the eyes are opened wide, and
the gaze is never turned from the bottle (especially
in the sixth and seventh months). If the child of six
months is very hungry, he turns the head and the gaze
vigorously and persistently toward the bottle, held before
him at a small or a great distance, and at once cries violently if it be taken out of the room. On the other
hand, he opens his mouth eagerly if the bottle be
brought near him. This object, and in general everything connected with it, has in the third quarter of the
first year by far the greatest interest for the infant, who
stretches out his arms toward it with sparkling eyes if
he has not had enough.

From the fifth month on, however, we succeeded in
diverting his attention temporarily from the taking of
food by means of new noises and movements (page 86);
in the last three months of the first year his eating was
not so hurried as before; hunger no longer prevailed so
much over all other feelings. This progress, apart from
the fact that under normal circumstances his hunger is
always appeased without delay, is also due to the increase
in the quantity of nourishment taken at a single meal.
The smaller the stomach, the oftener it becomes empty.
The more it can hold, the longer will hunger be post-
poned, there being no lack of nourishment. In healthy
new-born infants the stomach holds (according to
Beneke) only thirty-five to forty-three cubic centimetres; after two weeks, one hundred and fifty-three to
one hundred and sixty; after two years, seven hundred and forty (leaving out great individual variations).

Thus the intervals between the meals become gradually longer, and the meals less frequent, and there remains in the intervals more time for the infant to turn its attention to other things than food, since the child, the older it grows, sleeps so much the less and consumes its food so much the less rapidly. In the tenth week, to be awake and hungry three times in a night (from eight to six o'clock) is little; in the fifteenth week, the intervals between meals are prolonged in the daytime to three or four hours, against two hours at the beginning of life; and in the eighteenth week—and perhaps earlier —there are nights of ten to eleven hours without the taking of any nourishment at all. Great differences exist, to be sure, among perfectly healthy infants in this respect. Still, it is true of all that they are hungry more frequently at the beginning of life than in the second, and certainly in the third, quarter of the first year. If one busies himself too much with the child, allows too many new sense-impressions to act upon him, brings too much strain on his attention, then hunger arrives unseasonably, accompanied with crying, although during "play"—that is, in my case, during my observation of the child, and my experiments upon him—his cheerfulness may have been undisturbed. This sudden access of fretfulness and hunger I have often observed, and, indeed, even from the sixth week on. Later, however, viz., in the eighth and ninth months, the craving for food was less and less manifested by crying, and was often expressed by a peculiar cooing (*Girren*) with the mouth shut tight. This cooing, joined with movements of the larynx, always bore the character of desire, even for those who were not acquainted with its significance.

It does not seem to appear in many children. The origin of it is quite obscure. The child made the strange sound only when hungry, when he saw the food directly before him, which he could not at once take, because it was perhaps still too hot or not warm enough.

Notwithstanding the fact that the feeling of hunger is by far the strongest of all the feelings of the new-born and of the quite young infant, as appears from his whole behavior, yet it would be an error to suppose this feeling to be capable of producing a voluntary movement in the first weeks. I observed a child that, on the fourth and sixth days, obstinately refused, in spite of seven hours' abstinence from food, to take the left breast, whereas it took the right gladly every time, because the left was not so convenient for sucking, though it supplied milk enough. But even with the very convenient artificial nipple, this breast was often declined, and on the nineteenth day persistently, even after a fast of six to seven hours. On the other hand, the child sucked a long time at the skin near the nipple, then cried, and finally fell asleep, tired out with its vain effort. Manifestly in this by no means solitary instance the hunger is indeed great, but the knowledge that it might easily be appeased does not exist; and does not exist for this reason, because, at the first attempt to suck on the left side, the child's experience was that sucking was not so easy there as on the right. That this discrimination could be made so early as the fourth day of life is just as remarkable as the persistence with which it was held to by the infant, who regarded the difference as still existing in all following trials, even when the greatest convenience was attained.

4. The Feeling of Satiety.

Opposed in every respect to the expressions of the feeling of hunger and of thirst are the expressions of the feeling of satiety in the infant. The same food and source of food that were before desired with the greatest eagerness are now abhorred. When the child has sucked enough at the breast that yields milk in great abundance, so that his stomach is full, then he actually pushes the nipple away with his lips (third to fifth week). Just so, the child pushes out the mouth-piece of the nursing-bottle when he has sucked at it (fourth week). In the seventh month I plainly saw that the mouth-piece was vigorously thrust out with the tongue, almost with disgust. The head had already been turned away some time before, after the child had nursed abundantly. These movements are to be regarded as sure signs of the presence of the feeling of satiety. Other signs besides are early added to these.

As early as the tenth day, when the child had fallen asleep after eating his fill, I saw his mouth unmistakably take on the form of a smile, by which the expression of great satisfaction was imparted to the countenance. Later, this was frequently perceived. In the fourth week were added still other signs of the highest satisfaction, between the close of the child's feeding and the beginning of sleep : laughing, opening the eyes, then half-shutting them, inarticulate sounds, in which every person, even those who did not see the child, discerned satisfaction. In the first months, and even in the eighth, the expressions of pleasure and of discomfort are the most pronounced when the feeling

of satiety has come or just before. The appeasing of
hunger is the greatest pleasure; the increase of the
feeling of hunger and of the feeling of thirst, which is
not yet separated from that of hunger, is the greatest
discomfort for the healthy infant.

Yet I have not been able in any case to attain the
conviction that the infant is as yet capable, as Kussmaul thinks, of feeling nausea. Neither overfullness
nor vomiting, neither the greatest uncleanliness nor the
most repulsive, foul smell, calls forth in the child in the
earliest period the physiognomy associated with the
feeling of nausea. The repugnance to bitter substances
may, as Genzmer rightly observes, express itself even
without that feeling, although the corresponding defensive reflexes in the adult are accustomed to be associated with that feeling.

5. The Feeling of Fatigue.

In spite of the lethargy of the newly-born or of the
infant, it might seem doubtful whether he is easily
fatigued, because he *apparently* makes but little effort,
mental or physical. A closer consideration shows, however, that several causes of fatigue must be operative
directly after birth; that a feeling of weariness may
come soon after that event; and that the physiological
lethargy of the infant is connected with that feeling.

For the waking condition there is need of stimuli—
i. e., excitations of the sensory nerves. Now, if these
nerves are but little excitable, as is the case before birth,
and if few stimuli are present, then the opposite of waking—viz., sleep—will be persistent and sound. But
when after birth the excitability of the nerves and the

number of the stimuli are increased, by the very opening of the eyes and ears and the activity of the nerves
of the skin, then sleep is interrupted. The longer this
interruption lasts, the greater must be the accumulation
of the products of the activity of the central and peripheral portions of the organs of sense, on the one hand,
and on the other hand of the muscles, which contract
more strongly and more frequently in the waking condition than in sleep. Now, these materials of fatigue,
as I have attempted to show in my treatise on the
causes of sleep ("Über die Ursachen des Schlafes,"
Stuttgart, 1877), hinder prolonged waking, because they
withdraw from the blood the oxygen required for activity, in order to unite themselves with it, so that they
may be oxidized, and finally expelled. What are the
substances formed through the activity of the muscles
and the brain, and inducing the feeling of fatigue, we
have yet to ascertain.

In the new-born and the infant, whose muscles in
and of themselves are but little serviceable, and resemble the muscles of tired adults, as Soltmann proved by
comparative experiments upon animals, there are two
actions especially that require strong muscular effort—
viz., crying and sucking. The crying of the hungry
child is a sign of the waking condition that quickly
produces weariness. For, let the child have his cry out,
and he usually falls asleep soon, even without having
been fed. Sucking at a breast that contains little milk
is likewise tiresome; and I repeatedly within the first
three months saw sleep take possession of the child
while he was sucking thus at a scanty breast of the
nurse; and the sucking was frequently interrupted by

long intervals, even when the child must have been hungry.

Then there is the fatigue of the organs of sense. After the first two or three weeks are past, so that the attention can begin to be directed to something else than the milk, manifold changing impressions of light and sound, along with strong, cutaneous stimuli through touch and temperature from the beginning, act with rapidly fatiguing power upon the infant, especially when his relatives busy themselves too much with him. Thus, with my boy the hearing of piano-playing, in his eighth week, was followed by an unbroken sleep of six hours, whereas up to that time sleep had not once lasted so long.

But the weariness brought on by crying, sucking, manifold sense-impressions, is hardly sufficient to account for the brief duration of the waking periods in the first half-year, even if we make the largest allowance for the movements of the extremities, and add to that the labor performed by the respiratory muscles and by the heart. There must be still another cause that produces sleep, inasmuch as under normal conditions the greater part of the first two years of human life is actually spent in sleep. This other cause is, probably, the relatively smaller supply of oxygen (on account of the smaller quantity of blood and the less energy of the respiratory process) and the need of oxygen for growth; so that, on the one hand, less work is done and less warmth is produced; on the other hand, less oxygen can be spared for keeping up the change of matter in the ganglionic cells during the waking hours. We must also take into account the character of the food, which

regularly consists uniformly of milk alone in the period
of much sleep. Milk and whey in large quantities exert a somnific influence even upon adults. They contain sugar of milk, which, in the stomach produces lactic acid. This unites in the intestines with alkali, and
thus after every meal larger quantities, relatively, of
lactates must enter the blood in the infant than in the
adult. These become oxidized, and thereby withdraw
from the brain, according to the above-mentioned theory
of sleep, in great measure the oxygen required for the
waking condition, and for this reason, perhaps, the infant regularly falls asleep not long after each abundant
supply of milk. The milk may also contain somnific
materials from the blood of the mother. Finally, the
almost uninterrupted act of digestion of the milk,
scarcely ever discontinued more than two hours at a
time, may, by collecting blood in the vessels of the di-
gestive organs, withdraw from the brain temporarily,
larger quantities of blood (which are necessary for the
waking condition).

With these hypotheses accords the universal experience that in the first three months the duration of the
period of sleep between two meals is much shorter than
in the second three months, and that it continually increases. At first the period of digestion is shorter than
it is afterward, on account of the smallness of the stomach. I found the sleep of the infant the sounder and
more lasting, the more concentrated the milk was, other
circumstances being the same. Mother's milk, abundant and good, produces a sounder and longer sleep
than diluted milk of the cow, or scanty milk of the wet-
nurse. But even if the mother's milk be given exclu-

sively, the periods of sleep are shorter than in the first
weeks, the waking more frequent than later; yet the
whole time spent in sleep is longer. The frequent
waking is doubtless favored by other causes than hunger, especially by the greater uncleanliness of the early
period, and by wet—that is, by cutaneous irritation.

The notes I wrote down concerning the duration of
sleep in the case of my boy show clearly the decrease
of the duration of sleep as a whole, and the increase of
duration of the single period of sleep, from the first
day until the close of the third year. I extract the following particulars:

In the first month sleep lasted without interruption
not often longer than two hours; but of the twenty-
four hours, sixteen at least, and generally much more,
were spent in sleep.

In the second month, a three-hours' sleep often appeared; now and then a sleep of five to six hours.

In the third month the child often sleeps four hours,
frequently even five in succession, without waking.

In the fourth month, the sleep often lasts five to
six hours; the intervals between the times of eating,
three and four hours (against two hours at an earlier
period). Once the sleep lasted nine hours.

In the sixth month, a sleep of six to eight hours is
not infrequent.

In the eighth month, restless nights, on account of
teething.

In the thirteenth month, as a rule, fourteen hours
of sleep daily, in several separate periods.

In the seventeenth month, prolonged sleep began;
ten hours, without interruption.

In the twentieth month, prolonged sleep became habitual, and sleep in the daytime was reduced to two hours.

From the thirty-seventh month on, the night's sleep lasted regularly eleven to twelve hours, and sleep in the daytime was no longer required.

Thus, from the fourth year, the waking period is longer than that of sleep, and sleepiness does not come on so quickly as before. The child, when walking, no longer says, " swer " (" schwer ") for " müde " (tired), as he often did in the third year; and although the feeling of weariness sometimes asserts itself, yet drowsiness and sleep no longer follow directly upon it. The unwearied springing and running of older children is well known. The varied food taken at present, as contrasted with the milk-diet of an earlier period, unquestionably contributes to this, but chiefly the increased functional ability of the respiratory apparatus, of the blood, of the muscles, and ganglionic cells. The sleep itself is now in general more quiet, inasmuch as dreams, accompanied by movements and outcries, no longer occur so often.

I consider it as exceedingly important in the case of little children not to interrupt sleep artificially—to give them milk, it may be—and not to wake larger children either. By waking them a condition of real distress, accompanied with trembling and convulsions, is easily induced in perfectly healthy children, and a lasting depression of spirits generated. I know of no advantage to the child from being waked. It ought the more to be avoided, inasmuch as almost invariably a fright is given to the child, and all fright is absolutely harmful, whether caused by harsh address, or by threatening the child with the "black man," so called, or by catching the child, pouring water on him, and the like, in the way of fun. Older children like to show their superiority to younger ones by such misdeeds, and even ignorant nurses not seldom adopt such means. Thereby they arouse timidity, which may easily be increased by grewsome stories (" gräusige Geschichten ") and foolish tales, and then it leads early to a morbid excitability.

6. Fear.

The time at which a child first betrays fear depends essentially upon his treatment, in so far as the avoidance of occasions of pain prolongs the period that is marked by unconsciousness of fear; whereas the multiplication of such occasions shortens the period.

There is, however, an hereditary timidity, which manifests itself as opportunity offers. How happens it that many children are afraid of dogs, pigs, and cats, before they know the dangerous qualities of these animals? A little girl was afraid of cats as early as the fourteenth week of life (Sigismund). Thunder makes many children cry—for what reason?

If there is in this case the co-operation of ideas, either clear or obscure, of danger, or of reminiscences of pain after a noisy fall, or of disagreeable sensations at loud rumbling and the like (I observed that my child in his second year cried with fear almost every time that heavy furniture was pushed about), yet in the expressions of fear on the part of inexperienced animals factors of this sort are excluded.

A hen with her first brood, about a week old, was

frightened by Douglas Spalding, who let fly a young hawk. " In the twinkling of an eye most of the chickens were hid among grass and bushes"; and when the bird of prey touched the ground, at a distance of twelve yards from the hen, the hen attacked it, and would undoubtedly have killed it. I have repeated this experiment. A young kestrel, very lively, as large as a domestic cock, was by me held by the wings and brought near to thirty-three chickens, three and a half weeks old, hatched in the incubator and raised in an inclosed space, without intercourse with other fowls. At first they did not appear to notice the bird. But as soon as they heard its voice, they all became still and attentive, and moved but little. Then I let the falcon loose: instantly the chickens scattered in all directions, and concealed themselves. How, except through inheritance, did the chicks arrive at the point of hiding themselves at seeing and hearing the falcon? They had never seen it or its like before, and a mother could not have described it to her offspring. But when, after a long interval, I let a pigeon, instead of a falcon, fly away over the thirty-three chickens, they were just as much frightened; they scattered and hid themselves. On the other hand, they were not in the least frightened at their first sight of a hen which cackled loudly. The hereditary enemy must therefore be known through inborn memory. Yet I will not conceal that I do not regard the experiments, or this inference from them, as sufficiently conclusive (the check experiment with the pigeon prevents that), although no imitation by the chicks of the behavior of a hen was possible. When I put a kitten into a box in which there were eighteen

13

chickens not yet four hours old and two about twenty hours old, not one of the chicks made the least movement of flight. Even after the kitten had bitten a chicken, had been taken away, and afterward put into the box with the twenty chickens again, there was no stir at all among them; the one that had been bitten did not even turn away. The same thing took place on the third day. A turkey ten days old behaved as the chickens did in the above experiments. When he heard the voice of the hawk for the first time, and close to him, he "shot like an arrow to the other side of the room, and stood there, motionless and dumb with fear," for ten minutes, as Spalding reports. Chickens show unmistakable signs of fear in regard to bees also as a general thing, according to him, although they have not been stung. They bring the timidity with them, then, from the egg, as an hereditary property. Yet against this inference it might be urged that every sudden, strong sense-impression elicits the same symptoms as do the impressions that excite fear. The behavior of the inexperienced chickens was the same at the sudden appearance of the dove as at the cry and the approach of the falcon. But when I let the latter loose among a great number of fowls that were busily pecking, the warning cry of the cock at once sounded; and when the falcon made toward a hen, they all flew off, except one that prepared to attack the bird of prey. A peahen did the same thing directly afterward. We see from this that fear and courage are very unequally distributed among creatures of the same kind. Timidity and bravery are accordingly to be admitted as hereditary qualities.

The case must be similar in the human child, who is afraid of all sorts of things not at all dangerous, as well as of things really dangerous, before he knows danger of himself, and before he can be infected by the timidity of mother or nurse. It is altogether wrong to maintain that a child has no fear unless it has been taught him. The courage or the fear of the mother has indeed extraordinary influence upon the child, to the extent that courageous mothers certainly have courageous children, and timid mothers have timid children, through imitation; but there are so many cases of timidity and of courage in the child, without any occasion of that sort, that we must take into account, as in the case of animals, an element lying further back, hereditary. Thus, Champneys observed (1881) that his boy, when about nine months old, showed signs of fear for the first time, becoming attentive to any unusual noise in a distant part of the room, opening his eyes very wide and beginning to cry. A month or so later this child had a toy given him, that squeaked when it was squeezed. The child at once screamed, and screamed afterward again and again, when it was offered to him. But after some time he became accustomed to the squeaking; then he was pleased by it, and would himself make the toy squeak.

Among the observations that I made on my boy, a boy not particularly timid in his fourth year, but rather one who would defend himself against two or three older children together, are some that certainly are not to be referred to imitation, as the fear of machines and of small animals when near.

In the ninth month I observed him for the first

time crying, turning away, and drawing back from fear, when a small dog barked at the nurse, who was carrying my child on her arm. The same thing happened just a hundred days afterward, and again in the seventeenth month. In the second quarter of the third year the fear of all dogs is very conspicuous, although the child has never been bitten by such an animal, and, so far as can be determined, has never seen a dog bite a child. Even in the thirty-third month, his crying at the approach of even the smallest dog, of a few weeks old, is remarkable. Yet soon after this period the timidity was gradually overcome, and on one occasion the child, in my presence, actually took an apple out of the teeth of the dog, which had taken it away from him.

How little this fear of dogs, so late to be overcome, was a result of education, appears from the behavior of the child toward other small animals. To give pleasure to him, when he was two and a quarter years old, a number of very young pigs were shown to him. He at once became serious at the sight. But, when the queer creatures proceeded to suck at the teats of the mother that lay there perfectly quiet, then the child began to scream, to shed tears, to cling, and to turn away with fright. He thought, as it afterward appeared, that the sucking pigs were biting the mother. That he should himself be thrown into a state of genuine fear every time he was brought near them is the more strange, as they were all shut up in a pen with a high, strong fence about it. This fear became so great in the course of the fourth and fifth years in my child that he sometimes cried out in the night, and imagined that a pig was going to bite him. He seemed to see the animal as if it were actually there, and he could not be convinced that it was not there, even after his bed was brightly lighted up. The explanation offered by Heyfelder for similar cases may apply to some. He supposes that when children cry out in falling asleep, and believe themselves to be bitten by a dog, a sudden jerk of the leg or arm occasions a feeling out of which the imagination constructs the animal. But when a child that is sleeping in perfect quiet suddenly cries out, " Go away, pig!" and this without waking, we must assume that the dream-image appears without any external movement. A little girl was so afraid of doves in the seventeenth week and in the eleventh month that she could not make up her mind to stroke them; in the thirteenth month she ventured to stroke a dove, but immediately drew back her hand; in the fourteenth month her fear was overcome.

Just as remarkable as this fear of animals is the fear of falling at the first attempt to walk. Although the child never had fallen, so far as could be determined, he did not dare, in the fourteenth month, when he could not yet go alone, to take a step without support, and became fearful if he was not held. The child had before this bruised himself repeatedly, but in this case he cried from fear of falling, without having had the experience of being bumped in falling.

Two more examples: In the sixteenth month my child was afraid (to my surprise, for I thought to please him) when I drew tones of high pitch from a drinking-glass by rubbing with the finger, as I had done once at an earlier period (p. 47). His fear, which did not at that time—in the third month—appear, now increased

to the point of shedding tears, whereas the ring of the
glasses when struck was greeted with a cry of joy. Did
the unusual tone in the sixteenth month seem uncanny on
account of ignorance of the cause? Yet the same child
laughed at the thunder and lightning (in the eighteenth
and nineteenth months); another child even in the
thirty-fifth month did the same, and imitated cleverly
with the hand the zigzag movement of the lightning
(Gustav Lindner).

In the twenty-first month my child showed every
sign of fear when his nurse carried him on her arm close
by the sea (in Scheveningen). He began to whimper,
and I saw that he clung tighter with both hands, even
during a calm and at ebb-tide when there was but a
slight dashing of the waves. Whence the fear of the
sea, which the child is not acquainted with? The water
of the Eider Canal, of the Saale, of the Rhine, he was
not in the least afraid of in the same year. The great-
ness of the sea could not of itself excite fear, for the
symptoms of dread were shown only close by the water.
Was it, then, the roaring heard in advance?

The fear of persons in black, too (seventeenth
month), even when they are friendly, as well as the
fear of a deep voice, of masked faces, of strange faces
(Frau von Strümpell), (in the seventh month and in
the twenty-fourth week), is not derived from education (Herr Ed. Schulte). It expresses itself in this
way: The infant cries at the sight of strangers or at
hearing strange voices, a thing he did not do in the first
three months. On the other hand, the fear of punishment—a fear that has been bred in him—appearing
in the second year, may easily be distinguished from

natural dread. The child that for the first time disobeys a well-known prohibition does not cry, or tremble, or cling closer, or cower down, but he tries to get away. The fear of being chastised, however often it appears, through many successive generations, in the same form, at the same age, is always acquired anew. A proof of this I find, as do others, in the fact that my child is not in the least afraid in the dark, no doubt for the reason that he has never been punished by being shut up in a dark place.

How the special symptoms of fear, e. g., the characteristic trembling, are developed, is wholly unknown. It is asserted, in regard to little children, that they can not tremble (in fact, Darwin says this). But children just born, and those of four years, can tremble, as I have myself perceived. A perfectly healthy child, of good weight, not yet a quarter of an hour old, trembled almost incessantly, sometimes more, sometimes less, during my observation, although it was comfortably warm in the room (in the lying-in hospital). The child had already had a warm bath. Many just-born children, to be sure, do not tremble.

Many new-born animals—dogs, mice, rabbits, Guinea-pigs, and chickens, which I have often observed in regard to this point—tremble in a warm nest. But they have not at first the least fear at being laid hold of with the hand. The behavior of the chicken hatched in the incubator is very different in the first days of its life from what it is afterward; in the following days you have often the greatest difficulty in catching it. In the beginning it does not run away, though it knows how to run well enough; but later it runs away invariably.

Bird-dogs are likewise entirely without fear of man at the beginning of life, even after they can see. But, after they have once become acquainted with the whip, they manifest fear of man in the most marked manner— badger-dogs, in individual cases, in a striking degree, as Romanes reports, without their having ever been whipped, so far as appears. How inherited endowment is united here with individual experience we can not at present say, for lack of facts. But that fear of man is not originally present, but is introduced into many animals in common by inoculation through man's own agency, appears from the behavior of many animals, which in the wilderness unvisited by man are not in the least shy, whereas their fellows of the same species, where they are hunted, hide themselves with the greatest caution, or flee, even when they are not pursued, if they get scent of human beings. Of the graceful phalaropes, especially, I know this to be true, from personal observation. They have no fear at all of man in the uninhabited interior of Iceland, where I frequently observed them, whereas on the inhabited coast they are anything but tame.

So, with man also, it is, on the one hand, ignorance of danger, on the other hand, the becoming accustomed to it, that makes him fearless.

7. Astonishment.

It is exceedingly difficult to determine the moment when a human being is for the first time in his life astonished. *Surprise*, which manifests itself by a reflex movement of the arms, and that in the first week, after a sudden loud noise, is essentially different from *aston-*

ishment. And the great concentration of *attention* that the infant bestows on his own fingers, after he has begun his attempts at touching and seizing (in the fourth and fifth months), is different from the state of being overpowered by a high degree of astonishment at some new impression. But precisely at this period I could, not seldom, distinguish accurately the astonishment of the infant from that strain of attention—and this in the twenty-second week. When the child was in a railway-carriage, and I suddenly entered after a brief separation, so that at the same moment he saw my face and heard my voice, he fixed his gaze upon me for more than a minute, with *open mouth* (the lower jaw dropped), *with wide-open, motionless eyes,* and in other respects absolutely immovable, exhibiting the typical image of astonishment.

Just so he stared at a stranger (in the sixth and seventh months), who suddenly entered the room, for more than a minute, motionless, with open mouth and eyes. In the eighth and ninth months these symptoms seemed to be still more pronounced, and appeared not unfrequently at new impressions of sight and sound— not at new impressions of smell and taste—and in remarkable uniformity. E. g., the child was thus astonished in the thirty-first week at the clapping together of a fan; in the thirty-fourth, at an imitation of the voices of animals; in the forty-fourth, at a strange face near; in the fifty-second, at a new sound; in the fifty-eighth, at a lantern (after waking). I do not remember to have perceived along with this a raising of the eyebrows; but this may have been overlooked on account of its being slight at this early period. Often, when the mouth was opened, an *ah* was heard. The attitude of the astonished child was in every case that which he had in the moment just before the new impression. This attitude was retained, with eyes stretched wide apart and with the mouth very widely open. But when a less degree of astonishment than in the cases mentioned was felt, then in every instance a pulsation of the eyelid or a succession of such movements indicated wonder; the eyes, indeed, were opened wide, but not the mouth.

Toward the end of the second year, the symptoms of the highest degree of astonishment made their appearance, in general, more seldom than before, especially the dropping of the lower jaw. It took more, therefore, at this time, to turn the entire attention to a single impression of sight or hearing so powerfully that the lower jaw could not be kept up. The child had been astonished too often, and had become accustomed to the once new impressions.

The whole behavior of the child when astonished is completely original with him, not being in the least acquired by imitation or through training, for it was in the fifth month at latest that his astonishment was of the sort described. His immobility is the consequence of the sudden, powerful, new impression, and resembles the cataplexy of animals, caused by the arrest of the will through fright. For particulars, see my treatise on "Cataplexy and Animal Hypnotism" ("Die Kataplexie und der thierische Hypnotismus," Jena, 1878).

Individual animals, however, may be astonished at new impressions without being so frightened as to lose their will completely. I have repeatedly seen a bird-dog stand motionless before the stove-door, in which there was isinglass, after the fire had been kindled, staring at the flames and hearkening to the blowing noise and the crackling. The dog was astonished, as a child is at the fire in a stove, not yet knowing what it is. Astonishment is certainly not an emotion peculiar to mankind alone.

Animals experience also the mingling of fear and astonishment, just as children do, especially when some quite new and incomprehensible thing happens. Romanes gives us (1878) the following observations, made by himself, which he adduces as proofs that animals form concepts, but which I use as proofs that fear and astonishment are mingled when the understanding fails —i. e., when insight into the connection of new perceptions with old is lacking:

A dog was afraid of thunder, and became frightened when one day a noise like thunder was made in the house by pouring apples upon the floor of the garret. But when he was taken up there, and had seen what occasioned the uproar, he was again as lively as usual. Horses that are easily frightened behave in a similar manner, showing fear only so long as the cause of a noise remains unknown to them.

Another dog was in the habit of throwing dry bones about. Romanes one day fastened a long, fine thread to a bone, and while the dog was playing with the bone began to draw this away slowly, standing apart. The whole bearing of the dog changed; he started aside, and observed with terror how the bone seemed to move of itself. The same dog was frightened by soap-bubbles on the floor, but touched one of them with his paw, and when it vanished he ran away, manifestly horrified by the incomprehensible disappearance of the large ball.

In these cases, just as in the examples of the child above given (also p. 150), want of knowledge generates fear, but at the same time the novelty of the impressions generates astonishment. In the first case, fear came first and disappeared in astonishment at the recognized cause; in the second, both were present together; in the third, astonishment came first, then fear, on account of lack of comprehension.

If we were to try these three experiments with little children, we should certainly find many who would behave like the dogs—only it would not be easy to select those of the right age. There is no doubt that astonishment makes its appearance earlier than fear.

CHAPTER VII.

SUMMARY OF GENERAL RESULTS.

It is very difficult for the matured human being to place himself in thought in the condition of a child that has had as yet no experiences, or only vague ones; because every individual experience leaves in the brain, without doubt, after the first epochs of growth are successfully passed, an organic modification—as it were a scar—so that the previous condition of the sensorium in the newly-born. a condition as yet undisturbed by individual impressions—affected only by the traces of the experiences of past generations — can not be reconstructed without employing the help of imagination. For the mental state of each man is so much the product of his experiences, that he can not picture himself to himself at all as being without these experiences.

And yet I believe that, on the basis of the facts comprised in the previous chapters, something may be laid down as probable.

With regard to sense-activity in general, we may note, as in the highest degree probable, that before birth no sensation of light exists, no luminous image produced by pressure on the eye, or by pulling upon the optic nerve or the retina, and yet immediately after birth light and darkness are distinguished. It is certain that no sensation of smell is experienced before birth, and yet the newly-born react upon strong-smelling substances in the first hour of life. No human being, certainly, can hear before birth; but several hours (with animals half an hour) after birth reflex movements upon strong impressions of sound have been, in individual cases, regularly demonstrated by me. A sensation of taste, in the strict meaning of the word, can hardly be possessed by the child before birth, but directly after birth he behaves quite differently toward very bitter substances from what he does toward sweet. There remains, then, only the sense of touch, as a probably active one in the fœtal state. Yet the unborn human being, beyond a doubt, is not in condition to distinguish warmth from cold. Accordingly, unless general sensations may exist, it is only sensations of contact that the human being just born has experienced before he comes into the world.

In regard to the development of the separate senses, the following results are especially to be mentioned :

SEEING.—The human child can not see, in the proper meaning of the word, during the first weeks. At the beginning, the child merely distinguishes light from darkness, and discerns the change from one to the other only when a large part of the field of vision is illumined or shaded. But if the light object is much brighter than the surroundings, as the flame of a candle in a dark room, then it produces the sensation of light in the very first week, even if the object be small.

The discrimination of colors is in the first months exceedingly imperfect, and is, perhaps, restricted to the discerning of unequal degrees of light. The first colors to be rightly named are yellow and red, and the sensations of brightness, white, gray, and black ; green and blue, on the contrary, are not correctly named till much later. Probably the child of one year continues to perceive green and blue almost as gray, at any rate as not so different from each other as at a later period. A child will hardly name correctly the four primitive colors mentioned before the end of the second year ; while, on the other hand, every normal child will, in the fourth year, even without special training of the color-sense, recognize and name them better than the compound colors.

The winking of the eyelid on a sudden approach to the face is wanting in the first weeks, and is a reflex movement of the nature of defense, which originates only after a disagreeable feeling, in consequence of a sudden hitherto unobserved change in the field of vision, has been able to be developed. Accordingly, the rapid opening and shutting of the eyes is, from the second month on, a sign of perfected sight, especially a sign of the perception of rapid movements. Further, it is true in general, that the eyes are opened wider when impressions and conditions are agreeable than when disagreeable.

The eye-movements of new-born human beings are not co-ordinated, not associated as they are later in distinct vision, but are in the first days predominantly irregular ; yet it often happens that, among the manifold unregulated movements of the eyes, there even appear turnings of both eyes at the same time to the left, or to the right, or upward, or downward. These originally rare and not quite symmetrical eye-movements, soon become more frequent and quite symmetrical, and gradually displace the irregular movements entirely, because they favor clearer vision.

The "fixation" and distinct seeing of an object are slowly developed. In the first stage the child stares into empty space. In the second, he turns the eye frequently from an object that is in the line of his gaze, e. g., a face, to a remarkably bright object that emerges near by, e. g., the flame of a candle, and then stares at this. In the third stage he follows a slowly-moving object with eye and head, or with the eyes only.

The transition from staring to looking is complete ; that from looking to observing is attained in the fourth stage. Accommodation is now effected ; objects unequally distant from the eye are distinctly seen in succession, whereas, at the beginning, all seemed to be blended in the same plane. The contraction of the pupil comes with convergence of the lines of vision in seeing near objects, whereas, at the beginning, the contraction of the pupil to light, even without near vision, and without convergence, is noticed, and dilated pupils are often present along with convergence. The expression, when there are convergence and binocular vision of a slowly-moving object, is always "intelligent."

The longest delay of all in the child is in the gradual development of the ability to interpret what is seen. Transparency, lustre, shadow, are for years incomprehensible, and lose the mystery that clings to them only through very frequently repeated perception.

The thickness of objects seen remains long unknown, and the third dimension of space becomes a constituent part of perceptions late and imperfectly, in comparison with the first two (the length and breadth). The failures of attempts at seizing objects show how imperfectly (even in the second and third years) the estimate of distance still is; the erroneous interpretations of ordinary sight-impressions, as of steam and flame, prove that the establishment of a relation between the impressions of touch and those of sight is effected but slowly in the first years; and that in particular the perception of the difference between a surface-extension and an extension in three dimensions begins late and is established slowly. Yet the ability to recognize pictures of known objects and persons as such, is developed early.

As to the theory of space-perception, the facts prove directly that there does not exist in the human being immediately after birth a ready-made, inborn mechanism to be set in regular activity by impressions of light; but that the impressions themselves really develop the inherited mechanism, which is but incomplete at birth. In this the empirical theory is correct. The foundations only are innate, not the entire apparatus. And yet this proposition can by no means be admitted to be exclusive, to be invariably true. It is true for mankind; but, on the other hand, many animals that see at birth—especially chickens and pigs, but many others, too—bring with them into the world a mechanism for space-perception that is completely capable of performing its function—that needs only some luminous impressions in order to operate at once nearly or quite as perfectly as in the adult animal. In this case, which supports the most extreme nativism (see p. 34), the possibility of any considerable perfecting of sight by practice on the part of individuals is, it would seem, excluded, to begin with; the chicken, which, when just hatched, pecks accurately at a grain of millet does not learn to see much better through frequent seeing. Man, on the contrary, learns, from the time of birth on, to see better day by day, and, even in later life, can, by much seeing, vastly improve his visional apparatus in more than one direction. The hereditary mechanism is, therefore, still plastic in him— still highly capable of differentiation—because not so far advanced and one-sidedly developed as in the fowl, which is sharp-sighted immediately after being hatched, having a visual organ that is complete, and no longer so plastic, and also relatively much larger.

HEARING.—The hearing of the new-born child is so imperfect that it must be called deaf. All mammals are also incapable of reacting upon impressions of sound immediately after birth. The cause of this peculiarity is partly peripheral. Previous to respiration, air is wanting in the middle ear, and the outer auditory

14

passage is not yet permeable, the tympanum being set too obliquely.

Even after the sound-conducting parts of the ear have become open, from a quarter of a day to several days after birth, there is no discrimination of sounds; but before the end of the first week we notice, in normal children, the characteristic winking of the eyelid after a sudden loud noise. The starting at powerful sound-impressions, which continues for several months, proves the growth of the faculty of hearing. Meanwhile, although particular kinds of sounds, not previously observed, are perceived as different even in the first months of life—e. g., deep voices and high voices, hissing sounds and *s*-sounds, singing and speaking—still, it is three quarters of a year, at least, before a child *knows* the notes of the piano, and it is questionable whether he can learn to name correctly *c, d, e, f, g, a, b* before the end of the second year. Many children, notwithstanding, learn to sing before they talk, and all distinguish the noises and tones of speech long before they can produce them themselves. At the same time the intensity of the sound-impression made, in the case of great differences, is recognized by the attentive observer, by the varying liveliness of the reflexes, even in sleep. The direction of the sound is perceived by the child as early as the second and the third month.

The great superiority of the ear to the eye, from the psychogenetic point of view, is but slightly prominent upon superficial observation of the child that does not yet speak; but we need only compare a child born blind with one born deaf, after both have enjoyed the most careful training and the best instruction, to be convinced that, after the first year, the excitements of the auditory nerve contribute far more to the psychical development than do those of the optic nerve.

Further, many mammals and fowls are provided, at their entrance into the world, with a more developed, much more correctly-working auditory apparatus than that of man, and are far superior in perception of pitch, intensity, and direction of sound, to the human child; but in no animal is the cerebral portion of the organ of hearing capable of so fine differentiation after birth, for none reacts with anything near the precision with which the child reacts upon the subtile variations of intensity and quality of the sounds of human speech.

SENSIBILITY TO CONTACT is, in the first hour of life, much inferior to what it is later; the sense of *temperature* does not yet exist. The latter probably leads, but not till after repeated alternations of warm baths and the cooling off of the whole surface of the skin and of particular places, to discrimination of the sensations "hot, warm, cool, cold," inasmuch as the neutral point of the temperature of the skin, always the same before birth, can not at once be established.

To painful assaults that reach only a few nerves of the skin, the newly-born show an inferior degree of sensibility; yet it can not be doubted that they are capable of highly unpleasant sensations after they have exhibited unambiguous signs of comfort (in nursing and in the warm bath).

The inferior degree of sensibility to contact, as well as to temperature and to pain, in the newly-born, are to be referred (as with the fœtus) to the as yet incomplete development of the brain, not of the skin. On the contrary, the nerves of the skin are very excitable, no doubt because they alone, of all the nerves of sense, are very frequently excited before birth, the movements of the child causing contact at many points of the skin.

TASTE.—Of all the organs of sense that of *taste* is best developed in the new-born child at birth. Sweet is at once distinguished from bitter, sour, or salt, and the sour gives a different sensation from the bitter. Here we have one of the cases, rare in mankind, of innate capacity to distinguish among qualities in the same department of sense. Many animals can likewise immediately after birth distinguish sweet from other tastes. On the other hand, the ability to distinguish unequal intensities of taste is very slightly developed in the child at the beginning of life.

SMELL.—Probably the newly-born can not smell anything immediately on its entrance into the world, because the cavity of the nose has been previously filled up with amniotic fluid; and in the adult, when the cavity has been filled with liquid, there is for some time inability to smell, or a dullness of the sense of smell. But, after some hours, and it may be even in the first hour after birth, normal children can distinguish between agreeable and disagreeable smells. Of many animals, it is known that they do not delay to make use of their sense of smell when the nasal cavity has once been filled with air by breathing. And the normal child, too, early distinguishes clearly different kinds of milk; accordingly, he very likely distinguishes some odors at the end of the first day of life.

FEELINGS.—As to the feelings of the child in the first period of life, it is certain that they are not manifold, indeed (because the activity of the senses is still incomplete), but they may be very intense. Every sensation, when it is compared with a different sensation, produces a feeling. All feelings are either agreeable or disagreeable. In the first case, they awaken in the child the desire for a repetition of the sensation concerned, since the very lack of the agreeable produces discomfort; in the second case, the desire for repetition is not stirred. It is, however, a peculiarity of all agreeable feelings that, after a certain duration, they are no longer agreeable, doubtless because they depend upon excitations of the ganglionic cells, and these cells are soon fatigued when they are intensely excited—i. e., when the feeling is very vivid. In little children this is shown by the rapid change in what they think desirable.

The feelings that are not agreeable are either disagreeable or indifferent. The former are wont to be expressed by vigorous, loud expirations of the breath, by cries, and, even at the earliest period, by an unmistakable play of the countenance, especially by the shape the mouth takes.

Little as is known thus far of the emotions and feelings of the young child, one thing may, however, be declared as certain—that these are the first of all psychical events to appear with definiteness, and that they determine the behavior of the child. Before a sure sign of will, of memory, judgment, inference, in the proper sense, is found, the feelings have expressed themselves in direct connection with the first excitations of the nerves of sense, and before the sensations belonging to the special departments of sense can be clearly distinguished as specifically different. But through repe-

tition of feelings, opposed in character, are gradually
unfolded memory, power of abstraction, judgment, and
inference.

The most powerful agent in the development of the
understanding at the beginning is astonishment, together
with the fear that is akin to it.

Out of the desire of everything that has once occasioned pleasurable feelings is gradually developed the
child's will.

SECOND PART.

DEVELOPMENT OF WILL.

ACTIVITY of will is possible only after perceptions have been had. What is desirable must necessarily have been set off from what is to be repelled, through repeated comparison of sensations, before willing can show itself. For whoever wills, knows what he wills and what he does not will; has previously ascertained what is to him desirable and what is repulsive. The new-born child knows nothing of this, and hence has as yet no will. He has not yet had any experiences in regard to his own states; has not compared any sensations; perceived anything of the external world; and so has obtained no knowledge of what will be to him agreeable or disagreeable. He who wills has gained this knowledge through his own experience, and regulates accordingly his behavior—i. e., his movements.

In order to follow the very slow transition, accomplished not by steps but in a continuous flow, from the one condition to the other, all movements made by the human being while he is still feeble must, as far as possible, be observed, with the question in view, how far they may be expressions of a will.

I therefore put together, in this second part, my observations touching the movements of the child, and some conclusions that follow directly from them, bearing upon the formation of the will.

CHAPTER VIII.

THE MOVEMENTS OF THE CHILD AS EXPRESSIONS OF WILL.

It is only through movements that the will directly expresses itself. The possibility of recognizing the will of the child in his movements must, therefore, be established, and the manifold character of the child's movements be set forth, before we consider the observations upon the gradual development of will.

1. Recognition of the Child's Will.

Widely different as are the phenomena within the domain of will, that owe their origin directly to it, every expression of will is first recognized in movements, viz., words, acts, looks, gestures. Not every spoken sound, nor every act performed, nor every look or gesture, is the expression of an act of will: for sleeping persons can talk ; somnambulists do various things without willing, without knowing what they do; and expressions of countenance may be produced artificially, by electrical stimulus, in opposition to the influence of the will ; and infants that have no will often make gestures, the significance of which as expressions of will (to adults) is wholly unknown to them. But, conversely, it is true strictly and universally, that the will, in the ordinary sense, during its development, announces itself only through the language of words, acts, looks, and gestures.

After its first stages of development it can reveal itself indirectly, also, by the opposite means, to wit, by the suppression of these very movements. No one doubts that a man is capable of expressing his will indirectly by silence and by inactivity, without altering his countenance and without gestures, precisely by the inhibition of movements. In this, however, we have to do, not with a particular kind of willing which is to be classed with those positive expressions of will that have been spoken of, but we have to do with the exact opposite. It is clear that in all these cases in which the will has been already much developed beforehand, the person that inhibits the movement is in the state of non-willing, noluntas, or nolentia, in contrast with voluntas. To this state of being-unwilling belongs the voluntary inhibition of a movement, this inhibition being nothing else than the non-willing of the movement. Non-willing is not, however, characterized by the absence of symptoms of willing, as the mere negation of that, but is a peculiar condition of excitement in that it checks a movement, or is intended to check one.

The will-apparatus, or the complex organism of centro-motor structures of the highest rank, which is to be looked for in the cerebrum, must be so organized that, when it is in activity, some muscular contraction results ; when it is not active, either nothing happens, because there are no ideas (without prejudice to the possibility of immediate activity of will in case a motor idea presents itself), or nothing can happen, because the apparatus is brought to a standstill by other ideas. This last is the state of inhibition, which, as so-called voluntary inhibition or nolition, also controls, from the brain outward, motor centers of lower rank (in part).

To the state of willing is opposed, in general, the state of not-willing; in particular, the state of inhibition of a movement. Not-willing is the excluding or contradictory opposite of willing; inhibition in the physiological sense, the contrary opposite of willing. An illustration will make this clear. Take a bar of soft iron and make it magnetic by means of an electric current that incloses it, and it attracts another piece of iron; but let a second electric current of the proper strength, in a second spiral wire, circulate around the bar in an opposite direction to the first, and the bar no longer attracts the iron. When this second inhibitory current is interrupted, then the attraction is present again. Here the attraction of the iron represents a muscular movement in the condition of willing; the non-attraction represents muscular rest in the condition of not-willing; while in general a bar of iron does not attract another, so, too, in a particular case, a bar of iron encircled by two properly-graded electric currents having opposite directions, likewise does not attract another, but regains its magnetism at once when the second current ceases. Thus, when a child expresses no will—i. e., makes no voluntary movement—two cases are to be distinguished from each other: either the child has as yet no will, or he checks his movements with a will already much developed: he wills, namely, that a movement shall not be made. As soon as the inhibition or nolition passes away, movement appears again, in case the antecedents of it in the brain have not in the mean time vanished. For voluntary inhibition has influence in general only on those muscles the nerves of which are in organic connection with the cerebrum, the seat of the will.

This distinction between willing and voluntary inhibition may seem an idle one, but it is necessary, because it refutes the notion that one can will a non-activity. One can merely will-not-to-be, inhibit, prevent activity; for it lies in the nature of willing to be always positive. It can, therefore, be recognized only by positive expressions; where these are wanting, we are authorized to deny its actual presence, and we have then to investigate not-willing (or willing not-to-be, or not-to-act).

Now, according to experience, the expressions of will are four only—word, act, look, gesture. If, then, it is to be ascertained whether a child is in the state of willing, at least one of the four forms of expression must be proved by observation to be present. Failing in this, we must conclude that, invariably, at the time of observation, the individual observed was demonstrably not in the state of willing.

But, granting that we succeed, the inference as to the presence of the will continues still to be uncertain, inasmuch as in some circumstances the phenomena mentioned appear without will. Hence, we need more exact criteria.

In the first place, it is settled that all willing is recognized exclusively by movements of contractile parts of the willing being—in man and the higher animals by muscular contractions induced by excitement of nerves. But there are various classes of nervo-muscular movements, and in beings of low order without nerves

and muscles there are movements of contractile tissues
to which choice can not in advance be denied. Finally,
in all cases where a contractile tissue exists, direct stimulus of this is capable of producing contraction, which
may take precisely the same course as if, instead of the
artificial stimulus, the will itself had caused it.

In order to ascertain in the midst of these manifold
movements of contractile structures those to which the
predicate " willed" applies, we should be obliged to
have an objective sign once for all present in those very
movements, and wanting in all others. But such a criterion can not be given.

Only subjective means of distinguishing can be
given, and the four following are, in my view, characteristic :

1. Every willed movement is preceded directly by
ideas, one of which, finally, as cause of the movement,
acquires motor force.

2. Every willed movement is previously known in
general, or in its kind, to the one who executes it, and
it has—

3. An aim, more or less clearly represented in his
mind ; finally, the movement may—

4. Even at the instant of the rise of the voluntary
impulse, be inhibited by new ideas.

The three first-named signs accompany every willed
movement ; the last makes its appearance only after the
will is completely formed, and stamps the willed movements as voluntary in the stricter sense.

Every movement to which these four characteristics
do not apply is involuntary. Accordingly, all muscular
movements of man may, in fact, be distinguished as

willed and not-willed, voluntary and involuntary. Many
willed movements are executed by adults involuntarily
also—e. g., talking in sleep; many involuntary movements voluntarily, especially by actors; but, for all that,
the essential difference of the two remains. For the impulse to an involuntary movement has something added
to it when it is changed into a voluntary; and the impulse to a voluntary movement has something subtracted
from it when it becomes involuntary. This something
is precisely the purely psychical element of the previous
motor idea, the knowledge of the movement and of its
aim, and the possibility of its being inhibited by new
ideas.

When do these attributes appear in the child?

The answer to this question, as I shall attempt to
give it, presupposes that shortly before birth, and in a
higher degree immediately after birth, the motor centers possess a variable excitability, of such a sort that
in certain conditions, especially the first agreeable ones,
they supply fewer motor impulses; in certain other conditions—the first disagreeable ones—they supply more
such impulses. By this the irregular, manifold, inborn
movements of the very young babe are influenced necessarily—e. g., they are increased in the condition of hunger; and this influence appears as the manifestation of
an innate faculty of desire, so called. The movements
continue until the increased excitability (e. g., that
caused by hunger) is lessened. Then the assumed desire
seems satisfied. With repeated variation in the central
excitability (due purely to organic causes—nutrition,
supply of oxygen, etc.), the feeling that now appears,
of satisfied or unsatisfied desire, will work upon the

motor central organs in opposite ways, and will impart to the innate movements the character of longing or of repulsion. But these movements can not be transformed into willed movements until ideas are formed.

Thus the will does not arise out of nothing, and does not pre-exist as such, but is developed out of that desire, which on its part is not a fundamental, simple function of the ganglionic cell, but the result of the variations in the excitability of that cell by means of feelings and then of ideas. The will, as such, is not inborn, but it is hereditary: The variable excitability of the motor central organs, and, associated with that, a succession of primitive (impulsive) movements, which adults designate as movements of "longing," and ascribe to a faculty of desire; this is inborn in every one as the first germ of willing. The question is, When does this germ manifest itself in such a way that no doubt can exist of the presence of will?

Evidently we must, in order to find the answer, test the normal infant, proceeding chronologically in our experiments, to ascertain whether a new movement, as, e. g., the first grasping at an object seen, is accidental or intentional; i. e., whether the grasping movement is known to the child that desires as well as grasps, and whether its aim actually hovers before him. But even then the movement is not yet necessarily voluntary. It is so, however, when it can be omitted; say, on account of the idea of disagreeable consequences.

Although the discovery of the appearance of such activity of will in the child has an element of uncertainty in it, because it comes at a time when verbal language is still wanting, yet the determination of the first

instance of excitement in non-willing is much more difficult. Here, however, the earliest independent inhibition of accustomed movements presents something for
us to lay hold of.

Both taken together—the development of will in
the actually-executed movements of the child, and the
development of non-willing in the inhibition of frequently - repeated movements—furnish the foundation
for the formation of character. Both demand for their
investigation, above all, a careful observation of the
movements of the child from the beginning of its life.
No one has up to the present time even attempted this.

2. Classification of the Child's Movements.

A principle of classification for the movements of
the human being, sufficient for all actual cases, has not
yet been found. I must, therefore, attempt a new one,
in order simply that the movements of the child that
appear in the first years of life may be brought into
groups for a synoptical presentation.

If in this scheme of classification we regard the process immediately preceding the movement as the exclusive criterion of distinction, then there will be four
different kinds of movements, according to the com-
plexity of this process, to be separated from one another
—movements of the first, second, third, and fourth rank
—further movements may be derived from these, as
will appear in what follows.

The accompanying diagram will serve for illustration. It lays claim only to a general significance—i. e.,
it is true anatomically only of the relation of each case
to the following case :

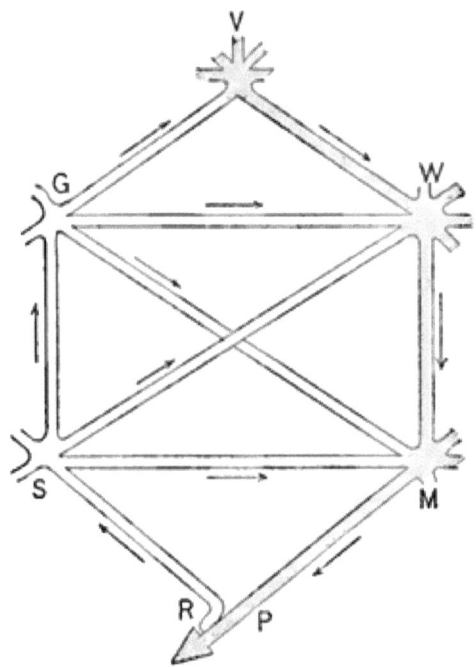

R represents the extremities of all the nerves of sense (in the eye, ear, mouth, nose, skin).

R S, the nerves of sense in their course (e. g., the paths of the optic nerve, auditory nerve, cutaneous nerves, in the upper portion of the pe- duncle of the cerebrum).

S, the lower sensory centers (e. g., optic thalami, corpora quadrigemi- na, corona radiata).

G, the higher sensory or emotional centers in the cerebral cortex (pa- rietal region).

V, the ideational centers in the cerebral cortex.

W, the higher motor or volitional centers (centro-motor and inhibitory) in the cortex also.

M, the lower motor centers.

P, the extremities of the motor nerves (muscles).

I. *Impulsive Movements.*—These may be distin- guished from all other movements by this, that they are caused without previous peripheral excitement, ex- clusively by the nutritive and other organic processes that go on in the motor centers of the lowest rank (M P). They are movements which the fœtus already executes, and earlier than any others, at a time when, as it can not possibly be incited to movement by peripheral stimulus, its centripetal paths are not yet practicable or not yet formed at all, and the ganglionic cells from which the excitations proceed are not yet developed. After birth such purely centro-motor impulses may continue long after complete development of the centers, especially in sleep. All these movements are unconscious.

II. *Reflex Movements.*—These require peripheral excitation—i. e., sense-impressions and centripetal, intercentral, and centrifugal paths (R S M P); they make their first appearance, therefore, in the embryo of the higher animals, after two sorts at least of centers of lower rank connected with each other are formed—sensory and motor. All reflex movements, in normal conditions, follow the sense-impression with great promptness and become conscious only after they have taken place.

III. *Instinctive Movements.* — These likewise require the presence of certain sense-impressions, and of at least three sorts of centers that have morphological connection with one another. Lower sensory, higher sensory, and lower motor centers must co-operate, in order that the simplest instinctive movement may take place (R S G M P). For these movements arise only after a sensation, and then an emotion, that supplied the motor impulse, have preceded. The instinctive movement must be preceded by a condition for which I find no more fitting designation than the word disposition (*Stimmung*). Yet the development of the ganglionic cells of the cerebral cortex is not required for all in-

15

stinctive movements—e. g., for sucking, which on that account comes near to the genuine reflexes. All instinctive movements have an aim, but are unconscious, as such, before and while they take place; and all are hereditary. Accordingly, when a human being or an animal executes a movement that was never executed by his ancestors, this movement can not be instinctive. This serves to distinguish instinctive from other movements, though it is to be borne in mind that many movements of the child may have been executed by his ancestors, which are not in the least instinctive. The ideo-motor movements of Carpenter are instinctive movements that lack the characteristic of heredity.

IV. *Ideational* (*Vorgestellte*) *Movements.* As the lowest form and the point of departure of this group, already characterized, are to be taken *imitative movements* or copies of others. These are necessarily dependent on sense-perceptions, and require at least four sorts of centers—lower and higher sensory, and lower and higher motor (R S G V W M P and V W M P; five, therefore, when G and V are separated). The centrifugal paths probably go, according to Meynert, all of them, from the cortex through the corpora striata and the lower portion of the peduncle of the cerebrum, but according to others directly also to the anterior columns of the spinal marrow. For the production of the most simple imitation, and so of the simplest ideational movement, the sense-impression must be previously elaborated as to time, space, and cause, i. e., wrought out to the formation of an idea, and this idea then works with motor force; it is determinative for the excitement of the motor centers and the muscles that reproduce the sense-impression. Imitations are, therefore, in the normal waking condition, always conscious; they can be unconscious only in various conditions of partial sleep. But in this case many conscious imitations have gone before. A participation on the part of the cerebral cortex is certain, whereas all movements of the first and second, and many of the third rank, take place without that.

From these four kinds of movement of the child may be derived all other centro-motor movements—passive and peripheral, caused by artificial stimulus of the motor nerves in their course are not considered—since we may suppose not only the expressive movements, but also the whole of the specifically voluntary, i. e., deliberate movements, to have arisen partly out of the frequent repetition, concurrence, and union of the four kinds named, partly from modifications of these according to the variation in the sense-impressions, feelings, and ideas. Physical causes only lie at the foundation of the first two kinds of movement; the last two have also psychical causes. Inhibitions of the discharges of motor impulses in the child whose will is completely developed, come to pass, as in the adult, in the following manner:

(1) R S M, (2) R S W M, (3) R S G M,
   (4) R S G W M, (5) R S G V W M,

and after very frequent repetition also without an immediately preceding excitement of the nerves of sense, R S, of which later.

No direct causes of the child's movements can be named beyond these four: (1), central, purely physical, stimuli; (2), peripheral, purely physical, stimuli; (3), feelings; (4), ideas. They correspond to the above groups. If, notwithstanding, the expressive, or expressional movements, and the deliberate movements, are hereafter treated by themselves, it is because of merely external reasons, in order not to complicate too much the presentation of the facts, a matter difficult at best. The intentional, voluntary, deliberate movements can not be separated physiologically from others, because no decisive objective criterion of distinction can be given; on the contrary, an involuntary movement becomes voluntary, simply by taking on something psychical, a particular activity of the central organs of the highest rank, which alters nothing in the movement itself (unless by incidentally delaying it somewhat and making it less harmonious). In truth, a physical difference no more exists between a voluntary and an artificial, electrical, nervo-muscular excitation than between the vibrations of the air from a vowel-sound sung and one artificially produced. The cock of the gun once set going, the shot follows invariably in the same fashion, no matter whether it was willed or not, whether it had an aim or not.

Only the muscular movements before birth, and in the earliest period after birth, take a somewhat different course from that of the later ones; for, according to Soltmann, the excitability of the motor nerves of the newly-born is inferior to that of adults, and does not surpass that in domestic mammalia until several weeks after birth. The muscles of the newly-born are like the wearied muscles of adults. With this is doubtless connected the peculiar sluggishness of the movements in the earliest period—a sluggishness that forms the greatest contrast to the vivacity of a later period, and that is interrupted in the transition period (as in the case of the marmot waking from his winter sleep) by surprising stretchings of the arms and legs, following one another almost in jerks.

CHAPTER IX.

IMPULSIVE MOVEMENTS.

ALTHOUGH the movements of the extremities in the unborn and the just-born child lack a characteristic mark by which these movements might at once be recognized as impulsive, they must, as must all later impulsive movements, be sharply distinguished from the reflex, the instinctive, the imitative, and other ideational movements, because they lack all the characteristic signs of the latter, as the following comparison will show :

The movements of the arms and legs of the fœtus and of the newly-born are of a *reflex* character, when a peripheral stimulus, be it only contact with the wall of the uterus, immediately precedes them. But how does the first movement of the embryo come to pass? That it can not be occasioned by passive contact has been proved to me by means of a close observation of the chick in the egg—the creature moves of itself, as I found, from the beginning of the fifth day. Here occur first only movements of the trunk, then also of the extremities and head—exactly as in the unharmed embryo of the trout, and like what occurs in the embryo of the frog in the egg—without the least change in the surroundings, and long before the reflex excitability is

present at all, the details of which are given in my book
on the " Physiology of the Embryo."

The cause of these remarkable primitive movements
of the trunk in unborn animals must exist in the animals
themselves, therefore, and can not be derived from a reaction of the superficial portions upon the central ones.
The same must be the case with the human embryo.

The impulsive movements are not *instinctive*, because they have no aim. They can not be designated
as directly useful or advantageous, appearing, as they do,
in an extremely irregular manner, nor can they, in general, be styled movements answering to a purpose. It
happens, in fact, that the very young child, by throwing
his arms and legs violently about, directly harms himself. In sleep he strikes his eye with his hand, rolls
himself aimlessly hither and thither when fast asleep,
so that he beats his head against the hard wood, and
wakes himself up, or cries out in a dream. Once I saw
my child (of sixteen months), when sound asleep, suddenly raise his left hand and put it against his left eye,
evidently by pure accident, so that the lid was raised.
The child slept on with one eye open—the pupil much
contracted—for a long time, and then removed his hand
without waking, just as accidentally, upon which the
lid dropped again. The eye did not move, notwithstanding the stimulus of the light. In this case the
convulsive raising of the arm first into the air and then
to the eye is to be called impulsive and almost dangerous, but not instinctive; besides, all purely instinctive
movements are co-ordinated, the impulsive movements
—the greater part of them—not co-ordinated.

The impulsive movements can not be *expressive*, for

the reason that, before birth, states of feeling which
might be expressed by these are not to be assumed, and
the presumable seat of such excitations in the brain—
in fact, the whole brain—may be wanting without the
appearance of the least change in the impulsive movements of the extremities, as I have proved in the case of
the animal embryo, and as has been demonstrated by the
movements of headless and brainless human abortions.
Neither does the attribute *voluntary* apply to them, because no ideas, as yet, exist of their possible results; nor
the term *imitative*, because a model is wanting. Moreover, Soltmann has proved, by many experiments, that
in the new-born dog, after manifold stimulus of the
cerebral cortex no movements at all of the muscles of
the extremities—the face, neck, back, belly, or tail—are
produced, but that, on the contrary, these appear only
from the tenth day, after the animals have got their
sight. Corresponding to this, the destruction of the
parts answering to the motor departments of the cortex in older animals had also no effect in creatures from
one to nine days old. No ataxy followed—no paralysis or disturbance of the muscular sense, or the like, even
up to the time when the electric excitability of the brain
existed. The muscular movements of new-born blind
dogs are thus, for this very reason, quite independent of
the gray cerebral cortex, as well as of peripheral stimulus—i. e., they are impulsive.

There is nothing left but to assume a cause of the
impulsive movements that is internal, given in the organic constitution of the motor ganglionic cells of the
spinal marrow, and connected, in the early embryonic
stages, with the differentiation and the growth of those

structures and of the muscular system. With the formation of the motor ganglionic cell in the spinal marrow and cervical marrow a certain quantity of potential energy must accumulate, which, by means of the flow of blood or of lymph, or possibly through the rapidly advancing formation of tissue, is, with remarkable ease, transformed into kinetic energy.

Difficult as it is to specify with certainty, in later life, movements of the human being that take place without peripheral excitement of any sort, direct or indirect, here we have them. And it is worthy of notice that impulsive movements, which outnumber others before birth and perpetually appear in all the newly-born, diminish even during the nursing period, and withdraw in proportion as the will develops, until finally, with ever-increasing voluntary inhibition of the original youthful impulse of movement, such muscular activity appears, in the adult, almost solely in dreamless sleep.

In the text-books hardly any notice is to be found of these peculiar centro-motor excitations, yet these are precisely of the very highest importance in the formation of the will. Alexander Bain alone has (1859) distinguished them definitely from other movements. He calls them automatic and spontaneous; but, as he reckons among these the movements that result from muscular sensations also, in young children and animals —movements which are to be referred to the condition of the muscles, and so to peripheral excitations—I can not entirely agree with him; for I give the name of "purely impulsive," and have given it (in my treatise "Psychogenesis," * 1880) exclusively to the muscular

---

* See "Jour. Spec. Phil.," April, 1881, for English translation.—ED.

contractions, proceeding from the fœtal constitution of the motor centers, that take place before centripetal stimuli operate, and so before muscular sensations can exist and assert themselves in stimulating movement.

The number of such movements is not great. Aside from those of the unborn, which are not to be taken into account here, the following may be specified: The out-stretching and bending of the arms and legs of the child just born, with movements sometimes quick, sometimes slow, generally non-coördinated, often co-ordinated, is nothing else than a continuation of the intra-uterine movements, and has, according to my observations, a striking resemblance to the extensions and flexions of the limbs of animals suddenly waking from their deep winter sleep. These, like sleeping children (and, indeed, in the first half of the second year it is still plainly marked), make genuine fœtal movements, which look as if they were directed against some invisible resistance. Convulsive motion is generally not so frequent in sleep as slow contractions, along with spreading and bending of the fingers, movements which likewise become more rare toward the end of the second year (probably with all sound children), and are from the beginning mostly asymmetrical.

The stretching of the limbs immediately after waking, which I have seen repeatedly in the second week, is often not distinguishable from these movements. It remains for years almost unchanged. In the twentieth month I saw it appear well marked, without being followed by waking.

The movements of the eyes before opening them at waking, especially the lateral turnings of the pupil, are impulsive. I have seen these movements, which can not be dependent on light, even in adults. The pupils moved rapidly under the lids this way and that, and indeed asymmetrically also. The lids, too, were meanwhile half opened, without any interruption of the snoring (in the second month).

The movements of the newly-born and of the infant in the bath, which has very nearly the same warmth as the amniotic fluid that perpetually surrounds the child before birth, can not be regarded as simply reflexive in character. We may, indeed, see in them already the beginning of expressive movements, especially expressions of pleasure, the more so since they are regularly accompanied by an extremely contented expression of countenance (protrusion of the lips also); but these movements in the bath are for a long time (so late as the fourth month)—the greater part of them—just as purposeless, senseless, and asymmetric as on the first day. Sometimes the trunk also takes part in them, with half twistings and raisings, and this as early as the second month.

There is nothing expressive in this. The infant is accustomed, also, as late as in the period from the fourth to the sixth month, just as on the first day, when he is left to himself, in the warm bath and in falling asleep, to give to his arms and legs by preference the same position almost that they had before birth. The position of the legs continues to be that of the fœtus even much longer. The muscular contractions required for that are impulsive.

A further impulsive muscular activity is brought to our acquaintance by observation of the play of feature, still empty of meaning, in sleeping babes. They very often move the facial muscles without waking, especially the lips and eyelids, and, indeed, for the most part, with bilateral symmetry, although grotesquely, and this without any interruption of their snoring.

Babes that are awake also strike very vigorously about them with their arms (in the third quarter of the first year) quite aimlessly, while for the legs, as a rule, more frequently, in bed and bath especially, there is a pretty symmetrical alternation of stretching and bending.

Yet it must be noted that the bilaterally symmetrical movement of the facial muscles and of the arms in reflexes appears very much earlier and is more pronounced than that of the legs. And the abductions, adductions, supinations, and rotations of the arms unquestionably appear plainly at an earlier period than do those of the legs in manifold variety. In the case of a very vigorous child, I saw that even in the first half-hour of its life the lips were protruded, and the mouth opened and shut, with perfect co-ordinate symmetry. The corrugation of the forehead, and the screwing up of the eyes, in the first hour of life, however, is not always impulsive; the latter, especially, is often of a reflex character. Only the strange asymmetrical grimaces of new-born children when awake are probably purely impulsive. In connection with this, I have been surprised at the immobility of the nose, which I have not seen moved earlier than in the seventh month; of course, I except the very early dilating of the nostrils by means of the levator alæ nasi, as a reflex and an accompanying movement in snoring, sucking, and difficult breathing.

Crowing and other similar exercises of the voice are in the first year to be regarded in many cases as discharges of accumulated motor impulses, which, as well as the squeaking of new-born animals, and the peeping of the chick in the egg, can not have their origin merely in peripheral excitement. Precisely as the muscles of the arms and legs, of the face and of the eyes, so those of respiration, of the tongue, and of the larnyx are set in activity without purpose by a centro-motor impulse. In the first year the exercise of the muscles is with all healthy children the beneficial result of such animation, which, considered in itself, seems entirely purposeless. An adult lying on his back could not make these persistent movements, that are made by the seven-to-twelve months child, without a decided feeling of fatigue ; and, when we consider that the child, in addition, turns his head attentively, and cries at every noise, at every change in his neighborhood, the total of the nervous excitements seems relatively much greater in the one-year-old child than in the adult, who makes fewer superfluous movements, and has become dull to ordinary sense-impressions.

Here belong, further, " accompanying " movements made by little children.

In individual cases it can hardly be determined whether movements wholly useless (like those described on pages 23 and 24). especially of the facial muscles, are merely impulsive, or are the remains of an extinct instinct, or are accompanying-movements. We have an example in the holding out of the little finger apart from the others at the first attempts of the child to carry the soup-spoon to the mouth without help. In the eighteenth month this graceful movement was executed by my boy without the least incitement, and without any one's having made the movement before in his neigh borhood, absolutely " of himself." Surprising as it seemed at the beginning—it occurred often from that time on—I can not admit that an imitation of unknown examples is at the bottom of this, because the child did not give the least attention to his finger, but, on the contrary, was wholly absorbed in carrying the contents of the spoon to his mouth. The extending of the little finger straight into the air probably came in as an ac companying-movement, but not in accord with the movement of the other fingers, without the cognizance of the child. In the third year it was only very rarely to be seen, and then also it was manifestly uncon scious.

Another still more surprising movement, wholly purposeless, and withal quite bilaterally symmetrical, was observed by me frequently in the first year, and even in the last month of it. When my child, namely, lying on his back on a soft couch, received the nursing-bottle which the nurse tilted for him holding it in her hand, he used almost invariably to stretch out his closed hands upward, with the lower arm bent at right angles to the upper arm, which rested on the cush-ion or the coverlet. And in this strange attitude the child remained until he had drained the bottle. If he was obliged (toward the end of the first year) to use one hand for giving the bottle a different direction or for holding it, then the arm that did not take part in this remained in its peculiar position. This has no resem-blance at all to the position of seizing; seems rather to be an accompanying-movement going along with extreme strain of the attention. When the child was allowed to drink out of a glass (in the sixteenth month) that was held to his mouth, he would then stretch out his hands and spread all the fingers, and while drinking would not cease from the muscular contractions necessary to those movements; this had a very peculiar look, and was more suggestive of grasping.

Further, all little children make unsteady accompanying-movements of various sorts, especially when they hear new sounds—music, singing. They like to move the arms up and down at such times. In play, too, when the cover of a pitcher is put on and off before their eyes, there is often a corresponding movement with the hand, executed while the cover is clapped to and subsequently (eighth and ninth months), after the first observations have once been made by the children. Here we have to do not with attempts at imitation, but with pure accompanying-movements. The child sees and hears or tastes something new, strains his attention, and has a feeling (an agreeable one) of gratified curiosity. This feeling leads to the motor discharge. Such a movement showed itself in my boy frequently in the fourth year, especially with new impressions of taste. His right forearm would go sidewise hither and thither from two to four times in a second, while he was tasting a new kind of food that he desired.

All accompanying-movements of this kind, which approximate to the reflexes, are no more purely impulsive, because they require a peripheral excitement, and because feelings co-operate in them. On the other hand, the movements of the head and legs in new-born puppies, and of most new-born mammals in general (movements called droll and comical on account of their striking awkwardness), are probably purely impulsive. And the trembling of these creatures in a warm bed belongs here also (p. 171).

CHAPTER X.

REFLEX MOVEMENTS.

THE fact firmly established by me in the case of numerous animal embryos, that no reflex movements can be elicited in early stages of development by however strong and varied stimulus, whereas movements, especially bendings and stretchings of the trunk, regularly take place from internal causes, proves the untenableness of a wide-spread view, according to which all movements of the newly-born are of a reflex character. The human being just born has, in fact, in many respects, a less reflex excitability than the infant manifests later, and yet he moves in a lively manner.

Notwithstanding this, many reflex movements of the newly-born are already strongly marked, answering to the reflex excitability that increases rapidly before birth in the last stage of the foetal development; and they have a very great psychogenetic significance, because through their frequent repetition the harmonious co-working of many muscles as means of warding off what might injure or be unpleasant is soon perfected, and the development of the will is made possible through these co-ordinations. Then, later, is manifested, in unmistakable fashion, the power of the growing

cerebral will-mechanism in the inhibition of reflexes.
These must, for this reason, have occurred previously
in great numbers, so that again and again harmful results have arisen, and the experience, e. g., has been
made, "Crying does no good, crying brings harm ;
better, then, keep down the violent, loud expiration."
Through logical operations of this sort—long before
gaining the power of speech—the foundation is laid for
self-control, which rests essentially upon the inhibition
of reflex movements.

The beginning of reflex muscular contractions comes
in the period before birth. For it is possible through
outward impressions, even by means of continued gentle
stroking (*Palpiren*), to produce and to augment movements of the fœtus in the more advanced fœtal period.
From my observations, I regard it as certain, also, that
rough handling during the birth, especially where the
amniotic fluid is scanty, may produce premature respiratory movements in the child, and thereby endanger its
life—a thing for midwives and physicians to heed. The
embryo begins early to swallow. The chick in the egg
makes movements of swallowing on the eleventh day ;
and before anything of the creature is visible—on the
twenty-first day of the brooding, according to my observations—can be brought, by means of a prick of a
needle, by cooling, and other harsh treatment, to loud
peeping; the prematurely-born rabbit may be made to
squeak by electric stimulation, provided only respiration
has begun. I have even seen the embryo of the Guinea-
pig in an unbroken ovary (in a warm, very much diluted solution of common salt) before a breath had been
drawn—the placental circulation being maintained—not

only make bilaterally symmetrical reflexes with the extremities on being lightly touched, but I have repeatedly proved, also, that in this case the touching of the lips, especially of the whiskers (*Spürhaare*), produces an extremely well-adapted movement of rubbing with the fore-paw of the same side—in the amniotic fluid—a movement, accordingly, which is, later, very frequent with the Guinea-pig, and which is proved by this observation to be absolutely hereditary. But if the touching of the lip or any portion of the skin is carried so far as to become pricking or pressure, then an inhalation takes place, and with that the reflex activity is modified.

A series of new reflexes begins also with the birth of the human being, through breathing.

The first cry of the new-born child was, indeed, formerly regarded as anything but reflex, yet it is in the highest degree probable that this first loud expiration is a pure reflex effect. Kant wrote (certainly without having himself observed children and animals just born): "The outcry that is heard from a child scarcely born has not the tone of lamentation, but of indignation and of aroused wrath; not because anything gives him pain, but because something frets him; presumably because he wants to move, and feels his inability to do it as a fetter that deprives him of his freedom. What can be the intent of Nature in causing the child to come with loud outcry into the world, when both for child and mother in a savage condition of nature, this is attended with the utmost danger? No animal, however, except man (as he now is), makes loud announcement of his existence at the time of his birth."

This remarkable view has been commented on in

16

various ways, and even at the present time many persons think that the whimpering and crying of the child just born have a higher psychical significance. All interpretations of this sort go to wreck upon the repeatedly established fact that new-born children without any brain at all cry out, and many healthy new-born children at their coming into the world, as Darwin reports, do not cry, but sneeze. In both cases the expirational reflex must be occasioned by a strong peripheral excitement— e. g., the sudden cooling off of the skin, and the rubbing of the back. For I have observed in the case of many new-born animals, especially Guinea-pigs, that they make their voice heard, with the same machine-like regularity as does the frog deprived of brain, if you simply stroke their backs. It is known, too, that many animals cry out during birth, and immediately thereafter. Calves especially bleat normally, not only directly after they have left the bodies of the mothers, but, as experienced farmers assure me, often even during birth. Goats often cry out directly after birth.

The purely reflexive movement of sneezing is frequent with the newly-born and with infants. It demonstrates the existence of a very firm connection, long hereditary, of the nasal branches of the trigeminus with the motor expiratory nerves, and is remarkable, as sobbing is, for the reason that it requires an inborn complex co-ordination of many muscles. In observations concerning reflex excitability, the sneezing of infants is a much better sign of the effect of stimulus than are other movements. On the thirty-eighth day I saw sneezing produced by some drops of lukewarm water that trickled over the forehead ; on the forty third day I saw that particles of witch-meal caused sneezing; on the hundred and seventieth mere blowing on the child had the same effect. Adults do not readily show such sensibility. In sneezing, the eyes even of little children are invariably closed (just so it is with apes, according to Darwin); why, is not satisfactorily explained. Donders found that the contents of the blood-vessels of the eye are lessened by the closing of the lid. The shutting of the eyes in violent expiration of breath seems from this to have a purpose. But it is purely reflex in character. F. H. Champneys, who observed his son throughout the first nine months, found that sneezing was always accompanied by violent movements of all the limbs, the legs being drawn up, and the forearms bent with the elbows pushed forward; noteworthy symmetrical accompanying-movements, which, however, do not appear in all infants.

Other innate forms of loud expiration of breath are common with very small children, as is well known, but are likewise of very little or no psychogenetic significance; thus, wheezing or snuffling, a phenomenon accompanying sucking; snoring (first observed by me on the twenty-fourth day), yawning with wide-stretched mouth, a striking habit in all infants in the early period, and which, merely as an augmented and intensified manner of drawing in the breath, helps to bring the respiratory apparatus, little by little, into regular activity, inasmuch as it probably comes on invariably after a succession of scanty inhalations, by way of compensation, after a stronger respiratory stimulus, or because the excitability of the respirational center has in the mean time increased. I once saw a child yawn on the seventh day

of its life, stretching its mouth very wide, and at the
same time screwing the eyelids together; and it kept this
attitude for some seconds. This child generally distorted its face in a remarkable manner when it had been
disturbed in going to sleep. But a direct physiological
connection of yawning with the dropping of the lids
and with sleepiness is not demonstrated, unless we count
as such the increased demand for oxygen, caused by the
fatigue of the respiratory muscles also, which may produce a deeper inspiration. Here, too, belongs the coughing that I, in one case, heard with perfect distinctness,
in the first hour of life. Clearing the throat is, on the
contrary, acquired, as Darwin rightly observes. Still,
in very young babes, who cough somewhere about the
fourth day, involuntary coughing has, as a matter of
fact, the same effect as voluntary clearing the throat has
later. The early involuntary pushing out of the nipple
by means of the tongue, after nursing, is, in fact, much
more adroit than the later voluntary spitting out of the
skin of a grape or gooseberry that has been crushed and
sucked out in the mouth. Yet the latter complicated
movement was executed quite skillfully in the nineteenth month (Sigismund).

Sobbing and sighing, two psychically characteristic
forms of expiration in later life, have in the infant not
the least expressional significance. Both make their
appearance late, under normal conditions. I observed
sighing in the seventh month, and that repeatedly after
the child had been brought from the recumbent to the
upright, half-sitting position. Sighing often appeared
in my child—even in the second year—when he was in
a contented mood, and this without its being an imitation.

The respiratory movements go on at the beginning of life, in general, without any relation whatever to the emotions. The heaving of the bosom in mental agitation, the holding of the breath under the strain of attention—these things do not take place in the very earliest youth. The respiration of the infant is, however, very irregular in the first weeks, so that there is an illusory appearance of such phenomena. In the newly-born, the breathing, now violent, now again quite weak, interrupted by intervals in which the breathing ceases, then rhythmical, then soon after alternately deep and light, approaches but slowly the later type.

At the close of the seventh week the number of respirations made by my boy in sleep was twenty-eight to the minute; in the thirteenth week twenty-seven. But for months yet the breathing was irregular. After four or five quick inspirations, would often follow a cessation interrupted by separate, deep breathings. The older the child, so much the more regular the movements of breathing and the less their frequency. During the teething-fever the number went up (in the ninth month) temporarily to forty and forty-two in a minute, and in the sixteenth and seventeenth months, during sleep, amounted to twenty-two and twenty-five a minute. From this period on, the character of it was predominantly regular: in the twentieth month it was twenty-two and twenty-three. But whenever there is a noise made that is not quite loud enough to wake the quietly-sleeping infant, then the frequency of the breaths immediately increases to twenty-five and twenty-six, to fall again soon to twenty-two and twenty-three. This extraordinary reflex sensibility of the respiratory apparatus I have often observed (p. 83). It is noteworthy because it proves the existence of a reflex arc from the auditory nerve to the inspiratory nerves (of the intercostal muscles and the diaphram).

The very slow consolidation of the entire respiratory mechanism in all infants is certainly connected with this great reflex excitability. In later life stronger and more numerous stimuli may operate without the least change in the respiration. Moreover, since breathing, like the activity of the heart, gradually settles into a regular rate without the participation of the will, it affords an excellent example of the development of a very complicated, co-ordinated, involuntary muscular activity of which no trace exists, under normal conditions, before birth. This co-ordination, however, as it begins directly after birth, in consequence of sufficiently strong excitement of the cutaneous nerves, as an imperfect periodical reflex, is not only hereditary but inborn, yet not so perfect as after it has been longer manifested.

Of reflexes not periodical those especially frequent in other departments are, in infants, vomiting, choking, and hiccough—all three inborn movements, which are performed at once in the same manner as they are later.

In choking, children of one to five days old stretch forth the tongue, with a reflexive elevation of the larynx, and make grimaces, as adults do when they wish by a choking movement to throw out a foreign substance from the œsophagus. The usual occasion of choking in infants seems to be accumulation of mucus, but it may also be produced by tickling the palate and the roots of the tongue, or by moistening them with bitter substances, on the first day (pp. 98, 121); nay, even by moistening the upper lip with bad-smelling substances (p. 131), and later by the sight of loathed food (p. 126).

Vomiting occurs both after overfilling the stomach with unsuitable liquid (even nurse's milk) and on putting the finger into the throat. In the fifth week I saw both cases, and observed how, without any external stimulus, the milk that had been swallowed shortly before sprang forth like a fountain, three or four inches high, from the mouth of the boy as he lay on his back. Eructation is not infrequent even in the first week.

Hiccough is observed to be very frequent in children in the first three months; much more frequent than in adults. I have observed it within the first twenty hours after the birth of the child. It can be stopped by putting upon the tongue half a spoonful of lukewarm sweetened water. After the swallowing of this small quantity, a very obstinate case of hiccough that I saw (in the tenth week) yielded; but I find no explanation for the effect of this simple remedy. For the diversion of attention is hardly sufficient here, since other sense-impressions do not produce the same result. The complicated mechanism for the movements of swallowing is inborn, and already performs its functions in man and in animals long before birth.

More important than all these typical reflexes, in their bearing on the genesis of mind, are the already-mentioned reflexive eye-movements and the movements of the limbs and of the head, following irritation of the skin, particularly by blowing and by tickling, and sound-impressions. Of the first sort frequent mention has been made in the first part of this book; in regard to the last I was in hopes of finding, by frequent observation of sleeping children, confirmation of the conformity to law that Pflüger discovered, such as exists in animals deprived of their brain. I was strengthened in my view after the first experiment (on the fourteenth day of my child's life), for, upon touching the *left* temple of the sleeping child, he started, and directed the *left* hand toward the place that was touched (law of the conduction on the same side for unilateral reflexes). This experiment, repeated at intervals, yielded the same result three times. In the same way, in the fourteenth week, when I touched the right eye on the inner corner with the finger-nail, the right hand of the child went directly to that spot and rubbed the eye; but, when I made the touch on the left, the left hand remained quiet. It is any way an accident that the little hand found exactly the right place, for in other cases it went by. When the child was awake, no convulsive, no reflex movement took place upon the same sort of contact, and the repetition of the touching of the sleeping child on other days had likewise often this negative result, or else irregular movements of rubbing as a consequence (p. 101). When in the seventh week I touched the *left* temple of the child as he lay quiet, his *left* arm remained motionless, but the *right* arm made an energetic movement forward, upward, and to the left, although the left arm lay perfectly free. Whence this contra-lateral response? Perhaps the sensorium was active and did not yet localize accurately, or the reflex path of the same side was less easily passable. Such unexpected responsive movements I have often perceived in the first two years, and that as late as the thirty-fifth month in a sleeping child, even when the tickling was on the left, the *right* arm lying under the body of the sleeping child and the left arm being free.

This observation is thus exactly opposed to that of Pflüger (1853), who tickled a sleeping boy of three years, on the right nostril, and saw that he raised the right hand in defense, and rubbed the right nostril. When tickled on the left, the child took the left hand. Then Pflüger laid both arms of the boy, who lay on his back asleep, gently near the body, held the left arm firmly with a light pressure, on a pillow placed upon it, and holding a feather in his free hand, tickled the left nostril of the little fellow. Immediately the left arm was moved, but could not be brought to the face. The child then made a grimace, and tried, after repeated tickling on the left, to press the left nostril with the right hand, "whereas he had at other times always chosen the hand of the same side, however much and however long he was tickled, until he awoke." The "always" can not hold good universally.

But I often saw the reflex of the same side in the second year also. Thus, in the seventeenth month, I touched the right nostril on the inside, while the child was asleep; at once the right hand went to it and rubbed, and, when I had touched the left nostril, that was immediately rubbed with the left hand. Then, on the repetition of the experiment, there was no longer any responsive movement of the sleeping child.

O. Rosenbach also has observed the action of reflexes in sleeping children, and has ascertained especially that some of them are lacking during sound sleep (those of the abdomen, the cremaster, and patella), but he does not give the age of the children.

At any rate, the experiments that I instituted suffice to show that, without detriment to the general validity of Pflüger's laws of reflexes, circuitous reflex routes must often be tried by little children, many experiences must first be had before those laws are manifested in their purity. Many times, to be sure, the experiments upon children sleeping soundly surprised me at once by their conformity to law. Yet simple experiments of that sort that I repeated upon several children, and the observation of the independent movements of arms and hands in the newly-born, have given me but few evidences of the existence of perfectly-developed inborn reflexes of the corresponding side after stimulus on one side. The trigeminus facialis reflex is such a case, since upon the touching of one eye, in the first hour of life, very often this one only is shut; another case is the spreading of the toes when the sole of the foot is touched (pp. 104, 225). The law of symmetry of the reflexes is recognized as valid for the just-born, in the dilatation of both pupils, when only one eye is shaded; in the closing of both eyes at the rude touch of one eye or one nostril; in movements of both feet when the sole of one foot is touched (p. 104); so likewise the appearance of the reflex in unequal degrees of intensity on both sides in bilateral reflexes following stimulus of one side is confirmed by the stronger movements of the eyelid (after the tickling of one nostril) as well as of the leg upon the irritated side (p. 104). But the law of inter-sensitive motor movement still needs proof; for, according to it, no reflex from the trigeminus to the motor oculi ought to occur. But if a child be waked by a touch of the eyelid, the raising of the lid seems to occur through reflexive action. The question comes up whether movements do not always take place before the opening of the eyes. I have not liked to experiment in regard to this, as I do not wake children without urgent reasons.

Further, in the case of two children, who in the first half-year suffered from local itching eruptions of the skin (milk-crust), the reflexive movements of the limbs were quite irregular and at the beginning absolutely unsuited, afterward not in all cases suited, to relieve the pain or the feeling of tickling; at all events, apart from the turnings of the head, which was the most tormented, and which was moved hither and thither like a pendulum when the arms were confined (fourth month). Many times when the arms had escaped from the tethers in the night, the face was scratched to bleeding in several places that were evidently not troublesome (fourth to sixth month). At every unguarded moment the hands went to the head; and the skin, even the sound part of it, was rubbed and scratched. These scratching movements can not be inborn, they must be acquired. The result of an accidental contact of the head and hand appearing in the diminution of the tickling sensation must have induced a preference of the movement of the hand to the head among all sorts of movements; for in the concurrence of all muscular movements those are preferred—i. e., most frequently repeated—which bring with them feelings of pleasure, and which remove whatever excites unpleasant feeling, while the movements that prevent feelings of

pleasure and those that cause unpleasant feeling become
more and more rare.

The mentioned reflexive reaching toward the head
had now, in one of the two cases before us, a peculiar association as its further consequence (in regard to the other
case there is lack of observation). When, namely, the
eczema became less and at last had entirely disappeared,
the lifting of the arms along with the carrying of the
hands to the head still continued, showing itself every
time that anything disagreeable occurred to the child, or
when he refused to do anything—e. g., when he did not
want to play any more or to play at all. Manifestly we
have to do here with a primitive process of induction or
generalization. Formerly that movement was regularly
executed in connection with the disagreeable cutaneous
sensation on the head (up to the sixth month); now that
sensation, indeed, is wanting, but the movement is so
firmly associated with the quality "disagreeable" of
that feeling, that it is executed even when something
else appears with the same quality (ninth month). Thus
individual expressional movements arise from acquired
reflexes, which disappear again later because they remain individual.

In direct contrast to the acquired reflex movements,
stands the inborn spreading of the toes that follows the
touching (tickling, stroking) of the soles of the feet,
which I saw just as plainly marked in new-born children five minutes after birth, and in the first days, as
in the fourth week. Darwin mentions that, after the
touching of the sole with a bit of paper on the seventh
day, the foot was suddenly jerked away, and the toes
curled up. I have not been able to find out under

what circumstances this reflex or the spreading of the toes at the touch of the sole of the foot occurs (cf. p. 104), but I observed that as early as the eighth week, tickling of the sole was followed by laughing. This so-called reflexive (" *reflectorische* ") laughing (p. 145) is not a regular, absolutely pure reflex act, because it is dependent upon the previously existing mood.

The reflexive starting, quivering, and stretching out of the arms at a sudden, unexpected, strong impression, especially a sound-impression, the starting back with the head and the upper part of the body at a sudden approach—fright, in fact—is wholly lacking in the first hours of life. The human child just born can not, properly speaking, experience fright any more than can animals just born, although many sensations, such as that of a dazzlingly bright light, are surprising and dis-agreeable to him. But this stage of inferior sensibility scarcely outlasts the first days in vigorous children; in some (born after their time) it may in the case of sud-den impressions (p. 80), have given place, even before the second day, to the susceptibility to fright that is more or less characteristic of the infant.

This has already been spoken of repeatedly, so far as the bilaterally symmetrical reflexes, occasioned by all sorts of acoustic, optical, tactile impressions (e. g., by taking hold of the child, or blowing upon him), espe-cially the extending and raising of the arms, the start-ing and the quick pulsation of the eyelid, are symptoms of being frightened (p. 82). Apart from the starting, which is not always regular, these reflexes are dis-tinguished above others by their perfect symmetry. *Both* arms are raised exactly simultaneously, *both* eyes

close for a moment after a sudden impression, even
when this is made only on one side (as in pulling at the
blanket on which the child is lying). This reflex mechanism, that unites the motors of the extremities with
the organs of sense, must have an easy action from the
beginning, although no direct advantage from it to the
child can be affirmed.

Another constant symptom of fright in children is
their silence. For example, when a child has had a fall,
screaming does not begin till after an interval. It is
probable that this condition of not being able to scream,
like that of apthongia or reflex aphasia, rests upon teta-
nic excitement of the motor nerves, especially of the
nerves of the tongue, in consequence of which every attempt to form a sound may result in spasm of the tongue.
In children this occurrence is by no means so rare as in
adults. Children, both before and after they have begun to learn to speak, do not begin to scream until some
time after the effect of the sudden impression; for this
reason, probably, because by that impression the will is
completely paralyzed, so that at first they do not even
get so far as to the attempt to form a sound. All the
muscles that at other times are voluntarily movable are
no longer moved becauses the impulses of will are wanting; so it is also with the tongue and the muscles of
the larynx. Even the reflex excitability is diminished.
Hence, probably. the silence of those frightened in the
first moment. The very strong excitement of particular centers brings with it an arrest of the other central
functions. Finally, the motor impulse becomes operative, but produces that spasm of the tongue, and not
till after that passes, screaming.

It takes a long series of experiences, which each individual must go through for himself anew, before such fright-reflexes and infringements upon the activity of the will can be controlled, and many persons never learn to control them. Still, it is of the greatest importance for the cultivation of the child's will to exercise children as early as possible in the conscious inhibition of reflex movements.

At the beginning, probably, no reflex is inhibited, but there exists a peculiarity discovered by Soltmann, which counteracts the disadvantages arising from this defect. The excitability of the nerve-muscle, namely, in cats, dogs, rabbits, gradually increases from birth on (in man probably until toward the sixth week of life, as it then about equals that of adults, or somewhat surpasses it). The inferior excitability of the motor nerves in the earliest period exerts a beneficial counter-influence to the tendency to convulsions after physiological stimulation. Here I must agree with Soltmann, and attribute to this factor, as he does, great importance, especially on account of the absence of will and of the inhibition of reflexes; but my experiments and observations upon new-born Guinea-pigs, and on those born prematurely, leave not the least doubt that in these animals inhibitions of reflexes take place through strong peripheral stimuli even before birth, or with the first drawing of breath. For when, in such a fœtus or new-born creature, I pinch sharply with the forceps any spot whatever on the skin after breathing has begun, the auricle does not react in the least, or reacts only very feebly upon the strongest impressions of sound; but if the peripheral stimulus ceases, then both auricles plainly

move at once upon the same acoustic stimulus. Here
exists, then, soon after the beginning of respiration (in
the prematurely and the normally born) an inhibition
of a reflex through strong localized cutaneous stimuli.
A paralysis of the reflex, or paraplegia, after contusion—
e. g., of a kidney—it has not been possible, thus far, to
produce in new-born creatures (dogs and rabbits). The
inhibitory effect of the excitement of the vagus upon
the activity of the heart is, on the other hand, present
in the new-born mammal.

It is highly desirable now to fix, by observation and
simple experiments, the date of beginning of inhibitions of reflexes in the human being. I saw a sixteen-
days-old child, that was screaming violently, become
quiet in an instant when it was laid face downward
on a pillow; and I have observed, even in very young
babes, the quieting effect of singing, making a hushing
sound, and playing on the piano. But in these cases
we have not to do with inhibitions of reflexes in the
strict sense of the term, but with the supplanting of a
feeling of discomfort, along with its motor consequences,
or a reflex activity, by means of a new impression. A
brainless new-born child, even, that was screaming violently, could be easily quieted, as Pflüger relates, by
letting him suck the finger. The cerebral activity of
the newly-born can not yet influence the reflexive
and impulsive activity of the spinal cord, because the
brain is not yet sufficiently developed. Soltmann has
proved, by experiments on new-born dogs, that at the
beginning of life no excitements pass from the brain
to the spinal cord, which would be capable of arresting
the reflex operations effected by the cord. And I have

no doubt that the very same thing is true of many other new-born animals. But it is not true of all, and whether it is precisely in the human being that immediately after birth no trace of the inhibition of reflexes exists, is doubtful. The Guinea-pig, which is much more mature at birth, comes into the world, according to the previously-mentioned observations, with a complete apparatus for inhibition of reflexes.

Genuine inhibitions of reflexes may first be observed with certainty in little children at the time when they no longer (as they do in the first six to nine months), without the least sign of self-control, excrete at once the products of nutrition when the accumulation of these stimulates them reflexively to do so. In all healthy infants this reflex excitability is great. But I lack observations as to when for the first time the reflex stimulus, that shows itself normally on the first day of life, is overcome, or the immediate response to it is at least delayed. At the beginning of the first year children are accustomed to scream after the evacuation; later, to scream before it, formally announcing it. In the latter case they have had the experience that the threats, the chastisements, and the natural disagreeable consequences of the immediate reflex activity cause more discomfort than waiting does. We have here one of the strongest effects of early training, as is proved by the behavior of animals and many insane persons.

The point of time at which control of the *sphincter vesicæ* begins, allowed itself in one case to be approximately determined. From the beginning of the tenth month, viz., the desire to evacuate the bowels was, in the daytime, in a healthful and waking condition, almost

17

invariably announced by great restlessness. If the child was then attended to, the evacuation took place invariably not till *several seconds* after giving him the proper position. The child needed so much time, therefore, in order to annul the inhibition by means of his now unquestionably authenticated will.

Here we have two proofs of the existence of choice: first, the inhibition of a reflex never inhibited in the first half - year, the non-willing of it; second, the removal of the inhibition, the willing of the reflex. The first inhibitory act, which, for that matter, does not last long when it is not regarded, seems to occur seldom before the last three months of the first year (sometimes much later). It is lacking, as a rule, when the child does not enjoy undisturbed health, when his attention is strongly claimed, and when he is tired. The overcoming of the reflex stimulus in sleep, which takes place independently of will by means of habit, requires for that very reason a much longer period of time. It is to be borne in mind, however, in this case, that a pretty strong pressure, like other peripheral stimuli, first interrupts the sleep, and thereby makes room for the influence of the will.

Those reflexes which during the whole of life are not inhibited by the will, appear, notwithstanding, to be in part more distinct in the new-born and the infant than in the following years of life. At least Eulenburg found (1878) in two hundred and forty-one children under twelve months the reflex of the tendon of the *patella* at the beginning not quite so frequent, indeed, as in adults; where it did appear, however, it was more distinct than it was later, especially in forty-one

children examined in the first month, and in sixteen (out
of seventeen) one day old. Later observations of the
same investigator and his assistant Dr. Haase (1882) confirmed the relatively more frequent absence of the knee-
phenomenon in one hundred and sixteen children from
one to twenty-four months old. In seven cases it was
wanting on both sides, in three cases on one side. The
foot - phenomenon was wanting, in fact, in the great
majority of the cases. It was distinctly seen only in
twenty-two out of the one hundred and sixteen children.
The osseous reflexes were still more rare (tibia reflex
observed in fifteen, radius reflex in fourteen of the one
hundred and sixteen). On the other hand the reflex of
the abdomen, of the nose, of the cornea, and of the
pupil were not missing in a single case. The ear-reflex
was only in five cases indistinct. (In seventy-eight boys,
from one to sixty months old the cremaster reflex was
lacking in twenty cases.) It appears from this that the
tendon-reflexes are not so easily inherited as those of
the skin and mucous membrane. The latter are more
useful to the organism.

The decrease of the general reflex tendency ("*Re-
flexdisposition*") in the earliest years is identical in
ultimate effect with the increase of an inhibition of reflexes. To be sure, the individual efficient factors in
both cases can not yet be isolated. The tendency to
spasms that has its origin partly in the lack of all reflex
inhibition in the earliest period, and the heightened
reflex sensibility easily to be established physiologically
in every teething child, which gives occasion for the
strangest grimaces, find their counterpoise only after
the development of the will—i. e., after far advanced

development of the gray substance of the cerebrum,
upon the removal of which there appear in animals reflex phenomena similar to those in new-born and quite
young individuals. But in older children, too (in the
fourth year) many reflexes are found, especially the
mimetic and the defensive (such as that mentioned,
p. 101—"shuddering"), more strongly expressed than
after their training has been carried further.

The pain-reflexes that are most strongly manifested
in later life are, according to the experiments of Genzmer, already in part mentioned, least developed precisely in the earliest period. Through observation of
some sixty new-born children, it was established by him
that they are, on the first day, almost insensible to the
prick of a needle, and in the first week they still have
an inferior degree of sensibility. Prematurely-born
infants were in the course of the first days so sharply
pricked with fine needles in the nose, upper lip, and
hand, that a little drop of blood flowed from the punct-
ure, and yet they gave no sign of discomfort; indeed,
often not even a slight quivering could be noticed. To
pricks that are acute for the adult, normal children responded after one to two days, seldom earlier, merely
with reflex movements as upon being touched. "The
pain-reflexes differ from those reflexes of touch in this,
that the movement is wont to follow the stimulus only
after a longer pause (up to two seconds), while in the
touch-reflexes the physiological period is considerably
shorter." The sensibility to needle-pricks was found to
be somewhat greater in children born after their time,
and it increases generally in the first weeks. It is of
great interest, in connection with this, that in children

of some weeks there followed occasionally upon a prick in the sole of the foot a distortion of the countenance without local reflexes. "They seemed to become conscious of the feeling of pain. In the first week this was never the case." A reflexive lachrymal secretion could not be produced at that period by any prick, but only by irritation of the mucous membrane of the nose; "at pricks on the skin of the face, the moisture of the eyes did seem, but only at times, to increase."

Now from all these facts it does not follow that the newly-born are sensible of no pain at all, but it follows that the pain-reflexes are still wanting when the painful impression is circumscribed—reaches but few nerves—as in the prick of a fine needle. Fifty simultaneous needle-pricks would doubtless bring pain-reflexes in their train immediately after birth. So much is made certain by my experiments on prematurely-born rabbits and Guinea-pigs, which responded, with unmistakable pain-reflexes, only to very strong local, and to weaker extended, painful assaults—to electric, thermal, mechanical, chemical cutaneous stimuli. Distortion of the face and loud screaming appear also in mature or nearly mature new-born human beings upon strong electrical stimulation of the skin, as Kroner found (1882).

It would be of great interest to draw up a list, as complete as possible, of the reflex movements of the newly-born, the infant, and the child not yet able to speak; to separate the inborn movements from the acquired, those capable of being inhibited from the purely physical reflexes and the pain-reflexes; and to test whether there is a single reflex that belongs to the human child alone. A thorough-going comparison of new-born chimpanzees and orangs with new-born negro children in regard to the reflexes would perhaps disclose no differences.

In the human infant there have been proved—to adduce only one sensory and one motor nerve as example—six different regular reflex movements from the optic nerve to the motor oculi alone, which appear in case of light-impressions, viz. :

1. Contraction of the superior rectus muscle of the eye in raising the glance, when bright light appears above; in the fourth week or earlier (p. 44).

2. Contraction of the elevator of the lid in moderate light; immediately after birth (p. 4).

3. Contraction of the internal rectus muscle of the eye (movement of convergence) at a moderately bright impression of light just before the tip of the nose; in the second week (p. 50).

4. Contraction of the inferior rectus muscle of the eye in lowering the gaze when bright light appears below; in the fourth week (p. 44).

5. Contraction of the muscle of accommodation at the approach of bright light to the eye; after the third week (p. 51).

6. Contraction of the sphincter of the iris under the influence of bright light; immediately after birth (pp. 4 and 51).

Anatomy has not yet discovered the paths of connection for any one of these six reflexes from the retina to the muscles of the orbit that are supplied by the motor oculi. And the same thing is true also of the mimetic reflex movements of the infant from the nerve of hearing, smell, and taste to the facial nerve, and from

the sensitive nerve of the face to the facial nerve.
Microscopic investigation has, in fact, thus far been
unable to demonstrate in a single embryonic reflex the
two centers—the sensory and motor ganglionic cells—
in full development. Complete ganglionic cells have
not been seen in the brain till after birth (p. 70).
Probably the paths of the embryonic reflexes are still,
in general, imperfectly isolated.

CHAPTER XI.

INSTINCTIVE MOVEMENTS.

THE instinctive movements of human beings are not
numerous, and are difficult to recognize (with the exception of the sexual ones) when once the earliest youth
is past. So much the more attentively must the instinctive movements of the newly-born and of the infant
and of the little child be observed. In order to understand them, accurate observation of the instinctive
movements of new-born animals is necessary. I will
first group and present some statements upon that point.

1. Instinctive Movements of New-born Animals.

Movements unquestionably instinctive are manifested
by chickens in the very first hours after leaving the egg
—in fact, even while they are still engaged in breaking
the shell. For what else was it but such a movement
when a chick that had worn an opaque hood from the
moment of breaking the shell until the lapse of some
days, moved its head, six minutes after it was unhooded,

in the right way to follow with its gaze a fly twelve inches distant? After ten minutes the insect came within reaching distance of the neck, and was seized and swallowed at the first effort. At the end of twenty minutes this chick was placed, on uneven ground, at some distance from a hen with which was a chick of the same age as the one under observation, in such a way that it could see and hear the hen. After chirping for about a minute, it ran straight to the hen (Spalding). The very young chick does not invariably succeed in seizing the insect or the kernel, at which it pecks, between its upper and its under mandibles, in such a way that the object can be swallowed, but almost all peck at it. Chickens one day old, and those of several days, according to my observations, often peck six, even nine and ten, times inaccurately, and very often toil in vain, with all sorts of movements of the head (p. 67), even after a successful seizure of the kernel, to swallow it.

Here, then, are in complete development—1. Head-movements at the sight of objects in motion. 2. Peck-ing, when these objects are capable of being reached. 3. Running or scudding (*Rutschen*), when the cluck of the hen is heard for the first time or she is for the first time seen. 4. Bill- and head-movements, when a small object is got ready for swallowing. All these movements may, indeed, fail to be made, even when the external conditions of their appearance are completely fulfilled, as I have several times seen in chicks from one to three days old hatched in the incubator; but they are not to be looked upon as acquired or voluntary, for they are still new to the chick itself, and are executed without a previous idea of the result. Otherwise, the little creat-

ures would not, as I have seen them do, peck at their
own nails. The very young chick, which has never yet
seen the movements mentioned, can have no self-acquired
idea of them beforehand, because no experience preceded them ; but its ancestors had the idea, and the
chick itself inherited, without knowing it, a memory-
image (Erinnerungsbild) of that. The chick thus acts
skillfully, and with seeming intelligence, not out of its
own deliberation, but through the inherited association
of the sensuous recollection with the motor recollection,
not through the idea of the movement itself executed
by the creature, this movement being rather involuntary. If the movement be omitted—under external
conditions otherwise similar—then, in the concurrence
of the inherited sensory-motor associations with one
another and with the new connections of sensation and
movement arising from individual sense-impressions,
another association has appeared in greater force than
those spoken of, or a new *feeling* prevails. Likewise
the diligent pluming of the down with the bill by the
chicken not yet one day old, and the scraping of the
head with the foot, that I saw on the third day (the
creature never having seen the thing done), and the
scratching, appearing on the second day (without a model
for imitation), can be nothing else than hereditary, instinctive movements. Spalding says forcibly: " The
instinct of present generations is the product of accumulated experiences of past generations. The permanence
of such associations in the individual life depends upon
the corresponding impression on the nervous system.
We can not, strictly speaking, experience any individual
fact of consciousness twice ; but, as by pulling at the

bell we can produce the same ring that we heard yes-
terday, so we are capable, as far as the established connection of nerves and nerve-centers holds, of living over
again our experiences. Why should not these modifications of the substance of the brain (which, persisting
from hour to hour, from day to day, make permanent
acquirement possible) pass on from parents to their offspring just like any other physical peculiarity? Instinct
is inherited memory."

It is no objection to this conception of instinct as an
hereditary association that not all the sensory-motor connections of the parents pass over to their posterity. For
very many of them are not firm enough The firmest
in the chicken are the movements of pecking, swallowing, peeping, running, scratching, and scraping, and the
beating with the future wings in scudding forward,
which last I saw very lively in the fourth hour, without
possibility of its being an imitation. Yet some of these
movements, long hereditary, may also vanish, or at least
may not appear, if the external occasions are wanting.
Chickens that were hatched by Allen Thomson upon a
carpet, and were kept on it for some days, showed no
inclination to scratch, because the stimulus that was exercised upon the soles of their feet by the carpet was
new, and was not adapted to set in activity their inherited mechanism for scratching. As soon, however, as
a little gravel was spread upon the carpet, the scraping
began at once (as Romanes reports). We see clearly
from this that chickens do not from the beginning of
their life scratch with the purpose of seeking grains of
seed. For the quite thinly spread gravel could not
furnish the prospect of finding such in the carpet. I

have even seen chickens that were hatched in the incubator, and then brought up in an inclosed space by themselves away from all other fowls, make vigorous scratching movements on smooth white paper without spots, especially in the fourth week of life, as if the brightness of the great surface might be scraped away. The scratching of fowls thus takes place without deliberation, after certain visual and tactile impressions, as a purely instinctive movement, like peeping, pecking, running, and flying.

Swallows do not *learn* to fly; they receive no instruction as to how they have to contract their muscles in order to speed through the air for the first time from the maternal nest, but they fly of themselves. The young redstarts, also, which I have observed daily before they were fledged, receive no directions for flying. But they exercise their wings in the nest before their first attempt at flight, often spreading them and making them whir. The first excursion is slower than the flight of the parents; the young creature flies downward, but it never hits against anything, and after a few days the certainty of its flight is worthy of admiration. Confidence grows with practice.

These flight-movements of quite young birds can not be voluntary movements; they are instinctive, precisely as is the pecking of the chicken that has been hatched a few hours, which, having come into the world alone in the incubator, without mother or companions, in the utmost quiet (without guiding noises), pecks at every single visible object capable of being pecked at, or at a spot or hole in the wooden floor on which the creature stands, as well as at its own nails, with astonishing address. Pecking is not, therefore, according to these observations of mine, set agoing by hearing, as has been suspected, when the noise made by the pecking of the mother was imitated with the finger-nail (Darwin). I have, in fact, observed that chickens between three and twenty hours old, hatched in the incubator, almost all of which had pecked at the yolk and white of egg put before them cut into small bits (after being hard boiled), and were now pausing—I have noticed that, when I let two large fowls close by them pick up the same food upon hard wood, noisily and persistently, the young ones were not in the least affected by the hammering of the bills, although they had hearing, for they started, at sudden loud noises, all simultaneously, like one fowl—a strange sight.

If a drop of water be put on the eye of a chicken on the twenty-first day, before the creature has left the shell, it shakes off the drop briskly, like a hen ; put the drop on the tip of the bill, and the chick makes many movements of swallowing, as I often observed.

All these movements are, like pecking, inherited. They appear, in fact, not exceptionally, but very frequently, when nearly the same conditions, internal and external, are fulfilled that were fulfilled when their ancestors executed them—executed them times innumerable. How easily in this case instinctive activity takes on the stamp of great individual intelligence is shown especially in the following observation made by A. Agassiz (1876): Very young hermit-crabs, not long after leaving the egg, rush with extraordinary animation for suitable shells that are given to them in the water. They examine the opening at the mouth, and take up their quarters inside with remarkable alacrity. But, if it chances that the shells are still occupied by mollusks, then they stay close by the opening, and wait till the snail dies, which generally occurs soon after the beginning of the imprisonment and the strict watch. Upon this the small crab pulls out the carcass, devours it, and moves into the lodging himself. What foresight! On account of the preference of the empty shells, the whole proceeding can not be hereditary. But the young animals are not instructed. They were from the beginning separated from their parents, and had no time or opportunity for experiences of their own. They must, therefore, have inherited their practice of waiting from their ancestors, as a rule of conduct for the case where a shell is occupied, and they can at once distinguish such a one from an empty one.

Now, precisely as it is true of these animals that are sagacious in one direction, and of the chicken, and, in general, of all animals, that they come into the world with a good share of inherited memory for movements (p. 71)—i. e., with instinctive motility (Motilität)—so it will be true of the human child. Which of its movements are instinctive? First, seizing.

2. Development of Seizing.

Of all movements of the infant in the first half-year, no one is of greater significance for its mental development than are the seizing movements. I have on this account observed these with special attention.

It is supposed by many that the moving of the hands hither and thither in the first days of life is a kind of seizing, since the fingers are carried not only to the face, but also to the mouth. Such a view is irreconcilable with the ordinary meaning of the word *seize* and with the facts. For seizing presupposes the perception of an object desired, and, in addition, a control of the muscles, both of which are wanting in the first days.

The first putting of the hand into the mouth has nothing in common with the later seizing, except that it requires a movement of the arm. The hand is not even *carried* to the face, but, in its random movements about, it gets to and into the mouth, as well as elsewhere, which, on account of the position of the arms in the fœtus long before birth, seems perfectly natural. Newborn children, left to themselves, keep this attitude, and move their hands to the face and to the lips, as they must have done already before birth. If the lips are touched, then sucking movements readily appear in the hungry infant; therefore nothing of purpose can be found in the early sucking of the child at its own fingers (observed by Kussmaul on the first, by me on the fifth, day), which is followed later by the biting of the fingers. The position of the arms and hands in the uterus is conditioned by the restricted space. Every other position would involve an enlargement of the superficies of the fœtus.

It appears, therefore, that we are not justified in seeing in the first approximation of the hand to the mouth, the beginning of seizing-movements. In the first days of his life the infant moves his hands about his face and into his eyes, in a very different way from that of seizing, which comes later as a gesture expressing a desire. Young infants, whose fingers have accidentally, in the random movements of the arms, come to the mouth, are not able, if anybody takes the fingers away, to put them to the mouth again. Nay, even if some one carries their fingers to their lips for them, the infants can not hold their own fingers there, in case gravity makes the arm drop (Genzmer). Later, however, babes are often seen to suck at their own fingers in sleep.

Neither does the fact that the infant, as I noted on the ninth day, when he is sleeping, does not, as he does when awake, clasp my fingers placed in his hand—neither does this fact indicate a seizing as a purposive movement; but the clasping is to be regarded as a reflex, just like the spreading of the toes when the sole of the foot is touched (pp. 104, 224). The proof of this I see herein, that the older child—e. g., of seventeen months—when I put my finger in the hollow of his hand during his sleep, does not clasp it either, but when I move my finger with a gentle rubbing movement back and forth upon the flat of his hand, he often clasps it quickly, almost convulsively, with his fingers, without waking. The foot behaves like the hand in this respect, in the earliest period, as it responds less readily in sleep. The absence of the clasping in sleep is thus to be ascribed simply to the insufficient excitement of the nerves of the skin, and the diminution of the reflex excitability in sleep; in no case is the clasping of the finger, by a child that is awake, intentional within the first two weeks.

The first grasping at objects, with manifest desire to have them, was seen by Sigismund in a boy nineteen weeks old; by me, in a girl in her eighteenth week, and in my boy in his seventeenth week.

The contraposition of the thumb, an indispensable condition to the completion of the act of seizing—which is said to be an easy matter for young monkeys, even within the first week of life—is very slowly learned by the human child, as I noticed ; he does not learn at all to place the great-toe opposite the other toes. It is a question, indeed, whether human beings born without arms, can learn to use the great-toe as a thumb, as the quadrumana do. I once saw a young man without arms make a drawing with his foot. But in doing it the pencil was held between the great-toe and the second, without contraposition, as one would hold it between the forefinger and the middle finger, in case one wanted to draw or write without the help of the thumb. Adults succeed easily in doing the latter, even without practice.

Having the opinion that possibly at the beginning of life seizing might be done with the great-toe as with the thumb, I tested hands and feet in the case of my boy in the earliest period, and I present here my observations concerning the development of seizing, in chronological order :

First to third day : movements with the hands to the face predominate.

On the fourth day, a pencil was decidedly not held firmly by the foot.

On the fifth day his fingers clasp my finger very firmly ; his toes do not. For the rest, his hands often move to the face, at random, without getting hold of it.

On the sixth day, the same. The hands even go into the eye.

On the seventh day, it appears that a thin pencil is

held with the great-toe and the other toes exactly as with the thumb and fingers. But in this there is no seizing; of a contraposition of the thumb there is just as little to be observed as of the great-toe, but in case of convenient position of the pencil between thumb and forefinger, and between the great-toe and its neighbor, fingers as well as toes are vigorously bent and the object is held.

On the ninth day the finger is not clasped by the sleeping child.

In the third to seventh weeks, the child has not yet clasped my finger with his thumb, but only with his fingers.

In the eighth week I am convinced that the thumb is still put around the pencil, as the fingers are, but it may more easily than before be bent passively for seizing, so that my finger is held firmly. The four fingers of the child's hand, directly without co-operation of the thumb, embrace my finger when I put it in the hollow of the hand of the child.

Up to the eleventh week no noticeable advance. If I put a pencil into the child's hand, he holds it firmly, indeed, but without heeding it (without knowing it, one would say of an adult, i. e., mechanically, as in absence of mind), and can not perfectly use the thumb in clasping. Another child, of exactly the same age, could not even clasp and hold the stick that was put into his hand.

End of the twelfth week: when the child was moving his hands about in the air, it often happened that my finger, held near, came into one of the little hands. On the eighty-fourth day I saw, in connection with this,

18

for the first time, a placing of the thumb opposite, so
that it looked just as if the child had purposely seized
the finger, which was not presented to him, but merely
held motionless within reach, and allowed to follow
passively the movements of the child's arm hither and
thither. This experiment was repeated several times
on the same day, with like result. Then first I gained
the firm conviction that the contraposition of the
thumb and the seizing of the finger, followed reflexively, without intention, as a consequence of the cutaneous stimulus occasioned by the contact.

In the thirteenth week, the thumb already follows
more readily the bending fingers, when a pencil is put
into the child's hand.

In the fourteenth week, seizing that is undoubtedly
intentional is not yet present, but the little hand holds
objects that come accidentally into it, or that are put
into it, longer and more firmly than at an earlier period,
and with a decided contraposition of the thumb, by
which many have doubtless been misled to suppose that
" proper grasping at objects " begins in this week—a
thing which certainly is not universally true. I, at
least, detected no trace of intentional seizing after objects seen, in the fifteenth and sixteenth weeks, and on
the one hundred and fourteenth day. While the babe
is nursing, however, a finger is reflexively clasped by
thumb and fingers more often than formerly. Others,
also, whose attention I directed to this point, confirm
my opinion that in the third month seizing is merely
apparent. It does not begin, as Vierordt also found,
before the fourth month.

In the seventeenth week (one hundred and seventeenth day) I saw for the first time earnest efforts to take hold of an object with the hand. It was a small rubber ball that was within seizing distance, but the child missed it. When now it was put into his hand he held it for a long time very firmly and moved it to his mouth and *to his eyes*, and that with a peculiar, new, more intelligent expression of countenance. On the following day, the awkward but energetic attempts to seize upon all sorts of objects held before the child were more frequent. He fixated the object—e. g., my finger—and grasped three times in succession at an object distant twice his arm's length from him, (p. 55)— and also fixated his own hand (cf. p. 109), especially when this had once successfully seized. His expression of countenance meantime indicated great attention. Again, after a day, the repeated grasping at everything that comes within reach of the arms seems to give the child pleasure. But wonder is mingled with it, for—

In the eighteenth week, in the attempts to seize, when they fail, his own fingers are attentively regarded. Probably the child has expected the sensation of contact, or if it occurred has wondered at the novelty of the sensation of touch. He continues to hold firmly, regard, and carry to the mouth objects once seized. But at this time the outstretching of the arms, as if to seize, becomes also the expression of the strongest desire. On the one hundred and twenty-first day the child, for the first time, stretched out both arms toward me at the morning greeting, and that with an indescribable expression of longing. On the day before, nothing of this sort was yet to be perceived. The progress from grasping at inanimate things to grasping at members of the family came suddenly.

In the nineteenth week the child took a bit of meat that was offered to him on the point of a fork and carried it with his hand to his mouth.

In the thirty-second week seizing with both hands, at the same time directing the line of vision to the object, was more sure and more frequent than before, the attention at the same time being more active. The child lying on his back, raises himself without help to a sitting posture and bends over forward, reaching out with both hands to lay hold of anything that is before him. The straining of the attention expresses itself especially by the protruding of the lips, which I saw besides on the one hundred and twenty-third day for the first time, in connection with the act of seizing.

During all this time the seizing is still imperfect, as the four fingers do not all work in harmony with the thumb. When the child sees an object that he wants, he generally spreads out all the fingers of both hands while stretching out the arms. But when he has clasped the pencil or my finger, it often happens that in doing so the thumb and one finger only are employed; frequently the thumb with two fingers or with three or with all. Very often, too, the co-operation of the thumb is entirely wanting. But the ability to seize accurately with thumb and fingers is so far developed that nothing more is wanting but the co-ordinating will to do it in every suitable case. Thus far it depends much more on the situation and form of the object and on the accident of the position of the hand, than it does on the purpose, how many and what fingers, as they bend in the act of seizing, actually take part in this act.

In the thirtieth week the seizing was noticeably quicker and more perfect, but the lack of certainty in getting hold of objects seized was still great. The hands still often pass by the object gazed at, with fingers spread. Grasping at objects at the distance of a metre becomes more frequent. Very often, probably always, whenever form, color, or luster has excited the child's gratification, the thing seized is at once carried to the mouth, the tongue is put far out, and the object licked. Probably we have here a case of primitive logical inference; up to this time sucking and tasting were the most important strong, agreeable, sensations the young being has known; when, therefore, he has a new agreeable sensation (e. g., of a bright color, a round, smooth body, a soft surface), it is brought into association with the lips and tongue, through which the pleasurable feeling at taking in the sweet milk was received.

The quick moving of the hands to a new object presented for the first time—e. g., a brush—must unquestionably be interpreted as a sign of desire. The parts of his own body, moreover, appear to the child as foreign objects. For in the thirty-second week, as he lies on his back, he likes to stretch his legs up vertically, and observes the feet attentively as he does other objects held before him. Then he grasps with the hands at his own feet, and often *carries his toes to his mouth with his hand.*

The child also expresses interest, by protruding the lips, his gaze being firmly directed to the object seized, presumably in the now discovered fact that the thing before seen and desired is at the same time the thing which is touched, and which yields new sensations. The bright, colored, long, short, appears now to him as also smooth, rough, warm, cold, hard, soft, heavy, light, wet, dry, sticky, slippery. The combination of two departments of sense in one object gratifies. Such an object is likewise his own foot seen and touched. In case the object seen and touched stands immovably firm, and so can not, like the ball and the toes, be brought to the mouth, the child tries, notwithstanding, in unmistakable fashion, to get hold of it, to pull it to him, and to bring it to his mouth, the source of his greatest feeling of pleasure, no matter whether it is large or small. At the same time it often happens, as I perceived to my astonishment on the occasion of his taking hold of a firmly-standing carved post, that the child (borne upon the arm) draws himself with the arms to the desired object and puts his mouth close up to it. The pleasure obtained in this way, also, through the touching of the object seen, which is the occasion of renewed seizing movements, is probably likewise the occasion of the desire to taste it. For now, after the nursing-bottle is presented to the child, he grasps at it with his hand; whereas he used to suck at it with arms inactive, he now tries to hold it fast, sometimes with the expression of eagerness. In this case the remembrance of the taste, or what in this regard amounts to the same thing, the gratification in the appeasing of hunger, stimulates the seizing movement. The order of succession originally is: tasting, then tasting and seeing, then seeing and desiring, tasting and desiring more, thereupon seeing, seizing, tasting. Through repetition of these associations, probably, the remembrance of the taste has, as it were, become amalgamated with seeing and seizing in general, until experience has taught that the things touched and seized have no taste or have a bad taste.

It is worthy of notice in this connection, that precisely during the first attempts at seizing, the greatest strain of attention, along with protrusion of the lips was observed, and later—in the thirty-fourth week, when the seizing was done more quickly—the mouth was opened before or directly after the seizing and then the object was put into it. At the first attempts the putting into the mouth followed without being intended beforehand, but now the hand is stretched out with the purpose of bringing the thing seen to the mouth, and the mouth is open; here it is to be borne in mind that the very thing that excites pleasure, the nursing-bottle, was especially often carried to the mouth. If the child at this period and afterward was allowed to carry a crust of bread to the mouth without assistance, it was often seen that in spite of accuracy in laying hold of the crust, it was carried not into the already-opened mouth, but against the cheek, chin, or nose—an uncertainty of touch that appeared still in the first attempts to eat with a small spoon, in the seventeenth month.

Failure to grasp, grasping too short, and grasping at objects very far off, disappear so gradually that I can not assign a definite period of disappearance.

Neither could it be ascertained at what time the putting of the fingers into the mouth and the grasping at the face without getting hold of any part of it ceased. Invariably, shortly before and after a tooth comes through, the child moves his fingers about in the mouth a good deal, keeping three or four fingers in the mouth. When alleviation had been experienced several times through chewing of the fingers, these no longer went accidentally—after moving about the hands in the air at random—but went regularly during teething into the mouth; and it must come, finally, through frequent repetition of the movement, to a reflex process, as the hand is brought near to every approachable place that feels pain. The first experience that biting the fingers, even before the teeth are there, moderates the pain or the tickling, appears as a consequence of the putting of the hand into the mouth; other painful impressions likewise become, therefore, later, the occasion of movements of the hand which may simulate seizing-movements.

In the forty-third week the child without help not only grasps properly with both hands at a nursing-bottle, but carries it correctly to the mouth; the same with a biscuit lying before him. He pulls strongly at the beard of a face that he can reach.

On the other hand, he grasped at the flame of the lamp in the forty-fifth week; in the forty-seventh, and later, at objects separated from him by a pane of glass, as if they were attainable, and that persistently, with attention and eagerness, as if the pane were not there. The discovery of the transparency of glass, which assuredly appears wonderful to every child, requires many such fruitless attempts at seizing.

The greatest progress in the movement of the muscles of the arm manifested itself at just this time, in the fact that often very small shreds of paper on the floor were grasped at and deftly laid hold of by thumb

and forefinger. But precisely this frequent play with
the bits of paper afforded occasion to observe the above-
mentioned uncertainty of the sense of touch when unsupported by sight. For whereas before this, when the
child used to take pleasure in biting pieces out of a
newspaper, these had to be taken out of his mouth by
some one, in the fourteenth month he could be allowed
to bite the paper to pieces undisturbed, because he now
of himself took out of his mouth with his right hand
every piece he had bitten off, and handed it to me. In
connection with this, I made the observation that the
shred of paper in the mouth on or near the lips was not
always found by the child when he touched with the
tips of his fingers. Without the guidance of the sense
of sight, therefore, touch was still quite imperfect.
Both senses united, on the other hand, did astonishing
things even much earlier than this, in spite of the failure to grasp, especially the failure to grasp far enough,
as late as the second year (p. 55), and the numerous
attempts to get hold of what could not be laid hold of
(p. 63). Thus I saw the child, at the age of ten months,
amuse himself, entirely of his own accord, by taking
deliberately from one hand into the other a long hair
that he had found on the carpet, and by gazing at it.

Of the many thousand nerve-fibers and muscle-fibers
that must come into harmonious activity in order that
such a movement may take place, the child knows nothing, but he directs already the whole nervo-muscular
mechanism with his will, which was generated by desire.
Before he is capable of this, the sensuous stimulus that
starts the seizing-movements must have been repeated
many hundreds of times, so that one and the same sensa-

tion often returned, an agreeable feeling arose, a perception at first indistinct, then gradually more and more distinct, and finally an idea of the objectivity of the thing seizable could be formed. Secondly, the movement of the arm, also, which, before as well as after birth, is directed to the mouth or the face, must have been very often repeated before it came to consciousness—i. e., before an idea of it could be formed, because in the beginning it was not perceived at all by the child. When, however, the desired object is represented in idea, and the movement of the arm is represented, the rapid succession of both representations favors their union, which calls into life the will. In fact, the distinct representation of the movement is not required any more at a later period, provided only that the aim is clearly recognized. Too much importance has often been attributed to the representation of the movement, the representation not being necessary beforehand except for a new purposive movement; this mistake has been made by W. Gude and Lotze; the representation of the aim remains the principal thing. For many voluntary movements—e. g., those of the eyes—are generally not clearly represented beforehand, at any period, while the end and aim of them fill the consciousness. At that time the kind of movement necessary to the attainment of the aim is known only in a general way.

But, in order to be able to execute a simple voluntary movement, such as reaching after objects, similar movements must previously have been often executed involuntarily, because only through these can muscular sensations or sensations of innervation be developed.

These are, however, necessary pioneers for the voluntary
motor impulses, and they play an important part in
other movements also besides the voluntary ones of the
child and of the adult, viz., the instinctive ones.   For
the memory-images of the innervation-sensations, or
muscular sensations, which the contraction of the muscle in contrast with its repose brings with it, determine
which muscles are to be contracted, and how strongly
each is to be contracted, after the kind of movement to
be executed is settled upon.

Now, if the repetition of a voluntary movement—
e. g., a seizing movement—occurs very often, then the
turning to account of those memory-images is hastened
and simplified to such a degree that, without the co-
operation of the brain-sensorium, the brain-motorium
alone sets the muscles in activity after a sensory impression has acted upon it.   Herein consists the chief
characteristic of the cerebro-motor acquired reflexes; to
these belongs also the grasping at a hat caught by a gust
of wind, at a later period of life.

But, on the other hand, in dreams—e. g., with the
child (and with the hypnotic subject) after exclusion of
the will—the sensory impression may affect only the
brain-sensorium in such a way that complex movements
go on just as if they were voluntary.   Such movements
Carpenter has called ideo-motor movements.   The cere-
bral-motor impulses are accordingly not purely reflexive,
as are those of the spinal reflexes, for in the latter no
center of higher rank, no brain-sensorium, no brain-
motorium, is originally concerned.

Moreover, for both these last there comes into consideration a cerebral inhibitory apparatus, which, want-

ing to the infant, arrests more and more easily, with his increasing development, the voluntary, or ideo-motor or purely reflexive (spinal-motor) movement that follows the sensory impression, and becomes manifest at the period when self-control begins.

That movement of the quite young child, which from the beginning is commonly called " seizing," originates, accordingly, in the following manner:

The moving of the hands hither and thither, especially to the face, is inborn, impulsive, determined by the position of the child within the womb.

The clasping of the finger laid in the hand in the first days is purely reflexive.

Then follows the " absent-minded " (in the adult) or " mechanical " holding fast of objects put into the hand as an unconscious, instinctive movement (in the adult, a movement that has become unconscious or no longer conscious; in the child, a movement not yet conscious).

Next is observed the holding fast of the object with contraposition of the thumb, when the object is so situated that the hand, moving hither and thither, accidentally grasps it. As the thumb now co-operates, the pure reflex has become complicated, and the central separation of the previously united impulses has been attained. As the holding-fast lasts much longer than in case of the reflex, and the attention, although only very imperfectly and transiently, is directed to the new experience of holding fast, the movement has now no longer taken place without the consciousness of the cerebral sensorium, but it is not yet voluntary; this kind of primitive holding-fast (not seizing) still approximates to the instinctive (ideo-motor) movements.

In the seventeenth to the nineteenth weeks the participation of the will of the brain-motorium in this act begins to attain its full force; the child does not yet stretch out its arm, but wills to hold fast the object that has accidentally come into his hand. He looks at it and forms an idea of it. From this fixation of the held object to the seizing of the object fixated is only a step. With that, willed-seizing is present, since the path of connection is at last passable from the brain-sensorium to the brain-motorium.

Years now pass before this seizing, which is indispensable for the development of the understanding (i. e., for having experiences) is perfected, and the voluntary inhibition of it by new, chiefly inculcated ideas, becomes possible.

Most of the voluntary inhibitions, the first acts of self-control, come into existence at a period that lies outside of the scheme of this exposition.

3. Sucking, Biting, Chewing, Teeth-Grinding, Licking.

Sucking belongs to the earliest co-ordinated movements of man; it is associated directly with swallowing, and has been repeatedly perceived even before the child was fully born, in case an object that could be sucked got into the mouth, and upon the upper surface of the tongue, at the same time touching the lips. When (December, 1870) I touched with my finger the tongue of a child, born at the right time, and moved my finger to and fro, or turned it on the upper surface of the tongue, three minutes after the head had emerged —the child was already crying feebly as soon as the mouth was free—the babe immediately stopped crying

and sucked briskly, but not when I merely touched the
lips or put the finger between them. Without doubt,
every normal child has become acquainted with the
swallowing of the amniotic fluid before birth, but has
hardly sucked as yet at his own fingers. Still, it is a
matter of absolute indifference, for the performance of
the act of sucking, whether liquid comes into the cavity
of the mouth or not, and the sucking for hours at empty
rubber-bottles—a vicious, highly reprehensible practice
—encouraged in Thuringia for the purpose of keeping
infants quiet, shows, just as the sucking at cloths and
at the fingers a few minutes after birth (according to
Champneys) shows, that swallowing is not required for
prolonged sucking. Yet under normal conditions, swallowing is the muscular action that attaches itself directly
to sucking.

Of what kind is this movement, which is to so
high a degree indicative of adaptation to an end? As
human abortions without brain, and puppies without a
cerebrum, can suck, the participation of the intellect,
any choice or purpose, is excluded in advance. But
since in the normal condition only the hungry, or, at
least, only the not completely satisfied infant, sucks
(the one that is full rejecting the nipple forcibly), we
have here something other than a purely reflex movement. For the absence of the sucking movement can
not be ascribed in the satisfied child to fatigue caused
by previous sucking, because frequently the act is not
renewed for a long time after the previous sucking has
been finished. No more is it an impulsive movement,
since it appears, in the waking condition at the beginning, only after lips, or tongue, or palate are touched by

an object capable of being sucked. The sucking movements of sleeping (dreaming) infants with empty, untouched mouth, however, show that the act may arise from purely central causes, after it has once been initiated through peripheral stimuli.

Accordingly, sucking must be classed among the instinctive movements. A scruple concerning this may easily be removed.

It has been maintained that young animals easily forget how to suck, if they omit sucking for some days. Such an assertion, however, relates either to such animals (like Guinea-pigs) as at the very beginning of life bite and chew, digest other food than milk, and soon have no more need to suck; or to the unlearning of sucking at the breast, which is somewhat less easily accomplished than is sucking from the bottle. In both cases, therefore, the question is not of a forgetting of the act of sucking—an act which yields great pleasure to older children also, as is well known, and even to adults (in smoking).

Of all the movements of the "suckling," hardly any is so perfect from the beginning as that which gave him this name. It is not so productive on the first day, indeed, as on the second; in fact, I found the efforts at sucking in the first hour of life, with healthy, new-born children, often quite devoid of effect (1869); when an ivory pencil was put into the mouth, they were found also non-coördinated; but again they may be quite regular, and, as has been mentioned, effectual, at the very moment of birth; they are based, therefore, on hereditary movements, which take place after two weeks with machine-like regularity, without imitation or training, and without other movements, except swallowing. The intermissions in sucking that occur with shorter intervals in the first days of life than at a later period, depend in part upon fatigue, in part upon the quicker filling of the little stomach, where the milk itself is not of unsuitable quality. On the other hand, I once saw a babe of seven days (not fully satisfied, no doubt) after ceasing to suck, keep up the movements of the mouth as in sucking.

It has long been known that children do not at once find the nipple without help, when they are placed at the breast, but only after several days (in one case not till the eighth day), thus later than is the case with animals. Like the latter, the very young child, before the nipple is put into the mouth, makes lateral movements of the head, which sometimes look like a groping about; the opening wide of the eyes before being placed at the breast and the keeping of them open during the nursing (very surprising in the first week, in a light not glaring) has, however, no connection with the finding of the nipple, since even those born blind, it appears, are no later in finding it. The action of the eyes is rather, in the first week, simply the expression of pleasurable feeling (pp. 32 and 143).

It often happens that, when the child is placed at the breast, the nipple does not get into the mouth; but the child sucks hard at the skin near it as late as the third week—a proof of the lack of discernment at this period. Yet the connection of the breast, as a whole, with nursing is known, for as early as the twenty-second day I saw the babe open wide its mouth at a distance of an inch and a half from the nipple. That the sense of smell is less decisive in the matter than the sense of sight is proved beyond question by observations upon infants whose eyes are bandaged, and upon those born blind. In animals born blind (dogs), the sense of smell is, on the contrary, recognized as an indispensable guide. The stretching out of the arms and the straining open of the eyes by the older infant, at sight of the breast at a distance, is against the participation of the smell. In the first period, the nipple is probably found by means of the sense of touch in the lips.

Besides, the sense of touch plays an important part in even the act of nursing, from the beginning. For it is not any object whatever put into the mouth that is sucked, but only certain objects, not too large, not too rough, not too hot or too cold, and not of a strongly bitter, or sour, or salt taste. In general, hungry children suck at their own fingers from the first days; if they are not hungry, they like to hold the fingers in the mouth, especially when teething, without sucking at them, and in the bath they suck at a sponge (in the eighth month), which they hold to the lips like a piece of bread.

Biting is not less instinctive than sucking. In the tenth month my child no longer sucked at the finger put into his mouth, but bit it almost invariably. Yet I can not give the exact date at which biting begins and sucking at the finger first ceases. In the seventeenth week the finger was already plainly bitten—i. e., compressed firmly between the toothless jaws; in the eleventh and twelfth months the child seized my hand, carried it to his mouth, and bit the skin till it hurt, as he did in general with the fingers of others which he

19

himself put into his mouth. Just so he tried at this period to bite to pieces a cube of solid glass. In the tenth month he had learned without instruction to crunch, with his four teeth, bread, which he then swallowed. After his teeth came, almost everything desirable was brought into contact with them as far as this was possible, and was then bitten, and he liked to smack his lips (eleventh month).

Before the infant gets his first tooth, he already makes frequent movements of chewing, which are especially multiplied after a hard bread-crust has been put into the mouth. The flow of blood that is increased before the teeth come through is, toward the end of the first three months, when driveling has begun, doubtless associated with disagreeable sensations, which are referred to the gum. But the fact that the toothless babe makes perfect chewing-movements—he who has never had in his mouth an object capable of being chewed, except his own fingers, that have often got in there—goes to prove that the function of chewing comes into activity, without practice, as soon as the requisite nerves and muscles and the center are developed. Chewing is a purely hereditary function; it is instinctive.

Another movement, absolutely original, and probably practiced for a while by all teething babes, is grinding the teeth. In the ninth month it affords the child great satisfaction to rub an upper and a lower incisor together, so as to be heard at the distance of a metre. The infant seems to be interested in the sudden appearance of his teeth in quick succession. For he makes comical movements of the mouth—e. g., protrudes both lips far out, makes perfect chewing-movements, and performs gymnastics with the tongue without the utterance of sound. But the grinding is practiced chiefly with four teeth.

Another movement that belongs here is absolutely original—licking. If this were not innate, how could the new-born human child within the first twenty-four hours of its life lick sugar? I have myself observed it, and have also seen licking for milk on the second and third days, and that hardly less adroit than in the seventh month. At this period not only are desired objects, whether stationary or seized, stroked with the tongue, but the lips of the mother in kissing; and, *vice versa*, the tongue is stroked with the objects.

All the movements of the infant here enumerated—sucking, biting, smacking, chewing, tooth-grinding, licking—must be designated as typical instinctive movements, like the pecking of the chicken. All are useful to him, for even the grinding with the first teeth is of use in making the child familiar with them. All are hereditary and involuntary.

4. Holding the Head.

All new-born children, and chickens just hatched, probably all new-born mammals, and all birds just hatched, are unable to hold the head up and to keep it balanced. It falls forward, to the left or the right, even backward, when it is held up straight by some one else. In this respect the helplessness of the human child is not greater than that of the chick hardly clear of the shell; but the latter learns in a few hours to control better the muscles required for holding the head than the child does in many weeks.

This muscular activity is especially adapted to help us in following the growth of the child's will. For weakness of the muscles can not be the cause of the inability to balance the head, because other movements of the head are quickly executed. At the end of the first and at the beginning of the second week I saw the babe, on being placed at the breast, continually make vigorous lateral movements of the head, which are made in like fashion by very young Guinea-pigs, calves, foals, and other animals in sucking. But during the first ten weeks no trace could be discovered, in the case of my boy, of an attempt to hold the head in equilibrium. In the eleventh week the head no longer bobs about, absolutely unsteady, when the child is made to sit up straight, but rather is balanced occasionally, although very imperfectly as yet. In the twelfth week the head often falls forward, also backward and sidewise, and is only for moments in equilibrium; yet a gain may be perceived from day to day in this respect, as the short duration of the holding erect becomes daily somewhat longer on the average. In the thirteenth week the head falls but seldom to one side, even when it is entirely free; rather is it for the most part tolerably well balanced. In the fourteenth week (in the case of another child not till the twenty-first) it falls forward also, but seldom (when the child is held up straight), and in the sixteenth week the bobbing of the head has altogether ceased; the holding up of the head is now settled for life.

In this important step is expressed an unquestionable, vigorous act of will. For the contractions of the mus cles that balance the head are at first not willed; they are not reflexive, not imitative, but impulsive, and then,

as the purpose of them soon becomes discernible, they
are instinctive. The benefit of these contractions is not
recognized by the infant, but the muscular feelings that
go with them are distinguished from other muscular
feelings by their agreeable consequences; since, for example, the child can see better when the head is erect,
and food can be taken more conveniently; therefore,
these muscular contractions are preferred. Among all
possible positions of the head, then, that of equilibrium
gradually appears oftenest in the upright position of
children, because it is the most advantageous, and when
children establish it we say they possess *will*. Adults
let the head fall when they go to sleep sitting, just as
infants do when awake. Their will is extinguished
when they cease to be awake. There is thus, during
the waking period, a certain outlay of will permanently
necessary for balancing the head, and the new-born and
the very young child, though awake, do not yet possess
this small quantum of will. We may, therefore, without
hesitation, refer the period of the first distinct manifestation of activity of will in the infant in this field to that
week in which the head, while he is awake, no longer
bobs hither and thither—i. e., the sixteenth week in the
case of my child, the only one accurately observed as
yet; in general, the fourth to the fifth month. R.
Demme observed—not so accurately, to be sure—one
hundred and fifty children in reference to this, and
found that "very powerfully-developed infants carry
the head properly balanced as early as toward the end
of the third or within the first half of the fourth month
of life; children moderately strong do this for the first
time in the course of the second half of the fourth

month; and more delicate individuals that fall somewhat below the normal standard in their nutrition do
not attain to this before the fifth or the beginning of
the sixth month of life." The statement of Heyfelder,
that even after six or eight weeks attempts were made
to hold the head erect, I can not confirm.

Observations are lacking, also, concerning the first
attempts of the infant, who at the beginning lies
straight or keeps the position it had before birth, to
lie on the side. One child did not accomplish it until
the fourth month, and only by great effort. When I
laid my boy, in the ninth and tenth months, on a pillow
face downward, the unusual position seemed to be extremely uncomfortable to him. He behaved in a very
awkward fashion, but turned over without any help, so
that after a minute or so he lay on his back again, or
supported himself on his hands. Something similar to
this happened, however, even in the sixth week of life.
The infant, when laid upon a pillow face downward,
propped himself even at that time on his forearms,
turning his head meantime to one side, without crying, thus exchanging the uncomfortable attitude for
one less uncomfortable. But in this there is as yet no
choice.

In the first three months no voluntary movement
appears. New-born children can not so much as free
the face by turning the head when any one covers
the face with his hand or lays them on a pillow with
the face downward. They cry and move the extremities
aimlessly, so that it can not be told with certainty
whether the new position is agreeable to them or not.
Some of them, indeed, retain for some time, without

moving, every position that is given to them—a thing which I have observed also in new-born animals.

5. Learning to Sit.

The first successful efforts to sit alone are referred (by Ploss) to the fourth month, or (by Sigismund) to the period from the seventeenth to the twenty-sixth week. Heyfelder also states, that vigorous children of five to six months sit with the whole of the upper part of the body erect. R. Demme found, on the other hand, that very powerfully developed children, "without specially remarkable strain of their muscular powers, could sit all alone toward the end of the seventh or at the beginning of the eighth month for several minutes." Those of moderate strength did not achieve the same thing till the ninth and tenth months; weakly ones in the eleventh and twelfth months.

With my child, who was vigorous, we succeeded with surprising ease in the first attempt to have him take a sitting posture contrived for him so that his back would be well supported. This was in the fourteenth week. In the twenty-second week the child actually raised himself to a sitting posture when he wanted to grasp at my face; but it was not till the thirty-ninth week that he could sit alone for any length of time; then he liked sitting, but not without a support. Even in his baby-carriage he needed that (in the fortieth and forty-first week still) in order to keep sitting. But although he could sit only for moments, at most, without any support, yet he always kept trying, manifestly to his own gratification, to maintain his equilibrium.

Finally, in the forty-second week the child sits up,

naked in the bath, without support, holding his back straight; so likewise in the carriage, where the clothes, coverings, and pillows essentially facilitate the balancing. The more difficult sitting upright in the bath, with its smooth sides, demands in the following period his entire attention. So long as his attention is not claimed by fresh impressions, the child does not fall to one side. He gains day by day in certainty in maintaining his equilibrium, so that after some days he sits for a full minute undressed in the bath, or in the carriage, without any support. From the eleventh month on, sitting becomes a habit for life.

In the beginning there appears along with this a peculiarity that is also found in monkeys, as was brought into notice by Lauder Brunton (1881). When, viz., little children are allowed to sit alone on the floor, they turn the soles of the feet toward each other, a habit that perhaps comes from the position of the legs before birth; for every child, when it is left to itself, undressed and unswathed, in a warm bed, takes for a long time after birth an attitude resembling the intra-uterine attitude—legs drawn up and arms bent and drawn in.

The sitting apparatus used by different nations in earlier times and at present—children's chairs with and without provision for locomotion—have been described by H. Ploss in his book "The Little Child from the Cushion to the First Step" ("Das Kleine Kind vom Tragbett bis zum ersten Schritt," 1881), and illustrated with cuts. These contrivances all serve rather the convenience of those who have the care of the child than that of the child itself. In fact, they are injurious when used too early. It is an important rule in or-

thopedy and in pedagogy that no child be habituated
to a sitting posture before he has of himself raised
himself with the upper part of the body from the recumbent position, in attempts to seize objects, *without
aid*—in other words, before he *wills* to sit.

That the time at which this is done is, as appears
from the above statements of different observers, very
different with different children—the earliest time being
generally in the fourth and the latest in the twelfth
month—is explained in part by the premature attempts
of the relatives to bring on the sitting by artificial
means; in part by imitation, where brothers and sisters
are growing up together—the latter, however, applies
only to the later stages; in part, finally, through muscular weakness also, unequal nourishment, lack of care,
or neglect. But, apart from all these influences, variation in the statements about the first sitting is caused
also by different conceptions on the part of the observers. The attempt to sit is still very far removed from
actual sitting; and this difference has been often overlooked.

6. Learning to Stand.

The first successful attempts to stand, in which my
child stood on his feet without support, but only for a
moment, were made in the thirty-ninth week. In the
following weeks he needed only slight aid, and he
seemed to prefer to occupy himself with learning to
stand rather than with learning to sit, although it must
have been more of a strain upon him.

In the eleventh month he can stand without any
support, and even stamps with his foot, but for all that
he is not at all sure on his feet. Only when chairs that

offer support, or watchful arms are close by, is the upright posture maintained longer than a moment.   In fact, until some time after the first year of life has been completed, the child does not stand for a longer time than that, except when he leans back in a corner.   I have not ascertained that in the numerous attempts, repeated daily, to have him stand, he actually fell down a single time in the first year ; and yet he gave us exactly the impression of being afraid of falling, as soon as he was to stand without leaning or being held.   Finally, however, at the beginning of the second year, the child could stand for some moments without a hand to hold him.   Then he gained gradually more confidence in himself through his efforts to walk, which were undertaken at the same time.

A little girl, who in the nineteenth week had raised herself for the first time alone to a sitting posture, could from the eleventh month on hold herself upright for some moments without any help, and could get up alone ; her sister could do it from the tenth month (Frau von Strümpell).

R. Demme found that only very vigorous children were able. at about the thirty-fifth to the thirty-eighth weeks of life, with slight support (given by taking hold of their hands or arms) to stand for some minutes ; and not before the fortieth to the forty-second week could they stand entirely unsupported for two or three minutes. Children of moderate strength arrived at this only about the forty-fifth to the forty-eighth week ; those more feeble not till the twelfth month or later.   These observations relate to one hundred and fifty Swiss children.

Sigismund puts the date of the first attempts to stand

at the eighteenth to the twenty-sixth week. "At that time children like much to stand, if they are grasped under the arms." But standing without support does not begin before the seventh month, and generally begins after the eighth.

Imitation co-operates in this, for in families in which several children grow up together the younger ones usually learn to stand somewhat earlier than the first-born does.

7. Learning to Walk.

Learning to walk is mysterious in its beginnings, because the reason for the alternate bending and stretching of the legs at the first placing of the infant upright is not apparent to him. But the possibility of learning to walk rests solely on the invariably repeated lifting and putting down of the feet by the child when standing or held erect. The flexions and extensions occur, to be sure, when the child is lying down, in bed or in the bath; but the regular bending and stretching which appear even months before the first successful attempt to walk, when the child, held upright on the floor, is pushed forward, is a different thing—it is instinctive. If infants could sustain life without coming in contact with human beings, they would of themselves doubtless adopt, but considerably later, the upright walk, because it is advantageous for command of the surrounding region through eye and ear. In the nursery, walking is almost always induced, and with unspeakable pains, earlier than can be good for children with regard to the growth of the bones. Children's go-carts (Kinderlaufstühle) and walking-frames (Gehkörbe) that favor such premature exercises are objectionable contrivances, because they help to make children bow-legged. Creeping, the natural preparatory school for walking, is but too often not permitted to the child, although it contributes vastly to his mental development. For liberty to get to a desired object, to look at it and to feel of it, is much earlier gained by the creeping child than by one who must always have help in order to change his location. Mother and nurses, in many families, prevent children from creeping before they can stand, through mere prejudice and even superstition, even when it is not the convenience of the elders, their disinclination to be observing watchfully the freely-moving child, that determines the unjustifiable prohibition. It can not be a matter of indifference for the normal mental development of the child not yet a year old, whether it is packed in a basket for hours, is swathed in swaddling-clothes, is tied to a chair, or is allowed to creep about in perfect freedom upon a large spread, out-of-doors in summer, and in a room moderately heated in winter.

When it is that a child tries to creep for the first time can not be accurately stated, just because he is generally hindered in such attempts. The date is besides very different for children of the same family, according to the nutrition and the firmness of the bones, the muscular power, and the desire of movement, which depend upon the nutrition. Some infants do not creep at all. Moreover, the manner of creeping is by no means the same in all children, nor do even European children all drag on both knees. My child dragged as a rule on one knee only, and used the other for an advance movement, putting forward the proper

foot, as Livingstone reports of the Manyuema children in
Africa. But like all children he learned to kneel down
only a long time after he could walk, whereas animals
a day old kneel of themselves (p. 68). So, too, it was
long after he could walk, that he learned to move forward on hands and knees.

The date of the first successful attempts to walk also
varies much, even with children of the same family,
with approximately the same nourishment. One weakly
child (according to Sigismund) could run alone cleverly
when it was eight months old, another at sixteen
months; many do not learn till after they are a year
and a half or even two years old. Much depends on the
surroundings. If a child grows up among other little
children, some of whom are walking, some learning to
walk, then he will, as a rule, be able to stand erect and
to run, without any support from the mother, earlier
than if he grows up alone. But in this case the frequent repetition of the instruction in walking may
shorten considerably the natural period. Thus Demme
saw (1882) out of fifty children two at the end of the
ninth month of life walk alone for some minutes—unsteadily, to be sure; on the other hand, seven not till
between the eighteenth and twenty-fourth month; the
remaining forty-one in the third half-year. A vigorous
female child with whom no experiments in standing
and walking were undertaken, began to creep with the
fifth month. "Up to the end of the tenth month she
moved forward very briskly on all-fours, like a monkey,
and up to this time, according to the express statement
of the trustworthy parents, she had made no attempt
to raise the body upright. With the fourteenth month

she began first to raise herself up by firm objects, and from the sixteenth to the eighteenth learned to walk properly without any assistance, keeping up meantime the frequent practice of going on all-fours. The girl was intelligent, and her development in other respects was regular."

In general, the first attempt of the child that can hold himself erect by means of firm objects, to stand free of support, to trot, to walk, comes into the time including the last quarter of the first year and the first three quarters of the second year, although proper walking-movements of an infant supported from above appear even in the second quarter of the first year. Champney's child was held upright for the first time at the close of the nineteenth week, so that the feet just touched the ground, and was moved forward. The legs moved themselves fitly all the time, in alternation. Every step was taken perfectly, and that without delay or irregularity, even when the feet were held too high; only, that when the boy was held too high, the alternating movement was interrupted, as the foot remaining in the air made a new step. The touching of the ground on the part of one foot seemed to furnish the stimulus for the movement of the other. These perfectly correct observations—out of the nineteenth week—support absolutely my view of the act of walking as an instinctive movement.

It was after the close of the first quarter of the second year that my child, standing unsupported on his feet, suddenly trotted for the first time around the table, swaying, to be sure, or staggering like a drunken man that wants to run, but without falling. And from

that day forth he could walk upright, at first only
rapidly, hardly except on a trot, as if the only thought
were to prevent the falling forward, and with arms extended in front — then slower and more securely.
Within the next ten weeks, however, the child went
over a threshold hardly an inch high, between two
rooms, only by holding on, and was often seen at this
period to fling with a jerk the foot that was put down
in advance, like a tabetic patient, or to lift it too high
and set it down too hard. The muscular sense was not
yet developed.

In order to give a clear idea of the gradually pro-
gressing development, I place together here a few more
observations which I made upon my child concerning
the first sitting, creeping, standing, walking, and running:

22d and 23d weeks.—Lying on his back the infant
often lifts himself up to a *sitting* posture, and is pleased
when he is *placed upright* on the knees of his nurse.

28th week.—The child of his own accord *places
himself upright*, but only on the lap of his mother,
holding on to her.

35th week.—The child, while being carried, places
himself on the arm and the hand of the nurse, and
looks over her shoulder.

41st week.—First attempts at walking. The child
was held under the arms so that his feet touched the
floor. Then he lifted his legs alternately and stretched
them imperfectly, in alternation. What induced these
movements in him is beyond finding out. Sitting and
standing without support are impossible.

42d week.—Whence it comes that the child, held

under the arms, his feet touching the floor, sets these to moving *forward*, and in the beginning *sidewise* also, now more regularly, is the harder to comprehend, for the reason that there is no pushing from behind, and usually nothing is before the child that he would desire. The inclination to walk is very great. From this time on the child *sits* without support.

43d week.—Whereas the child at the beginning put his feet irregularly over, by, and before each other, he now *lifts* the foot high up and generally puts it down firmly on the floor without crossing the legs. These remarkable movements occasion him the greatest pleasure. If he is very restless, he is speedily quieted if he is placed with his feet on the floor and held so. He begins then at once, without the least urging, *to move himself forward.*

45th to 47th weeks.—The exercises in walking, practiced almost daily, were at this period entirely omitted, in order to ascertain whether that which had been hitherto attained would be forgotten.

At the end of the forty-seventh week, however, the child when held up places his feet remarkably correctly, and seldom over each other; but the needed estimate of the amount of muscular force to be employed is still lacking, for he often lifts the foot too high, and puts it down too hard.

48th week.—The child often stands now a moment without support and stamps with his foot. He takes hold of a chair and *pushes* it forward somewhat, with only the slightest support.

49th week.—If the child is left to himself on a soft blanket, surrounded with pillows, he can not raise himself without help, and he can not stand more than an instant without help.

50th week.—The child can not yet of himself place himself upon his feet, when he is sitting or lying, nor can he walk without help.

53d week.—The child can *creep*, or rather drag himself along somewhat, but can not walk alone.

54th week.—He can *walk* when held by *one* hand. When creeping on the carpet, he moves but little and slowly from his place, and this with *asymmetrical* movements and stretchings of arms and legs.

57th week.—He hitches along hither and thither quite nimbly on hands and knees, but walking without being led (by one hand) is quite impossible.

60th week.—The child can raise himself alone from the floor by a chair, first to his knees and then to his feet. But he can stand all alone only a few moments; always clings tightly when he is put down.

62d week.—The child is still unable to stand longer than a moment without being supported, or at least touched. This inability depends no longer on the difficulty of maintaining the equilibrium, but on the lack of confidence in himself, for the only time when he is still unable to stand is when he knows he is not held. But when, without his knowledge, I have withdrawn from his back the support of my hand, having gradually reduced the pressure, then he *stands* for several seconds upright, and *without support*. Just so in the—

63d week.—The child still walks only when he can hold on with both hands (on the sides, fifty-five centimetres high, of a rectangular wooden structure of one

20

and a quarter metres length on the side, made by me on purpose for my child in 1878, and cushioned).

64th week.—When the child is led by one of his arms, so loosely that the arm is as if put through a loose ring, he walks properly and steadily; he can therefore walk without being held; but if he is left entirely free from one's touch, then he does not walk, but falls or stumbles into the arms of the person sitting or standing before him. Co-ordinating ability is not lacking, therefore, but self-confidence; whereas the inability to speak depends on lack of co-ordinating power. By altogether too frequent support, by too much telling how and showing how, by training, independent development is hindered and self-confidence is smothered in its origin.

65th week.—The child can not yet walk alone, indeed; but when he clasps only one guiding finger with his thumb and finger, he strides swiftly and securely forward. He raises himself, if he is laid down, first to the knees, and while he holds fast to something he *stands up*, but can not stand up without holding on.

66th week.—Suddenly—on the four hundred and fifty-seventh day of his life—the child can run alone. The day before, he was entirely unable to take three steps alone—he had to be led if only by means of a stick, perhaps a lead-pencil. Now, he ran alone around a large table, unsteadily indeed, and staggering and not holding his head in a stable position, but without falling. On the following day the little traveler is manifestly pleased at his new accomplishment, runs staggering, at random, with arms now hanging down, now lifted as if he wanted to hold on, now mute, again crying out,

"Hey! hey-ey!" (this he continued to do for months), and laughing. He likes to hold on by the furniture. On the day following, the child frequently stops during his hasty walking, and stamps, changing position from one foot to the other without any help. On the four hundred and sixty-first day he can walk *backward* also if he is led, and without leading can *turn round* quickly and cleverly. In walking he strikes about him at random with his arms. At the end of this week he can, *during his walking*, already direct his attention to other things, move his hands hither and thither for pleasure, hold objects and look at them during the *slow* walking, which has just been learned.

67th week.—Although a fall appears inevitable frequently in his walking alone, yet it rarely occurs—in the first five days of walking scarcely more than three times. In falling forward, both arms are now stretched straight out, which must be instinctive, as a falling person has not yet been seen by the child. In falling backward there is no protective movement. Whether the arms were extended at the *first* fall I have not been able to settle.

68th week.—The act of walking no longer requires so great attention as at the beginning. During his advance his look is already turned sidewise; and he even chews, swallows, laughs, and calls out. Walking is already becoming mechanical.

70th week.—The child raises himself from the floor alone—i. e., he stands up himself.

71st week.—Now first can a threshold—only an inch high, at the door between two rooms—be stepped over without help (not yet invariably, in the seventieth week, the child holding by the wall and the door-post). If he is sitting, he can now stand up without help.

77th week.—One day the child ran, without intervals of more than five seconds, nineteen times around a large table, calling out meantime, "Mamma!" and "Bwa, bwa, bwa!" Great liking for running.

78th week.—If he is holding something in his hands, then he walks over the threshold an inch high without holding on by anything.

85th week.—The thresholds are stepped over quickly without hesitation. In *running* he inclines forward, as if, at every step, falling were consciously prevented by carrying forward the center of gravity.

89th week.—Running is still somewhat awkward—with asymmetrical movements of the arms—so that it looks as if the child must fall. But a fall is very rare.

In the twenty-fourth month the child turns of himself, *dancing* in time to music; also beats the time with tolerable correctness, when he hears a hand-organ or a bag-pipe.

In the twenty-eighth month he first learned to "go on all-fours"—that is, on hands and feet (playing "bear"). Before this he had (in creeping) dragged himself along on hands and knees, never on hands and feet. In this period came the first exercises in *jumping*, which were continued to the point of exhaustion. In this month, too, and in the previous one, begins pleasure in climbing (on tables, chairs, benches).

In the thirtieth month, *mounting a staircase* of twenty-five steps without help—the right hand, on the

balustrade, rather directing than holding. After ten
days the same, with both hands free in the air.

In the thirty-fourth month, the first gymnastic exercises, which, like climbing and jumping, afford extraordinary pleasure. Also the throwing of any kind of
objects (out of a window); the hurling of stones into
the air or into a pond; the moving or setting in motion
of objects within reach (on the table) are absolutely original, and must consequently be traced back to hereditary
tendencies to produce changes in movable objects.

On the whole, it appears from the observations concerning sitting, standing, creeping, running, walking,
jumping, climbing, throwing, which are rapidly but
unequally developed in all children in like fashion,
that these movements are predominantly or exclusively
instinctive. They are not imparted by education. If
any one insists on saying that they are learned, he must
admit that they are only in the smallest degree learned
by imitation; for a child that sees no one drag himself
along, jump, climb, or throw, will without fail perform
these movements, even when he is not trained. The
progenitors of man must have found these especially
useful, so that they grew to be fixed habits and became
hereditary. At the same time, as it appears, those harmonious movements remained oftenest in use which,
like those of the muscles of the eye that are used
in seeing (p. 35), are of most service with the least
strain.

CHAPTER XII.

IMITATIVE MOVEMENTS.

To determine as exactly as possible the date of the first imitative acts is of especial interest in regard to the genesis of mind, because even the most insignificant imitative movement furnishes a sure proof of activity of the cerebrum. For, in order to imitate, one must first perceive through the senses: secondly, have an idea of what has been perceived; thirdly, execute a movement corresponding to this idea. Now, this threefold central process can not exist without a cerebrum, or without certain parts of the cerebrum, probably the cortical substance. Without the cerebral cortex, certain perceptions are possible, to be sure; many movements are possible, but not the generation of the latter out of the former. However often imitation has the appearance of an involuntary movement, yet when it was executed the first time, it must have been executed with intention —i. e., voluntarily. When a child imitates, it has already a will. But the oftener a voluntary movement is repeated, always in the same way, so much the more it approximates reflex movement. Hence many imitative acts, even in the child, occur involuntarily quite early. But the first ones are willed. When do they make their appearance?

If we make, for the infant to see, a movement that he has often practiced of his own accord, he can make a successful imitation much earlier than is commonly supposed. Such a movement, which I employed as suitable for early imitation, is the *pursing of the mouth*, the protruding of the closed lips, which often occurs, (even in adults) along with a great strain of the attention.

This protruding of the lips occurred with my child on the tenth day of life (in the bath, when a burning candle was held before him at the distance of a metre); in the seventh week it was decidedly marked at sight of a new face quite near him; in the tenth week, at the bending and stretching of his legs in the bath. It was as if the letter *u* were to be pronounced—and yet the child was wholly unable to imitate this movement so easily made by him (as late as the fourteenth week) when I made it for him under the most favorable circumstances. At the end of the fifteenth week appeared for the first time the beginnings of an imitation, the infant making attempts to purse the lips when I did it close in front of him. That this was a case of imitative movement is shown by the imperfect character of it in comparison with the perfect pursing of the lips when he makes the movement of his own accord in some other strain of the attention. Strangely enough, the imitation was attempted on the one hundred and fifth day, but not in the following days.

Further attempts at imitation occurred so seldom and were so imperfect, notwithstanding much pains on my part to induce them, in the following weeks, that I was in doubt whether they might not be the result of accidental coincidences. Not till the seventh month were the attempts to imitate movements of the head, and the pursing of the lips already spoken of, so striking that I could no longer refer them to accidental coincidence. In particular the child often laughed when one laughed to him (p. 145). The attention is now more and more plainly strained when new movements are made for the infant to see—he follows these with evident interest, but without coming to the point of an attempt at imitation in a single instance. This indolence was the more surprising, as even in the seventeenth week the protruding of the tip of the tongue between the lips (customary with many adults at their work) was perfectly imitated once, when done by me before the child's face, and the child in fact smiled directly at this strange movement which seemed to please him. Imitative movements thus appear in the fourth month, which in the seventh, and even the ninth, do not succeed or are quite imperfectly achieved. Yet in the tenth month correct imitations of all sorts of movements were frequent, and it is certain that these were executed with distinct consciousness; for, when he is imitating movements of hand and arm frequently repeated before him—e. g., *beckoning* [in the general sense of making a sign] and saying—" Tatta "—the child looks fixedly at the person concerned, and then often suddenly makes the movement quite correctly.

Beckoning (*Winken*) is in general one of the movements of the infant acquired early by imitation. In my child it appeared for the first time at the beginning of the tenth month. When he was going to be taken out, his mother used to make a sign to him, and now he likewise made a sign, almost invariably, in the doorway, with one arm, frequently with both arms, yet with an expression of face that indicated that he moved the arms or arm without understanding, upon the opening of the door. The proof of this lies in the fact, that when I enter the room, the child, so long as the door is in motion, makes that movement which he at first only imitated, and does it regularly—no hint of leave-taking in it therefore. The beckoning movement is made also at other times—e. g., on the opening and shutting of a large cupboard; it has, therefore, completely lost its purely imitative character. The movement consists essentially of a rapid raising and dropping of the extended arm; it is not, therefore, genuine beckoning. Not till after some weeks were motions of the hand added, and this more skillful imitation made it seem as if the machine-like movements that were made at the opening of the door were less and less involuntary, were more and more intentionally performed as genuine signs of leave-taking. But at this period (tenth month) such an action is not yet admissible; for when I make the same beckoning movement for the child without opening the door, he repeats it often in a purely imitative fashion without deliberation, though, to be sure, the eye has an expression of great strain of attention, on account of the difficulty of comprehending so quick a movement.

Not every imitative movement can be so clearly perceived to be willed as can this one. When one enters a room in which there are a good many infants, all quiet, one can easily observe the contagious influence of crying. For, if only one child begins to cry, then very soon several are crying, then many, often all of them. So, too, when one single infant (in the ninth month) hears other children cry, he likewise, in very many cases, begins to cry. The older the child becomes, the more seldom appears this kind of undesirable imitation; but even in children four years old, quite aimless imitative movements may often be perceived (as in mesmeric patients) if the children are observed without their knowledge. For example, they suddenly hold the arms crossed, as a stranger present is doing, and bow as he does at leaving.

A little girl in the last quarter of her first year imitated, in the drollest fashion, what she herself experienced in her treatment by the nurse, giving her doll a bath, punishing it, kissing it, singing it to sleep; and before the end of the first year she imitated the barking of the dog and the bleating of the sheep (Frau Dr. Friedemann).

Another female child imitated the following movements in a recognizable manner: in the eleventh month she threatened with the forefinger if any one did so to her, used a brush after she had seen brushes and combs, used a spoon properly, and drank from a cup, and made a kind of cradling movement with her doll, singing, " Eia—eia." In the thirteenth month the child made the motion of sewing, of writing (moistening the point of the pencil in her mouth) and of folding the arms. In the fifteenth month she fed the doll as she was fed herself, imitated shaving, on her own chin, and reading aloud, moving her finger along the lines and modulating her voice. In the eighteenth month she imitated singing, and made the motion of turning a crank like a hurdy-gurdy player when she heard music; in the nineteenth she went on hands and feet, crying " Au, au!" (ow, ow), in imitation of a dog; in the twentieth she imitated smoking, holding a cane firmly with her fingers exactly as is done in smoking a pipe. Her younger sister, in her fifteenth month, first imitated the movement of sewing and of writing; while the elder, in the nineteenth month, after repeated attempts at imitation, sewed together two pieces of cloth, without instruction, drawing the needle through correctly (Frau von Strümpell).

Toward the end of the first year of life the voluntary imitative movements, more numerous than before, are executed much more skillfully and more quickly. But when they require complex co-ordination they easily fail. When (at the beginning of the twelfth month) any one struck several times with a salt-spoon on a tumbler so that it resounded, my child took the spoon, looked at it steadily, and then likewise tried to strike on the glass with it, but he could not make it ring. In such imitations, which are entirely new, and on that account make a deeper impression, as in the case of puffing (*Pusten*) it would happen that they were repeated by the child in his dreams, without interruption of his sleep (twelfth month), a proof that the experiences of the day, however unimportant they appear to the adult, have stamped themselves firmly upon the impressionable brain of the child. But it takes always some seconds before a new or partly new movement, however simple, is imitated, when it is made for the child to imitate—e. g., it was a habit of my child (in the fourteenth month) to move both arms symmetrically hither and thither, saying, " ay—ĕ, ay—ĕ " (altogether differently, much more persistently and rapidly, than when beckoning). If some one made this very swinging of the arms for the child to observe, with the same sound, there was always an interval of several seconds before the child could execute the movement in like fashion. The simplest mental processes of all, therefore, need much more time than they do later. But imitations of this kind are almost always performed more quickly when they are not sought, when the child-brain is not obliged first to get its bearings, but acts spontaneously. If I clear my throat, or cough purposely, without looking at the child, he often gives a little cough likewise in a comical manner. If I ask, "Did the child cough?" or if I ask him, "Can you cough?" he coughs, but generally copying less accurately (in the fourteenth and fifteenth months). The bow too tightly strained shoots beyond the mark.

Here, besides pure imitation, there is already understanding of the name of the imitated movement with the peculiar noise.

This important step in knowledge once taken, the movements imitated become more and more complicated, and are more and more connected with objects of daily experience. In the fifteenth month the child learns to blow out a candle. He puffs from six to ten times in vain, and grasps at the flame meantime, laughs when it is extinguished, and exerts himself, after it has been lighted, in blowing or breathing, with cheeks puffed out and lips protruded to an unnecessary degree, because he does not imitate *accurately*. For it can hardly be that a child that has never seen how a candle can be blown out would hit upon the notion of blowing it out. Understanding and experience are not yet sufficient to make this discovery.

I find, in general, that the movements made for imitation are the more easily imitated correctly the less complicated they are. When I opened and shut my hand alternately, merely for the purpose of amusing the child, he suddenly began to open and shut his right hand likewise in quite similar fashion. The resemblance of his movement to mine was extremely surprising in comparison with the awkward blowing out of the candle in the previous instance. It is occasioned by the greater simplicity. Yet, simple as the bending of the finger seems, it requires, nevertheless, so many harmonious impulses, nerve-excitements, and contractions of muscular fibers, that the imitation of simple movements even can hardly be understood without taking into account the element of heredity, since unusual movements, never performed, it may be, by ancestors—say, standing on the head—are never, under any circumstances, imitated correctly at the first attempt. The opening and shutting of the hand is just one of the movements by no means unusual, but often performed by ancestors. Still, it is to be noticed that at the beginning the imitation proceeded very slowly, although correctly. On the very next day it was much more rapid on the repetition of the attempt, and the child, surprised by the novelty of the experience, now observed attentively first my hand and then his own (fifteenth month).

Of the numerous more complicated movements of the succeeding period, the following, also, may be mentioned, in order to show the rapid progress in utilizing a new retinal image for the execution of an act corresponding to it : A large ring, which I slowly put on my head and took away again, was seized by the child, and put by him in the same way on his own head without fumbling (sixteenth month). But, when it is a case of

combination of a definite action of the muscles of the
mouth with expiration of the breath, innumerable fruitless efforts at imitation are made before one of them
succeeds, because, in this case, a part only of the working
of the complicated muscular action can be perceived,
while the rest must be found out by trial. Thus, the
child could not, in spite of many attempts, get any tone
out of a small hunting-horn. He put it to his mouth,
and tried to imitate the tone with his own voice. Suddenly the right manner of blowing was hit upon accidentally, and from that time was never forgotten (eighteenth month).

After the child had seen how his mother combed
her long dark hair before a glass, he took a hand-mirror
and a comb and moved the comb around on his head,
combing where there was no hair. So, too, he would
now and then seize a brush and try to brush his head
and his dress, but took special pleasure in brushing also
all kinds of furniture. More than once he actually took
a shawl, held it by a corner to his shoulder, and drew it
behind him like a train, frequently turning around while
doing this. He also put a collar round his neck; he
tried to dry himself with a towel, but without success;
whereas the washing of the hands with soap, without
direction, was imitated, though not with much skill, yet
tolerably well; none but very complicated imitative
actions these, and all of them, in the case of my boy,
belong to the third quarter of the second year—an exceptionally important period in mental genesis—the
same is true of seizing. holding things before him, and
(what was observed by Lindner in the sixth month) the
imitation of reading aloud from a newspaper or pam-

phlet, the feeding of deer—holding out a single spear of grass to them—scraping the feet upon entering the house (as if the shoes were to be cleaned).

But how little real imitation and understanding of the act itself there was, even in this period of perfect external imitations, appears from the circumstance that a map is held, as a newspaper, " to be read aloud," before the face, and upside down. Now, too, the child likes to take a pencil, puts the point in his mouth, and then makes all sorts of marks on a sheet of paper, as if he could draw.

Just as remarkable is the lively interest in everything that goes on in the neighborhood of the child. In packing and unpacking, setting the table, lighting the fire, lifting and moving furniture, he tries to help. His imitative impulse seems here almost like ambition (twenty-third month).

Toward the end of the second year various ceremonious movements, especially those of salutation, are also imitated. The child sees how an older boy takes off his hat in salutation ; immediately he takes off his own head-covering and puts it on again, like the other boy.

All these movements last enumerated are distinguished from the earlier ones by this, that they were executed or attempted by the boy unsolicited, without the least inducement or urging, entirely of his own motion.

They show, on the one hand, how powerful the imitative impulse has become (in the second year); on the other hand, how important this impulse must be for the further mental development. For, if the child at this age passes the greater part of his time in company inattentive to manners, or unrefined, then he will imitate all sorts of things injurious to him, and will easily acquire habits that hinder his further development. It is, therefore, of the greatest importance, even at this early period, to prevent the intercourse of children with strangers, and to avoid everything that might open wrong paths to the imitative impulse.

The imitative movements of the muscles of speech, the child's imitations of sounds, syllables, and words are treated of in detail in the third part of this work. The first answer of the infant to the language addressed to him by his relatives, which is said to be made, in individual cases, as early as the eighth and ninth weeks (according to Sully, 1882), is no attempt at imitation, but a directly reflexive movement, like screaming after a blow, etc. Singing has already been mentioned as one of the earliest imitated performances. It is true of these, as of all later imitations, that the first imitation of every new movement is voluntary on the part of the child, and, in case an involuntary imitation seems to occur, then either this has already been often repeated as such, or it is a movement often practiced without imitation. The accuracy of the imitation depends little, however, upon the co-operation of a deliberative cerebral activity. On the contrary, children of inferior mental endowment among those born deaf sometimes possess (according to Gude) a purer and more distinct enunciation than those more gifted.

CHAPTER XIII.

EXPRESSIVE MOVEMENTS.

EXPRESSIONS of countenance and gestures arise chiefly, as is well known, from imitation. Not only persons born blind, but also those who become blind at an advanced age, are distinguished from those who have sight by their lack of the play of feature. Their expression of countenance shows only slight changes; their physiognomy appears fixed, uniform; the muscles of the face move but little when they are not eating or speaking. Little children also lack a characteristic play of feature, hence the difficulty of making portraits of them, or even of describing them. Different as is the contented face from the discontented, even on the first day, different as is the intelligent face from the stupid, the attentive from the inattentive, the difference can not be completely described. In the second half of the first year children act after the example of the members of the family. Speak gravely to a gay child of a year old, and it becomes grave; if it is sober, and you show a friendly face, the child in many cases brightens up in an instant. Yet it would be premature to conclude from this that all the means of expression by the countenance are acquired solely through imitation. Some mimetic movements, of which we have already spoken, are of reflex origin. The same is true of gestures. Others may be instinctive.

As every gesture is wont to appear in association with the expression of countenance appropriate to it, when it has a language value, it seems advisable to treat

21

together expressions and gestures which together form
pantomime, and to separate the purely expressive muscular movements of the infant from its other movements, in our attempt to trace their origin.

So long as the child can not yet speak words and
sentences, it effects an understanding with other children
and with adults by the same means that are employed
by the higher animals for mutual understanding, by
demonstrative movements and attitudes, by sounds expressive of emotion or feeling, of complaining, exulta-
tion, alluring, repelling, or desiring, and by dumb looks.
These very means of expression are employed by the
child when it entertains itself in play with inanimate
objects.

Of the expressive movements of the child I have
especially considered, as to their origin, smiling and
laughing, pouting and kissing, crying and wrinkling of
the forehead, shaking the head and nodding, shrugging
the shoulders, and begging with the hands, as well as
pointing.

1. The First Smiling and Laughing.

The first smiling is the movement most often misunderstood. Every opening of the mouth whatever,
capable of being interpreted as a smile, is wont to be
gladly called a smile even in the youngest child. But
it is no more the case with the child than with the
adult that a mere contortion of the mouth fulfills the
idea of a smile. There is required for this either a feeling of satisfaction or an idea of an agreeable sort. Both
must be strong enough to occasion an excitement of the
facial nerves. A smile can not be produced by a mere
sensation, but only by the state of feeling that springs

from it, or by the agreeable idea developed from it, however vague it may yet be.

Now, as has been shown already, the number of sensations associated with a pleasurable feeling in the first days of life is very small, and an idea, in the proper sense of the word, the new-born child unquestionably can not have as yet, because he does not yet perceive. The child that is satisfied with nursing at its mother's breast, or with the warmth of the bath, does not smile in the first days of life, but only shows an expression of satisfaction, because for the moment all unpleasant feelings are absent. But how easily such a condition of comfort manifests itself by a very slight lifting of the corner of the mouth, is well known. If we choose to call this a smile, then even sleeping babes smile very early. On the tenth day of his life I saw my child, while he was asleep, after having just nursed his fill, put his mouth exactly into the form of smiling. The dimples in the cheeks became distinct, and the expression of countenance was, in spite of the closed eyes, strikingly lovely. The phenomenon occurred several times. On the twelfth day appeared, along with the animated movements of the facial muscles, a play of features in the waking condition, also, that one might take for a smile. But this play of the muscles of the mouth lacked the consciousness that is required to complete the smile, as does the smile of the sleeping child. On the twenty-sixth day, first, when the child could better discriminate between his sensations and the feelings generated by them, did the smile become a mimetic expression. The babe had taken his milk in abundant quantity, and was lying with his eyes now open and now half-closed, and with an indescribable expression of contentment on his countenance. Then he smiled, opening his eyes, and directed his look to the friendly face of his mother, and made some sounds not before heard, which were appropriate to his happy mood. But the idea had not yet arisen of the connection of the mother's face with the mother's breast, the source of enjoyment (p. 46). Nor can we at this period assume an imitation, by the child, of the smile of the mother, because at first inanimate objects (tassels) are smiled at, and before the fourth month no imitative movements at all were attempted.

Not only the first-mentioned very early movements of smiling, but also this perfect smile is connected with a condition of contentment, and there is no reason to regard it as less hereditary in character than is screaming with pain, which no one would refer to imitation.

Later the child smiles when he is smiled at, but not always by any means. Strangers may smile at him in ever so friendly a manner, yet the wondering little face, usually merry, now sober, remains immobile. The first imitations of the smile in children are not so free from deliberation as the smiles of many adults, which through training and the conventional forms of greeting have degenerated into mere formality.

The original smile of satisfaction at new, agreeable feelings, a smile which may continue even in sleep, and which appears only in a cheerful frame of mind, remains in force still later. By an unusual expression of intensity in the more brightly gleaming eye, as well as by lively movements of the arms and legs, most plainly by laughing and smiling, the infant manifests his satisfaction—e. g., in music (in the eighth week)—without any one's giving him in any other way the least occasion for it.

The date of the first smile varies very much, therefore, according as we take for a smile a spontaneous expression of pleasure, or the communication of an agreeable condition, or the satisfaction at a pleasing idea ; here belongs the first imitated smile, and the statements that the first smile appears in well-developed children about the fourth week, as the expression of pleasure (Heyfelder), in the sixth to the eighth week (Champneys), in the seventh and ninth week (Darwin), or that in the seventh to the tenth week (Sigismund) the babe smiles for the first time, are as indefinite as the statement that, at the end of the second week, his mouth takes on a lovely expression like a smile. It depends essentially on the nature of the occasion of the smile at what date the first smile shall be fixed.

One child first smiles at its image in the glass in the twenty-seventh week ; another, in the tenth (see below) ; the one observed by myself, in regard to this point, in the seventeenth week, and not at all till that time. It was rather a laugh than a smile that surprised me on the one hundred and sixteenth day, whereas even on the one hundred and thirteenth the image in the mirror was regarded with a fixed and attentive look, to be sure, but without any sign of satisfaction. In these cases it is simply the joy at the distinct, new perception—an idea, therefore, that occasions the smile ; in other cases it is pleasure in impressions of agreeable tastes, of softness or warmth, or joy in pleasing sound, or simply the feeling of satiety (fourteenth week), and then it is usually accompanied by a peculiar sound, which is always much softer in the first months than the expressions of displeasure. But, when the quite young child does not feel well, or is hungry, it can not smile any more. The surest sign of convalescence is the reappearance of this significant movement of the mouth.

From the smile to the laugh is but a step, and the laugh is often only a strengthened and audible smile. The first laugh upon a joyous sense-impression is, however, essentially different from that which springs from the heightened self-consciousness at the perception of the ludicrous; and the limit of time given for that, of six to seventeen weeks, is surprisingly late. Pliny thinks no child laughs before the fortieth day. I observed an audible and visible laugh, accompanied by a brighter gleam of the eye, in my child, for the first time, on the twenty-third day (p. 32). He was pleased with a bright, rose-colored curtain that was hanging above him, and he made peculiar sounds of satisfaction, so that I was first led by these to pay attention to him. The corners of his mouth were drawn somewhat upward. At this period no laugh yet appeared when the child was in the bath, but there also the expression of the little face with the widely-opened eyes was that of great satisfaction. Laughing appears at first simply as an augmentation of this expression of pleasure. It is often repeated in the same way in the fifth and sixth weeks—in the eighth especially—at the sight of slowly-swinging, well-lighted, colored objects, and on hearing the piano.

The child's laugh appeared for the first time, in the period from the sixth to the ninth week, as a sign of joy at a familiar, pleasing impression, his eyes being fixed on his mother's face. But the laugh at the friendly nodding to him (p. 62), and singing (p. 84), of the members of the family, was then already much more marked, and was later accompanied by rapid raisings and droppings of the arms as sign of the utmost pleasure (sixth month). This last childish movement continued for years as an accompanying phenomenon of laughing for joy. But it is to be noticed that this laugh first began to be persistently loud in the eighth month (in play with the mother); every one could then at once recognize it as a laugh without looking in that direction. In this the child made a peculiar impression of gayety upon every one who saw him.

Loud laughing at new objects that please, and are long looked at, is still frequent in the ninth month; so also at new sounds in the fifteenth month (p. 89); then follows laughing at the efforts to stand with support. In the last three months of the first year, however, the character of the laugh appears to become different, as it becomes more conscious. The child laughs with more understanding than before. But he with a laugh grasps at his own image in the glass, and makes a loud jubilant noise, in the eleventh month, when he is allowed to walk, although he must be held firmly when doing so. At the end of the first year, to these independent utterances of pleasure had been added the purely imitative laughing when others laughed. Yet self-consciousness manifested itself also in this, through vigorous crowing with employment of abdominal pressure. Roguish laughing I first noticed toward the end of the second year. Scornful laughing and lachrymal secretion during continuous laughter I have never observed in children under four years of age.

From the sum total of my observations in regard to the smiling and laughing of infants, it results unquestionably that both are original expressive movements, which may be distinctly perceived in the first month, which by no means take place the first time through imitation, and which, without exception, from the beginning express feelings of pleasure ; in fact, my child laughed in his sleep at the end of his first year of life, probably having a pleasant dream, and did not wake on account of it.

The reasons are not yet known why feelings of pleasure are expressed just in this manner—i. e., by uncovering the teeth, and even before the teeth are present, by lengthening the opening of the mouth, along with lifting the corners of the mouth, by peculiar sounds and a brighter gleam of the eye (secretion of lachrymal fluid, without its going so far as the formation of tears), and lively accompanying movements of the arms (p. 145). The causes must be hereditary. But Darwin rightly urges that they do not operate so early as the causes of crying and weeping, because crying is more useful to the child than laughing. And if he saw two children distinctly smile for the first time in the seventh week, we ought to infer from that not so much a failure to notice earlier attempts as the existence of individual differences. That he perceived the first decided laugh in the seventeenth week shows how unlike individual infants are in this respect. Probably much depends on the surroundings and on the behavior of the family. But in all children the expression of pleasure begins with a scarcely perceptible smile, which passes very gradually, in the course of the first three months, into conscious laughing, after the cerebral cortex has so far developed that ideas more distinct can arise. In the second month is perceived also the reflex laughing that follows tickling (p. 145) which I could besides (in the third year) distinguish almost invariably from expressive laughing by the sound alone, without knowing what was going on, although I was in a neighboring room when I heard it. This "thoughtless" laugh sounds, on the contrary, exactly like the child's laugh often heard continuously at this time, which occurred when he heard and saw adults laugh at jests unintelligible to him, and which was long continued without any meaning in it. Laughing incites still more to imitation and is more contagious than crying. The laughter of man seems even to have an enlivening effect on intelligent animals (dogs), which draw the corners of the mouth far back, and spring, with an animated gleam of the eye, into the air. I had a large Siberian dog that laughed in this manner. It is known that monkeys also laugh. These facts favor the hereditary character of the movement of laughing— all the more as tickling of the skin of the arm-pit excites laughing in children and monkeys in the same way, when they are gay, as Darwin informs us. But if a crying child is tickled in the same manner, it does not laugh.

2. Pouting of the Lips.

A peculiar expression of children and of many adults is the protruding of the lips when the attention is strained. I have seen old men, in playing on the piano, and in writing, protrude the lips in a still more striking

manner —even putting out the tongue—than infants that
are beginning to seize, and children that are examining
a new toy. The external occasions of this remarkable
alteration of the shape of the mouth may vary to whatever extent, yet they all agree in this, that after the
first week they introduce a vigorous strain of attention.
Yet the protruding of the lips appears long before the
development of the ability to examine objects. I once
saw a new-born child in its first hour of life protrude its
lips which were as yet untouched (p. 207); but this protrusion was without the movement of sucking; it appeared along with many other movements of the facial
muscles, and I should be inclined to explain it as purely
impulsive. My child showed it on the tenth day of his
life, distinctly, in the bath, when there was a lighted
candle before him; and from that time on with extraordinary frequency until his fourth year. His lips were
protruded almost like a snout, as in sucking (p. 98),
then drawn back and again protruded (sixteenth
month). The movements of the tongue exhibited by
many children in learning to write, were not observed by
me till much later than the protrusion of the lips; they
appeared along with attempts to do with effort some new
thing. Here it is worthy of notice that even in merely
looking at an object without taking hold of it himself,
the lips are pursed (fifth week, p. 56, and seventh week
p. 45, also the tenth month, p. 63); later more protruded,
when a testing (forty-fourth week, p. 55) or inquiring
observation (forty-seventh week, p. 50) is combined with
touching, in which the aim is to follow a moved object
in various directions, or to put an object in motion or
turn it around, to empty a box and fill it, or to open and

shut it, or to put a number of small objects of the same kind, e. g., buttons, into rows and rolls or into envelopes (first half of second year).

In this the protrusion of the lips is quite different from the pouting of sullenness. The protruded lips of the cross child, resembling those, still further protruded, of the cross chimpanzee, which I observed in the zoological garden at Hamburg, as Darwin describes it and gives a picture of it, appear much later than this narrowing of the opening of the mouth that is combined with prolonged fixing of the gaze, and that lasts (with children not yet two years old) several minutes. It looks as if the vowel *u* were to be pronounced, whereas the children, whose hands are busy, are absolutely silent. Whence this expression? I will try to give an explanation of it. That this excitement of the facialis is hereditary is a fixed fact; for in the case, very carefully observed by me—a strongly marked case too—it can not have been acquired by imitation. My child neither associated intimately enough with other children nor saw pursing of the lips in the adults about him, and could not imitate it before the fifteenth week (see p. 283). But if it is hereditary, then it must be referred to the progenitors of man. All animals direct their attention first to food. Their first test is applied to things that may be reached with lips, feelers, snout, tongue. All testing of food is attended with a predominant activity of the mouth and its adjuncts. Especially in *sucking*, which first awakens the attention of the newly-born, is the mouth protruded. Later, when new objects, that excite the attention, come within reach, they are carried to the mouth, because the thing that was alone interesting previously, food, came to the mouth. The inference, that what is interesting belongs to the mouth, is first shaken by the experience that many beautiful and interesting objects do not go into the mouth or are disagreeable within it. But the association of the first movement of the mouth arising from sucking, the protruding of the lips, with strain of the attention, is confirmed by too frequent repetition of the taking of food, the most interesting occurrence to the infant, to be lost as quickly as is the carrying of new toys to the mouth. It is therefore not only transmitted to the child, but often remains for years, even into old age, and manifests itself in an extremely striking fashion when the attention is on the strain, at anything unusually interesting; particularly in case some personal activity, such as writing or drawing, causes the strain.

A particular kind of protrusion of the lips, different from the foregoing, takes place in—

3. Kissing.

This belongs to the very late acquired expressive movements, which, in general, do not seem to be inherited. As it is unknown to many nations, it is to be called conventional.

How little the child understands the significance of the kiss, although it is kissed by its mother probably more than a thousand times in its first year, is plainly apparent from many observations.

A little girl in the fourteenth month kissed "quite audibly the cheek or hand (stroking it at the same time) often from a pure fit of tenderness," but many times in order to obtain something or to pacify some one. In the fifteenth month this child kissed her mother one day twelve times in succession, entirely of her own accord; her sister kissed her mother's hand at the beginning of the fifteenth month without solicitation some eight times in succession; her brothers and sisters used to kiss one another, at the age of three and a half and one and a quarter years, for amusement (Frau von Strümpell). Another female child returned a kiss from the tenth month on, without any movement of warding off (Lindner); all this was learned.

I put together here, in brief form, some notes concerning my child:

11th day.—When the babe was kissed by his mother on the mouth, he fairly seized one of her lips with his, and *sucked* at it as if he had got the breast, putting out his tongue.

32d week.—The child no longer sucks at the lips when he is kissed, but *licks* them as he licks objects in general that please him.

33d week.—When he is kissed, the child no longer licks the lips, but allows himself to be kissed on the mouth without response or opposition. In the following months, also, there is no trace of an attempt to return the kiss, although signs of affection are not wanting. For in the fifty-first week the child hands to his mother the biscuit he is himself about to eat.

12th month.—The opening of the closed mouth that takes place in kissing is tolerably well imitated.

13th month.—The child has absolutely no idea of what a kiss signifies. Kisses are not agreeable to him, for he always turns away his head when he is kissed, no matter by whom.

15th month.—The words, "Give a kiss!" produce a drawing near of the head, and often a protruding of the lips. This proves an understanding of the words only, not of the thing.

19th month.—When strangers want to be kissed by the child, he holds off; accordingly, he is fastidious in his choice in regard to approach.

20th month.—The child shows by touching the face, especially the cheek, with his face, that proximity has come to appear to him as essential in kissing. Herein lies already an imperfect return of the kiss. The child also bends his head when some one says, "Kiss," toward the face of the speaker, without opening the mouth as hitherto, but does not always put out his lips.

23d month.—The child now knows the significance of the kiss as a mark of favor, and is fastidious in his choice in giving a kiss as he is in giving his hand. In kissing, his lips are put forward closed, and then the mouth is somewhat too widely opened after the contact.

34th month.—The feeling of thankfulness is awakened. When one has done something to please the child, he sometimes kisses, and has a gracious, thankful air, but says nothing.

At first, then, the lips of the mother, when she kisses her child, are treated like the finger held to the mouth, or like the breast, as objects to be sucked; then they are licked, as by a puppy; next, the kiss is endured; further on it is refused; soon afterward it is awkwardly, and only on request, returned; and, finally, it is spontaneously given as a sign of thanks and of affection—and this by a boy who is not in the least tender and is not trained. Assuredly this tedious schooling in learning to kiss furnishes the best evidence how little justified we should be in designating the kiss as an hereditary privilege of humanity.

4. Crying, Weeping, and Wrinkling the Forehead.

It is a fact long since familiar that newly-born and quite young babes do not weep—i. e., there is no external secretion of tears, however vigorously they cry. Later, children cry and weep at the same time, and can cry without weeping (e. g., in jest), but not till much later are they able to weep without crying out.

The date of the first external lachrymal secretion varies surprisingly in different children. Darwin puts together some observations on this point, from which it appears that in two cases the eyes were wet with tears for the first time at the end of the third and the ninth week; in another case tears flowed down the cheeks at the end of the sixth week. In two other children this was not the case as late as the twelfth and the sixteenth week; in a third child, however, it happened in the fifteenth week. One of his own children shed tears in crying in the twentieth week, but not yet in the eighteenth, and in the tenth the eyes were moist in violent crying. At the end of the eleventh week with this same child an accidental, rude touch of the eye with a rough cloth produced a flow of tears in this eye, but not in the other, which was merely moist. Champney's child shed tears for the first time in the fourteenth week.

I have seen tears flow from the eyes as early as the twenty-third day, in my boy, while he was screaming

lustily. Soon afterward, crying with shedding of tears,
and whimpering, formed the most important sign of
psychical events of different sorts.

What Darwin reports, that usually babes do not shed
tears before they are two or four months old, is not true
of German children in general. Not weeping, but sobbing, comes so late, and even later, for the first time;
and some causes of weeping, as willfulness, grief, anger,
can not operate at first, because in general they are still
wanting; whereas pain is expressed by tears from the
first, when once the secretion of tears has begun. Yet
it is easy to prove that little children in the second and
third years weep much more easily and shed more tears
at impressions that cause displeasure than do children of
six months or a year. I suspect that in this matter more
depends on the excitation of the lachrymal nerves through
emotional cerebral processes than upon compression of
the gland in screaming, as Darwin thinks. For in the
first place there sometimes appears, as Genzmer observed,
in children just born, upon touching the mucous membrane of the nose, "an increased lachrymal secretion,"
which proves that through excitement of the nerves,
especially reflexive excitation (and that without compression), lachrymal secretion may occur before weeping; secondly, tears may trickle over the cheeks in great
drops without any compression of the lachrymal gland,
without screaming; and in the second year also appears
crying without weeping—that is, compression of the
lachrymal gland without lachrymal secretion. My child
cried in his sleep, evidently dreaming, without shedding
tears, and without waking, as early as the tenth month;
another child (Lindner) in the eighteenth week.

Of crying—with tears (*Schreiweinen*)—in little children, on the other hand, two alterations of countenance are extremely characteristic, the observation and explanation of which offer many difficulties—viz., the drawing down of the corners of the mouth, and the wrinkling of the forehead.

The peculiar form of the mouth, arising from contraction of the depressors of the corners of the mouth, directly before and after a fit of crying, has already been spoken of in the description of childish expressions of discomfort (p. 149).

The wrinkling of the forehead is, indeed, likewise observed without exception in crying with the eyes held tightly together, but is in the beginning an impulsive movement frequently occurring without a fretful mood. I saw it on the first, second, sixth, seventh, tenth days (cf. pp. 2, 23, 36), exactly as in many monkeys, frequently appear without any assignable outward occasion. On the contrary, in young infants, the corrugation of the forehead is lacking just when we should expect to perceive it—judging from adults—e. g. (p. 24), at raising the glance (in the eighth and twelfth weeks). It is surprising, too, that in the first two weeks the horizontal corrugation of the brow appears much oftener than afterward. In the fourth month I saw for the first time in my child slight horizontal furrows in the brow when he was looking upward, but in the third quarter of the first year not invariably as yet; in the last three months invariably. Distinct vertical furrows, which lend a somber expression to the childish physiognomy, are always present in crying with tears, as has been mentioned, but often occur without that (plainly

22

in a boy of nine weeks; in my boy, in the seventh month).

A girl, one of twins, only six days and some hours old, was seen by me to wrinkle the brow twice very decidedly—once with, once without a simultaneous movement of the skin of the head. The mother said, "The child has serious thoughts." And, in fact, it looked peculiarly precocious, to see the skin of the forehead both times laid in deep, parallel folds, which extended over the whole breadth of the forehead, and the face take on a very serious expression. In this case, as in all similar cases, it does not, however, appear safe to attribute to the wrinkling of the brow the significance of an expressive movement, because the psychical states are as yet wanting that are expressed by horizontal folds of the brow.

The distinct wrinkling of the skin of the forehead in astonishment I have seen for the first time in the twentieth month. I have often seen, also, when new tricks were done before the child (in the fifteenth month), the characteristic transverse folds as an accompanying movement of laborious attempts at imitation. Yet we look in vain for physiological explanations of these facts. Darwin, who saw his children wrinkle the forehead, from the first week on, as an invariable antecedent to tearful crying, has expressed the conjecture that this expressive movement, inherited from of old (contraction of the corrugators), originally serving to protect the eyes when impressions were to be warded off, was finally associated with unpleasant feelings in general. The vertical folds that accompany effort would harmonize with this, but the transverse folds that accompany astonishment are connected with the wider opening of the eyelids.

That a purely reflexive corrugation of the brow—the vertical folds—occurs together with that early expressive movement in the first days, is certain. In the fourth year I saw, moreover, an actual contraction of the corrugators of a child fast asleep take place, sometimes without the least movement of the eyelid, when I let bright lamp-light fall upon the closed eyes, in a place otherwise dark. The sleep was not interrupted by it, nor even the snoring. This reflex may, like the screwing up of the eyes in the same circumstances, be inborn, like the corrugation of the brow after sound-impressions and contact in the first week.

5. Shaking the Head and Nodding.

Shaking the head as a sign of denial or refusal is in like manner practiced by many children early, without instruction and without opportunity for imitation. A forerunner of this expressive movement, which signifies dislike, disgust, much earlier than it does denial, is, as Darwin also declares, the sidewise movement of the head, the turning away when food is refused, whether the breast or the bottle.

Much in the same way, the head is turned to the window (p. 3) even in the first days (pp. 41, 42), and then toward objects moved (pp. 48, 49), but with a contented expression; later, in the direction of a new sound (pp. 84, 85, 88). In general I found, from the first day on, sidewise movements of the head without any reflex excitement (p. 260) frequently in my child (Von Ammon is wrong in the opinion that the infant does not move the head at all in the first days). The head-movements are, in fact, quite lively when the babe is placed at the breast, or is in the bath, or is lying down. They are sidewise movements, not nodding, absolutely irregular and "natural." At the beginning, however, the turnings of the head are, strangely enough, not always in harmony with the movements of the eyes (p. 36), which makes them seem "unnatural."

Further, I saw in the first week in my child regularly, when it was placed at the breast, a vigorous turning sidewise in both directions, almost a shaking of the head (cf. pp. 153, 260). On the eighth day of his life, when he for the first time took the breast without any help whatever, these lateral movements of the head made it seem just as if the child were trying to find something. On the twenty-seventh day, however, they took place just the same, when the bottle was put directly to his mouth; a strange association, caused possibly by this, that in the very first days the head is somewhat directed by helping hands, so that the nipple comes into the mouth. Later the head-movement, that has been always followed by the stream of milk, becomes for the infant a necessary preliminary condition of the taking of food, and is retained by him, although in connection with the bottle it is useless. Accordingly we have here not a case of an acquired movement of the head, one that has been learned, but an instinct that occasions the head-movements in sucking at the finger as well as in nursing at the breast.

It has been already mentioned that many mammals likewise move the head vigorously hither and thither when they begin to suck, so that we may assume an

hereditary factor in mankind; the more so, as the turnings of the head were to be observed, very vigorous
even in the eighth week, and invariably when the babe
was placed at the breast, several times a day, before the
nipple was firmly grasped. In spite of the great haste
and greediness in sucking, these unnecessary previous
movements were never forgotten. They are, as to their
causes, different from the reflexive turning of the head.

When any one seats himself at the bedside of the
child, the child's head is regularly turned toward him
(fifth week). This is followed by the reflexive turning
around at new sound-impressions (eleventh week), and
when any one leaves the room noisily (twenty-second
week).

All these lateral head-movements are not in the
least forerunners of the denying or refusing shake of
the head—are not in any way related to it; although
they very frequently agree with it perfectly in appearance, if all the external circumstances and the physiognomy are left out of the account. The manifold variety
of the lateral turnings of the head in the infant, from
the first day, is astonishing. And yet the peculiar turning away of the head comes in as a well-marked expressive movement as early as the fourth day. My child
refused to nurse at the left breast, which was somewhat
more inconvenient for him than the right. He refused,
turning his head away decidedly from it, and on the
sixth day he screamed besides. On the seventh we first
succeeded in overcoming his opposition. Yet a single
averting of the head remained as a sign of refusal. It
appeared almost invariably after the infant had nursed
his fill and had thrust the nipple out of his mouth—a

thing hardly to be accomplished by a reflex mechanism (very plainly done in the first as in the seventh month). The child was so dominated by the feeling of satiety that food was repulsive to him.

This single averting of the head to the left or to the right, according to the position, manifestly means " No more!" is, therefore, of the nature of refusal. But after the child had learned to balance his head there came, for the first time, numerous and very rapid turnings of it, exactly like the shaking of the head in denial by adults (in the sixteenth week). Then appeared also a nodding, but more seldom. It no more signified affirmation than the lateral turnings in that early period signified denial. This is rather an instance of exercise of the muscles simply. The turning away of the head in refusal, when the child had drunk enough, persisted. In the sixth month arm-movements were added, which seemed like movements of warding off, without my being convinced, however, that they were so. Rather was it many months before the appearance of unquestionable arm-movements of warding off, such as take place in the case of adults when something is held before the face too long. The child that does not want the offered object raises his arm sidewise from one to three times in refusal, and turns his head away toward the opposite side. This deprecating arm-movement (distinctly marked in the fifteenth month) may well be an acquired one, that is, imitated, as we may attribute to the child at this period a capacity of observation that would suffice for this. At any rate the raising of the bended arm is not in the beginning associated with the turning away of the head, and the nurse may in like manner have protected herself frequently when the child has put his hands into her face. To be sure, the execution of a defensive movement is quite early associated with an idea of defense. When the boy (in the eighteenth month) tries in anger to hit with his foot some one who has refused him a key that he wanted, we can not find for such a re-enforcement of the refusing head-movement any model that he has imitated; still less can we find one for his striking about him with arms and legs, throwing himself at the same time on the floor and screaming with rage (just like what I saw in the case of a chimpanzee from whom an apple that he wanted was withheld). There occur in children as early as the tenth month similar fits of rage (p. 323), in which the face becomes red in case their desire is not complied with (Frau von Strümpell).

Neither is the half-closing of the eyelid, when the head is turned away in refusal, to be traced to imitation. It did not occur invariably. I saw it in the eighth month distinctly in my boy when disinclination was expressed. Especially was antipathy (not fear) expressed by such turning away of the head at the approach of women dressed in black, no matter how friendly they were, up to the third quarter of the second year, and even the second quarter of the third year.

Long before this period, however, a repeated turning of the head, or a shaking of the head in denial, had arisen out of the simple averting of the head; this came through training. It appeared mostly in the thirteenth month when any one said, "No, no!" but there was no nodding at the "Yes, yes!" and there was no success in imitating nodding in the fourteenth month, in spite of much pains. Afterward the imitation often succeeded (in the sixty-fourth week), but the nodding of the head along with "No, no!" was also sometimes observed, and the shaking of the head with the "Yes, yes!" the meaning thus being confounded (a paramimy). In fact, it was months before the meaning of the affirmative inclination of the head was firmly impressed, after the negative one had been long practiced. When, on the four hundred and forty-fifth day of his life, the first movement had been correctly imitated for the second time—on the day before for the first time—the child made a peculiar movement of the hand in time with nodding of the head, a genuine supination, looking, the while, very attentively indeed at the head of the person before him—an unconscious accompanying movement, therefore. That the inclination of the head, learned with effort, meant "Yes" was wholly unknown to him; and yet, in the sixteenth month, the negative head-shaking meant for the child not only "No," but also "I do not know," and, in the seventeenth month, "I do not wish." This gesture continued now, while the nodding of the head in affirmation seldom occurred, unless it was specially asked for. It was not till the fourth year that an affirmative nod of the head meant "Thank you!" The difference is the more surprising as both movements have been frequently regarded as original. But children use the voice for denying and affirming much earlier than they do the inclination and turning of the head, and this whole exposition shows that these movements have not from the beginning an antagonistic relation to each other, but the sidewise turning away of the head, at first in refusal, later in denying, is inborn, reflexive-instinctive, while the inclining and nodding of the head in affirmation or assent, or in the expression of thanks, which appears much later, must be called an acquired gesture of unknown origin.

6. Shrugging the Shoulders.

Little children show, at a very late period, a quick raising of the shoulders, corresponding to the shrugging of the shoulders in the adult. In the fifteenth month I saw my child, without any assignable cause, shrug his shoulders for the first time, just as adults do, only, perhaps, somewhat more quickly, and he did this in similar fashion on several days. For a moment it seemed as if the child's clothing were causing a disagreeable irritation of the skin; but the knowing expression of countenance did not at all harmonize with this. And the shrugging of the shoulders also occurred when I stood before the child and said, " Yes, yes!" As I had nodded then affirmatively, the child nodded also (four hundred and fifty-ninth day).

This led me to the conjecture that the shrugging of the shoulders might already express inability, and I was soon confirmed in this, for, on the following day even, this gesture was the answer to my question, " Where is your ear?" in reply to which the child, after some hesitation, touched his eye. In the sixteenth month this signification was beyond question; for if I ask, " Where is your eye, ear, nose, forehead, chin?" and the child does not know some one of these, then, to my surprise, he shrugs his shoulders. At the same date there often follows upon this expressional movement another, of waiting. When waiting—e. g., for a biscuit dipped

in hot water to become cool—the child plants both arms
at the same time symmetrically against his sides, in such
a way that his hands come against his hips with fingers
bent, the back of the hand touching the hips. The
whole attitude is that of waiting—not in the least of
demanding—and is probably imitated, which can not be
said of shrugging the shoulders. This became, moreover, in the second quarter of the second year, decidedly
a sign, in the same sense as a shaking of the head in denial, of refusing, and of not knowing and of not being
able. It must be counted among the as yet inexplicable
hereditary expressive movements. Darwin also declares
himself in favor of the hereditary character of the movement, but he did not see it in any very young English
child, and reports it only in the case of two sisters
(grandchildren of a Frenchman) who shrugged their
shoulders between the sixteenth and eighteenth months.

7. Begging with the Hands and Pointing.

Putting the hands together in the attitude of begging belongs to the earliest gestures of German children that are acquired by training. This movement is,
at the same time, one of the first of which the child understands the significance as language, and of which he
makes use. He soon finds that the begging position of
the hands brings him the desired food quicker than crying, and for this reason he makes the gesture of himself
always when he wants anything, whether it be a biscuit,
a toy, or a change of place. If continued crying, for a
longer or shorter time, has proved wholly useless, then
it is suddenly discontinued, and the child hastily puts
his hands together in a begging attitude (fifteenth

month), in case this childish trick happens to have been previously taught him. He also begs in this fashion without crying, and by making sounds of longing, with outstretched arms—e. g., when he desires the repetition of some new sort of fun. When some one had poised a spoon on the end of his nose, the (fourteen and a half months old) child laughed, seized the spoon, observed it carefully, put it from one hand into the other, and then handed it to the person with an indescribably beseeching tone of voice. Upon the repetition of the experiment he was again delighted.

Long even after learning the significance of the spoken "*Bitte*" ("I beg," or "Please"), which my boy pronounced "*bibi*" up to the twenty-second month, the accompanying raising and holding together of the hands did not cease; and what was especially surprising, when the child wished the continuance of a sight that pleased him, or of piano-playing, or when the railway train in which the child was traveling stopped, then he would strike his hands together repeatedly (twenty-third month), so that in a literal sense he manifested his applause and his desire for repetition or continuance by clapping the hands, just like a gratified public at the theatre. Nay, even in the tenth, as also in the seventeenth, month, this movement took place in sleep, no doubt, during dreaming.

It seems natural to assume that adults utter their applause by hand-clapping for the reason that the noise is greater; but the putting of the hands together in prayer in Christian churches, as well as the lifting of the arms in prayer by Mohammedans, agrees with the begging gestures of children. These express only indirectly, by hand-clapping and also by noiseless putting together of the hands, their satisfaction so far as they thereby beg for repetition.

How it comes about that very small children are artificially taught, along with the "giving of the hand" (even in the twentieth to the twenty-fourth week sometimes [Lindner]), to raise and put together the hands (not the feet), when they are to beg for anything, is not hard to understand. This gesture is indeed acquired by each individual through imitation and training, but probably has its foundation in this, that in the act of seizing, the arms are extended, and the hands, when the desired object is grasped, place themselves about it. Begging is also ultimately a desiring. And if we follow the history of the development of the seizing movements from the beginning (p. 241), we are easily convinced that the arms, which must be extended for seizing, are, when this has been many times successful, extended in case of every strong desire (with and without sounds expressive of desire), because the thing desired is regarded as capable of being seized. What I have stated as to the interpretation of the retinal images (p. 62) confirms this view.

At first the child expresses his desire only by crying; after he has begun to seize, also by stretching out the arms (in the case of my child for the first time on the one hundred and twenty-first day); then, by extending the arms and putting the hands together. These hereditary expressional movements, originating in the practice of seizing, are made use of by educators, in order to teach the praying, begging attitudes, with folding of the hands, which in the beginning are not in the least understood by the child; he simply finds by experience that the joining of the hands along with the raising of the arms is sooner followed by the fulfillment of a wish than crying is, and for this reason he adopts the gesture. When, now, with the development of the faculty of sight, new objects that can not be seized are better distinguished from their surroundings, then the child manifests his lively interest in them—especially in moved and moving objects, e. g., horses—by this very gesture; he opens his mouth, breathes loudly by starts, fixates the object, and stretches out his hands (eighth month). Often at this period one can hardly tell whether the child means to *seize* or to *point*. When, before he can speak, at the question, " Where is the light?." he turns his head to the light, he thereby shows his understanding of the question as to the direction (ninth month); but when (in the fourteenth month) he lifts the right arm besides and points to the light with outspread fingers, then he has executed the gesture of *pointing*, absolutely distinct from desiring.

For the understanding of mental development it is an important fact that this pointing is already employed with perfect correctness before the first attempts at expression in words. A little girl of eleven months, who could not yet speak at all, answered the questions, " Where is papa ? " " Where is Nannie ? " etc., correctly, without a single mistake, by movements of the eyes and by indicating direction with the finger (Frau von Strümpell).

Later, this pointing is used as the expression of a wish, as it is by the deaf and dumb—e. g., my boy in the ninetieth week, at sight of the milk-pitcher, pointed

at it with his hand, and directly after at the milk-bottle
with the same hand—in fact, to my surprise, with the
forefinger, the child unmistakably having the purpose
of getting the milk poured out. Whence comes all at
once the use of the forefinger in place of the spreading
of all the fingers for pointing? Imitation alone hardly
offers sufficient occasion for it; still less does the experi-
mental touching. Rather, the whole complicated combination of " fixating," opening the mouth, raising the
eyelids, lifting the arm, extending the fingers, must rest
upon hereditary co-ordination, which, in case of hunger,
has showed itself useful in obtaining food; so that *pointing* is thus to be traced back to *wishing to seize*. As is
regularly the case in the tenth month, so in the second
year, often the desired object that is pointed at is carried to the mouth, and as much as possible chewed up,
after it is obtained.

From the success of the arm-movements expressing
desire in case of hunger, soon arises the notion that
these movements will also gratify other kinds of desire.
Thus the child (in the twelfth month) sitting on a chair,
when he desires to change his position, stretches out
both arms longingly (cries if no attention is paid to
him), and rejoices when taken up, as he does on getting
an apple or a biscuit. In such cases, not unfrequently
—e. g., in the fourteenth month—a " paramimy " is
observed, since, instead of the begging position of the
hands, one of the other little performances acquired by
training and not yet understood by him, is executed—
e. g., the hand is moved toward the head as an answer
that has been learned to the question, " Where is the little rogue?" (*Trotzköpfchen*, "headstrong "). Here, with

the experience of success upon stretching out the hands blends the experience of the agreeable (of friendliness, it may be—of granting his requests) upon the right performance of those little tricks. The likeness of the results leads to confounding of the means.

But the more the voice is differentiated, so much the more surely is a sound united with the gesture in the first three months of the second year. Thus, with the extending of the hands the begging sound *"kay-ŭh"* (in the case of my child) was joined, this being associated with the look and the forward inclination of the body, as the expression of the strongest desire. But it passes away and is lost, since with the growth of the understanding the gestures become more firmly established, and are no longer confused with one another. Later still, the speaking of the words learned takes the place of the gestures, which they make less and less necessary. In the fifteenth month, by striking with a ring I made three glasses sound, the tones of which formed a chord. The child was pleased, laughed, and when I paused, he took the ring, handed it to me again, and directing toward the glasses his arms, eyes, and head, announced with his own peculiar *hay-ŭh*, his wish for a repetition. Here, as yet, no *word-language existed, but the language of gesture could not be misunderstood.*

When no response is made to a persistently-expressed desire, then there may easily happen in lively children a regular fit of rage; they throw themselves on the floor, strike out when taken hold of, and scream furiously and most angrily (observed by me for the first time in the seventeenth month). But it may also happen if, e. g., the child pulls some one by the hand and wants to be accompanied, that, on being denied the request, the child sheds tears of sorrow in place of being angry (twenty-third month). The spirit of invention may also be aroused, as in the following case: The child (of twenty-two months) wishes to sit at the table. No one listens to his entreaty or takes notice of his imploring gesticulations. Thereupon, he goes into the corner of the room, tries, with a great effort, to get a heavy chair, does not rest till it has been placed at the table, strikes with the flat of his hand on the seat of the chair, thus expressing plainly, without words, what he wants, and exults when he has been put up on the chair.

Besides the expressive movements discussed in this chapter, there are, in early childhood, several more that deserve a thorough investigation. They are generally hard to describe, however, although they are often easily understood, even when the child does not, as yet, speak a word. For the child's attitude, the direction of his look, the movements of his fingers, in varying combinations, make already a finely-developed *mute language*. Some examples may illustrate this.

In the fourteenth month affection is expressed by a gentle laying of the hand upon the face and shoulders [of others]—this movement is presumably acquired by imitation ; anger and disobedience (willfulness) by very obstinate straightening of the body ; this, in fact, in the tenth month even, when the child is laid down ; shame —when he has soiled himself—by peculiar crying, with tears ; pride (in a new baby-carriage in the nineteenth month). by a ridiculous bearing. The variety in the expression of countenance, when in the second and third years the separate passions gradually awake, is, however, indescribable, and, on account of the transitoriness of the phenomena, is hardly to be reproduced pictorially. Jealousy, pride, pugnacity, covetousness, lend to the childish countenance a no less characteristic look than do generosity, obedience, ambition. These states could not be recognized by the expression of countenance unless each of them had its own expressional movement, and, in fact, these movements appear in greater purity in the child, who does not dissemble, than they do in later life.

It is beyond the limits of this work to trace the connection of these mental states with the play of feature and with the growth of the will. Very many more observations must be instituted in regard to children before the influence of imitation and of inheritance upon the voluntary inhibition of emotional outbreaks, and upon the voluntary inducing of a state of mind at once self-contented and not disturbing to others can be understood.

CHAPTER XIV.

DELIBERATE (ÜBERLEGTE) MOVEMENTS.

THAT it is a very long time before we can perceive in the child a movement that is independent, proceeding from his own deliberation, follows from the foregoing chapters. Before *motives*, i. e., *reasons*, for movement can be added to the purely physical centro-motor impulses, to the peripheral reflex stimuli, to the inclination to imitate, to instinct, to the feelings as causes of muscular movements, not only must the motor experiences mentioned have been had countless times, but the

23

senses and the understanding must be a good deal developed. For he who moves no longer merely in *direct* dependence on his temporary feelings, moods, and mental and physical states in general—he who *represents to himself before the movement how the movement will be; in a word, he who acts must already have perceived very many movements of others and have felt very many movements of his own, in order to be able to originate in his mind a correct image of the purely voluntary, deliberate, or intentional movement that is to be executed.*

I should not be able to name any movement of the first three months to which this necessary condition applies well enough to exclude every doubt as to whether the movement might not be instinctive (and therefore inherited), or reflexive, or impulsive.

The *tactile* movements with the hands—not the feet —that occur in the first months, and have the appearance of *seeking,* are just as little voluntary as are the later *pulling* and *scratching* at the skin of a face touched; they are, as belonging to seizing, instinctive. Even *stamping* with the foot (in the eleventh month), pushing along a chair, at the same period, stretching the body out straight and stiff, as means of preventing being laid down by force (in the tenth month), as well as the much later movements of throwing, can not be styled intentional muscular movements, founded on independent deliberation. Rather do some plays, which are not to be referred either to imitation or instinct, either to reflex stimuli or emotions, point to the germination of choice and deliberation after the awakening of the function of causality. Thus my child, in the eleventh month, used frequently to strike a spoon against a newspaper or

against another object held in his hand, and to exchange
both objects suddenly, moving the spoon with the other
hand, which gave exactly the impression of testing
whether the noise proceeded from the one arm only, or
would arise likewise in case this arm were motionless
(p. 87). The restless *experimenting* of little children,
especially in the first attempts at accommodation (p. 54)
[of the eye]—even quite insignificant practices (like the
crumpling of paper from the third to the sixth month),
are not only useful but indispensable for the intellectual
development. Moreover, it is essential to consider, in
regard to the cultivation of the will, because thereby
the understanding is gradually awakened, how ineffi-
cient most of the early, unrepresented, non-coördinated
movements were, and how useful, on the contrary, are
the co-ordinated movements with definite aims. Only
when both occur together, the representation of the
movement and the expectation of its result, is deliberate
movement possible, which, unfortunately, is too often
prevented through training from showing itself early.
Often even in the second year we can tell only with
difficulty, or can not tell at all, whether the child acts
independently or not—e. g., when (in the sixteenth
month) he opens and shuts cupboards, picks up from
the floor and brings objects that he threw down. When,
on the contrary, at this period, he holds, entirely of his
own motion, an ear-ring that had been taken off, to the
ear from which it was taken, I am inclined to see in
that already a sign of deliberation—understanding and
choice—whereas in the mere making of noise—it may
be by opening and slamming-to the cover of a box, or
by the eager tearing of newspapers—there is rather the

co-operation of pleasure in noise and movement with
gratification in the putting forth of power, than of deliberation and choice. Yet it seemed to me worthy of
note that my child one day (in the fourteenth month)
took off and put on the cover of a can not less than sev-
enty-nine times, without stopping a moment. His attention, meantime, strained to the utmost, indicated
that the intellect was taking part. "How does this
noise happen?" the child would surely have thought, if
he had been able to speak; for he often enough asked
later, "What makes that?" when he heard a strange
noise.   But even the child not yet acquainted with
speech might think thus, like an intelligent brute animal, only the latter would not lift the cover so often of
his own accord.

It can not be doubted that the child wills and thinks
long before the acquirement of speech; but independent activity joins itself to the unintentional, involuntary
muscular movements quite imperceptibly, after long,
incomplete manifestation of the power of co-ordination.
The feelings that are determinative for all mental development, feelings of pleasure and displeasure, the attempts to seize that which excites desire—food, above
all—and to keep off that which causes discomfort, must
be looked upon as starting-points of the continuously-
advancing development.

In this respect the history of the development of
seizing, which has been portrayed, is a contribution at
the same time to the knowledge of the development of
volition. Especially the independent taking of food,
that begins after the first attempts at seizing, offers interesting transitions from the imperfectly co-ordinated

to the perfectly harmonious movement of the muscular apparatus of arm, mouth, tongue, and œsophagus. I group some observations concerning this point, made upon my own child, which show that the will is present before the co-ordination is complete.

5th month.—Meat offered with a fork is seized with the hand and carried slowly to the mouth; many times incorrectly, but once properly.

9th month.—Whatever can be brought to the mouth is put upon the tongue with astonishing celerity. In this operation fewer errors were made than before.

11th month.—The child, every day, of his own accord, takes a biscuit from the table with the hand, carries it correctly to his mouth—previously he often put it to his cheek or chin—bites off a bit, chews it fine, and swallows it; but he can not yet drink from a glass.

12th month.—Very seldom is there a failure to hit the mouth at the first trial with the biscuit. At the beginning of this month, too, the child can drink from a glass, only he still breathes into the water while drinking.

18th month.—The full spoon is carried to the mouth with tolerable skill.

19th month.—If the spoon is laid on the left side of the plate, then, after a little consideration, he takes it with his left hand, and no difference is noticeable between his use of the left and the right hand in eating.

20th month.—The child carries the spoon with food in it to the mouth more and more cleverly, quickly, and surely. For all that, he can not yet, without help or guidance, alone take food with the spoon—can not get it into the spoon. He does not always bestow attention enough on it; often pauses and grasps at shining objects of all sorts, when the things about him are such as he is not accustomed to.

In the months following, the child, being purposely remanded to his own resources, perfects himself in this line of action. What has been reported is, however, enough to show that intention is present long before co-ordination is perfected. Will, knowledge of consequences, representation of the whole movement—these are clear before the movement can be correctly executed. The reverse is the case with the characteristic pleasure taken by all boys in throwing; they hurl all sorts of things out of the window without a thought of the consequences.

This difference, often overlooked, between *willed* and instinctive movements of children, may be demonstrated in many other forms of movement, especially if the manner of playing, or the occupation from day to day, from week to week, is watched. But I have already presented so many particular instances, and the observations are so easy to make, if only time enough is given, and if several normal children are compared, that it seems unnecessary here to multiply examples. Only the movements of the tongue, which are the most important sign of the developed will, will be more fully treated as the foundation of learning to speak, in the description of that process (in the Third Part).

It suffices here, in order to ascertain approximately the date of the beginning of the manifestation of will, and of deliberation, in one child at least, to put together some of the movements treated in the previous chapters with reference to the questions: when the inborn movements are no longer purely impulsive; no longer purely mechanically reflexive; no longer purely instinctive; and when movements undoubtedly willed appear without the admixture of the others.

It holds good universally, that *willing can not take place until after the forming of ideas.* Up to that period the child is will-less, like an animal without a brain. After the beginning of the ideational or representative activity of the brain, a period is still necessary for the association of the idea or representation of a movement and the idea of an object (desired) as the aim of the movement. In this period of transition—from the incipient causative activity which changes the perceptions arising from sensuous impressions into ideas, to the combination of two ideas—a sensory and a motor— fall the movements of the infant that are the hardest to understand, those that have still a mixed character.

The following provisional synopsis is intended to help in determining the limits of this period in both directions:

MOVEMENT.	No trace existing.	First attempts.	With deliberation and effect.	Remarks.
Head-shaking	....	4th day.	16th week.	In refusal.
Holding the head.	10th week.	11th week.	16th "	
Seizing	114th day.	117th day.	17th "	
Raising the upper part of body.	12th week.	16th(?) week.	22d "	Lying on back without help.
Pointing..........	4th month.	8th month.	9th month.	
Sitting.......... ..	13th week.	14th week.	42d week.	Without being held or supported.
Standing	21st "	23d "	48th "	Wholly without support.
Walking..........	40th "	41st "	66th "	Alone, freely.
Raising one's self.	13th "	28th "	70th "	Without being held or helped.
Stepping over a threshold.	65th "	68th "	70th "	Without support.
Kissing..........	11th month.	12th month.	23d month.	
Climbing	24th(?) "	26th "	27th "	Without being held or helped.
Jumping	24th(?) "	27th "	28th "	

After this, will-power begins to show itself in co-ordinated movements of the larger muscular groups in the sixteenth and seventeenth weeks; so, too, the first imitations (p. 283) were successful, and, for the first time, his own image in the mirror was regarded with attention (twentieth chapter); willed contractions of the muscles of the eye, however, take place somewhat earlier (p. 46). Unquestionably deliberate, voluntary turning of the gaze to new objects I did not see, indeed, until the sixteenth week.

Thus, in the case of my child, the only one as yet regularly observed in the first months with reference to his movements, we shall have to postpone the beginning of the active manifestation of the will—i. e., of the activity of the cerebral cortex in the co-ordination of the muscles chiefly used later—to the fourth month. But, according to many experiments on other children, this very date probably holds good pretty generally, whereas later, in sitting, standing, walking, climbing, jumping, talking, the greatest variations as to time appear.

The first deliberate movements take place only after the close of the first three months.

Were there still need of proof that infants can not earlier execute voluntarily any movement whatever, on account of the as yet insufficient development of the cerebrum, it would be furnished by such facts as have been observed in microcephalous human beings. For in them the cerebrum remains deficient, and the will is not developed.

But that deliberate movements are made at the beginning of the second half-year, is proved by an instructive experiment that G. Lindner made upon his little daughter of twenty-six weeks. While the child at this age was taking milk as she lay in the cradle, the bottle took such a slant that she could not get anything to suck. She now tried to direct the bottle with her feet, and finally raised it by means of them so dexterously that she could drink conveniently. " This action was manifestly no imitation ; it can not have depended upon a mere accident; for, when, at the next feeding, the bottle is purposely so placed that the child can not get anything without the help of hands or feet, the same performance takes place as before. Then, on the following day, when the child drinks in the same way, I prevent her from doing so by removing her feet from the bottle; but she at once makes use of them again as regulators for the flow of the milk, as dexterously and surely as if the feet were made on purpose for such use. If it follows from this that the child acts with deliberation long before it uses language in the proper sense, it also appears how imperfect and crude the child's deliberation is; for my child drank her milk in this awkward fashion for three whole months, until she at last made the discovery one day that, after all, the hands are much better adapted to service of this sort. I had given strict orders to those about her to let her make this advance of herself."

Other examples of deliberate movements made before the ability to speak exists are given later, in the Third Part. To this category belong also the attempts at imitation, rare, indeed, but well marked, that are observed in the fifth month ; likewise, the first imitations of sounds and the attempts to repeat the speech of others, of which something will be said farther on.

CHAPTER XV.

SUMMARY OF GENERAL RESULTS.

In order to explain the formation and growth of the child's will, there is needed, above all, a careful observation of the muscular movements of the newly-born and of the infant. The inborn movements of every human being are of various kinds, but are of the same nature a short time after birth as they are a short time before birth—only freer than in the embryo, on account of greater room for motion, and modified by respiration.

These inborn, absolutely will-less movements are *impulsive*, when they are conditioned, as in the embryo, exclusively upon the organic processes going on in the central organs of the nervous system, especially in the spinal cord, and take place without any peripheral excitement of any of the sensory nerves. To these belong the remarkable, aimless, ill-adapted movements of the arms and legs of children just born, and their grimaces. All the motor nerves of the whole organism seem to take part in these impulsive muscular contractions. The opening of the eyes and the lateral movements of them, the rolling of the eyeball, the closing of the lid, and many contractions of the facial muscles immediately after birth, prove the excitement of the oculo-motorius, of the trochlearis, of the motor-trigeminus branches, of the abducens, of the facialis; the movements of the tongue show excitement of the hypo-glossus; the arm-and-leg-movements show excitement of the spinal motors without any assignable or admissible peripheral stimuli.

The inborn movements are, on the contrary, reflexive when they occur only upon peripheral impressions, such as light, sound, contact. In these, also, most of the motor nerves seem to be concerned, and, indeed, in general, in the manner that the laws of reflexes which have been found in brainless animals would lead us to expect. The reflexes of the newly-born are, however, slower in their operation at the beginning than after frequent repetition, and in individual cases show deviations from the condition found in full-grown men and animals. These deviations are probably to be referred partly to this, that the reflex-paths are developed to an unequal extent, so that a roundabout way sometimes offers less resistance to the reflex excitement than does the direct way. Hence, perhaps, the contra-lateral reflexes. From all the organs of sense, in the first days, reflexes go forth—viz., from the optic nerve, auditory nerve, olfactory, gustatory, the sensory branches of the trigeminus, and the cutaneous nerves, upon the whole surface of the body. But the stimuli must, in general, be stronger than at a later period, or (at least, in the skin and retina) must affect a greater number of extremities of nerve-fibers simultaneously, in case distinct reflexes are to take place. The reflex excitability of the skin of the face is relatively greater from birth on, than that of other parts.

A third kind of inborn movements is the *instinctive*, which, indeed, likewise occur only after certain sensory peripheral excitations, but neither with the mechanical uniformity of the reflexes, nor with the constancy of those, even when reflex excitability is present. Rather is there need of a special psychical condition, which may best be styled "disposition" (or "tone"). At any rate there is required an activity of those central organs of the nervous system, through which feelings have their existence. If the disposition, or the feeling is wanting, then the instinctive movement is not made, even under the strongest or most appropriate stimulus—as in the case of laughter, when the sole of the foot of a child in a sorrowful frame of mind is tickled by a stranger. A good example of the typical, instinctive, inborn movements of mankind is presented in sucking. With this is allied licking. In new-born animals, especially chickens just hatched, many more complicated instinctive movements appear, however, since perceptions producing directly a motor effect are followed by highly expedient co-ordinated movements; especially perceptions of sight. The eye of the bird, during the whole embryonic period, is much larger in proportion to the brain than that of man, and can furnish accurately localized impressions immediately after the bird is hatched. These impressions are, by means of an hereditary mechanism, at once (in pecking) turned to account, and thereby deliberate movements are simulated. In fact, however, no movement of a new-born animal or child is deliberate ; none voluntary.

Willed movements can not take place until the development of the senses is sufficiently advanced, not only to distinguish clearly the qualities belonging to the separate departments of sense, not only to feel every impression, to localize the sensation, and to compare it with other sensations, to note its antecedents and consequents

—in a word, to perceive, but sufficiently advanced also
to recognize the cause of the perception, whereby the
perception becomes a representation, a mental picture
or idea. Without the power of representation there is
no will; without the activity of the senses there is no
representation; thus the will is actually, inseparably
bound up with the senses. It disappears when they are
extinguished; it is wanting to the person who is fast
asleep.

From this dependence of all will upon the senses, it
by no means follows that a developed activity of the
senses invariably brings with it the development of the
will; on the contrary, something else is required for
that. The representations, or ideas, formed in the first
months of human life, by means of innumerable perceptions, must, in order to have a motor effect in general,
find on hand a large number of movements, upon which
they now operate with determinative force. It is only
upon the central sources of the motor nerves, which
have for a long time and often been excited, impul-
sively and reflexively or instinctively, that an idea can
operate to co-ordinate or to modify. And this motor
influence of ideas is greatest when the idea itself is
that of a movement, particularly that of a movement
leading to a desired object or a goal striven for. Only
after the lapse of the first three months do such willed
movements take place; but not in such a way as if a
wholly new psychical agency suddenly appeared in the
child as by inspiration; rather does the development
of the will go on very gradually. Only to the spectator
the transition seems sudden, from the will-less child to
the child that wills, if he observes seldom. The first

successful combination of a motor idea with the idea of an object or an aim, as in the case of the first successful attempt to seize—that is what seems sudden. But what is surprising here is the *result*, because that was wanting before in the numerous similar attempts. In fact, both the movements that are now willed, and the perceptions that also become willed later, were long ago and often made; at first without being willed, as a result of the heightened excitability of the central organs of the nervous system, and of the increasing paths of association; then each one for itself, which gave rise to ideas; and finally both together. The movement itself runs the same course in both cases. The willing of the movement is merely the willing of one of the impulses, as W. Gude well observes; one of the impulses that the child has already often allowed to operate in himself or that he had to let operate. But all this is true only of the first act of willing.

After the child, in the second three months, has begun to execute willed movements in greater number, he soon finds that the earlier combinations of muscular contractions no longer suffice for his desires, which have, in the mean time, become exceedingly manifold. Hence becomes necessary, on the one hand, a *separation* of nervo-muscular excitations hitherto combined; on the other hand, an *association* of those hitherto separated. In this, for the first time, is manifested the direct participation of the intellect in the occurrence of voluntary movements. The ordinary childish performances, the first attempts at imitation in the fourth month, and the greater independence in the taking of food (e. g., taking hold of the bottle) are proofs of this; but the essential character of the will is not to be found either in separation alone, i. e., in the effort to make muscles contract separately that have hitherto always contracted together, or in association alone, i. e., in the effort to make muscles contract together that have hitherto always contracted singly. The will is neither co-ordinating only nor isolating only, but both; and, what is most frequently overlooked, in both departments it performs nothing absolutely new. As Gude has shown, it can not "call forth primary movements." It finds completely co-ordinated movements—inborn ones, in fact— like sucking, swallowing, already on hand, as well as typically isolated movements—e. g., the lifting of the eyelid with the look downward—which later it in part can not call forth at all, in part can call forth only after an enormous amount of practice.

In this important fact, that the will, as a reciprocal action of motor ideas, can alter, isolate, combine, repeat, strengthen and weaken, hasten and delay existing movements, lies, at the same time, the key to the understanding of the difficulty of *learning*.

On the one hand, the abundant material of inborn impulsive, reflexive, and instinctive movements, which are mingled together in the first three months and are influenced by the increasing activity of the senses, favors the development of will, since it alone supplies the requisite representations of movement; on the other hand, however, this very material renders more difficult the manifestation of the directing power of the will. For the more that certain nerve-paths have been made easily passable by frequent repetition of movements, the greater will be the resistance to the combinations of these with others, and to the employment of isolated tracts; the best proof of this is furnished in the accuracy, never afterward reappearing, of children's imitations (in the fourth year) of the accent, pronunciation, intonation of words given to them from foreign languages and from various dialects of their mother-tongue. The first imitations are the first distinct, represented, and willed movements.

In order to give accuracy to the proposed outline of the development of will in the child, we have yet to set forth briefly its bearing with regard to four problems. To every perfect activity of will are indispensable desire, muscular sensations, voluntary inhibition, and attention.

Desire, in the ordinary meaning of the word, presupposes ideas. Therefore, when it is said of the newly-born that it desires something (or even that it is searching for and wishes something), this form of expression is false. The child's relatives merely infer from its movements, attitude, position, situation, a condition of discomfort, displeasure, or discontent (in case of hunger, thirst, wet), and out of their own subjective state reason to the existence of a similar objective state in the child. In fact, however, the behavior of the newly-born, like that of the unborn, is intelligible without the assumption of any mental process whatever when we consider that, with the greater excitability of the central nervous organs in the spinal cord and the medulla oblongata, not only do reflexes—after refrigeration, wet, and the like —occur more easily and more frequently, but instinctive movements also, like sucking, and especially impulsive movements, are multiplied, e. g., crying; but now, in the case of hunger and other disagreeable states,

that excitability is, in fact, increased.   After the removal of the causes of the discomfort it is diminished,
and then the mobility is likewise diminished.   Thus the
child behaves as if it desired, although it does not desire.
But the repetition of the alternation of great mobility
along with discomfort—less mobility along with comfort
—during the first days, leaves behind in the central
organs traces that make possible, or favor, the association of the remembrance of movement with the sensuous impression (milk, warm bath, etc.) that relieved the
discomfort.   Then the thing that relieves the discomfort is perceived and represented, and now, for the first
time, a movement of " desire " is made.

The *muscular sensations* probably begin to be developed before birth, with the movements of the child.
They must be present in all later muscular actions, even
the purely impulsive, and they exert their influence in
the performance of all those which take place only when
a psychical factor co-operates—hence in all instinctive
movements and all represented movements, consequently in voluntary ones also; for if it were not so, then it
would remain incomprehensible how, in the successful,
often extremely complicated, harmonious contractions
of the most different muscles, just the required degree
of contraction, and no more than this, is attained.   But
from this it does not in the least follow that they determine the will itself, especially as they do not regularly
enter into the consciousness.   They belong rather to
the machinery of nervo-muscular excitement, and to the
impulse to it, upon which alone the will can operate.
They remain below the threshold of the will when they
do not generate ideas.

24

The *voluntary inhibition* of a movement pre-sup-poses willed movements; it therefore appears in the child only after well-advanced development of the rep-resentational or ideational stage. It is based on an ex-citement in the state of non-willing, and is produced in the child through ideas as to the result of a movement. When the child's will is completely at rest, the rise of no movement is arrested by it; a muscular contraction may occur at any moment. But when, in this state of rest, ideas are formed which prevent the motor ideas awakened by sense-impressions or memory-images from operating on the motor centers of highest rank, then this state is called *voluntary inhibition*. It does not come to a manifestation of will—i. e., in this case; the child does not will, because in him an inhibitory process takes place that neutralizes the motor ideas. When he is asleep he does not will, because there are no motor ideas and no inhibitory ones. I understand by ideas here, as always, psychical facts that are bound up with organic processes in the ganglionic cells of the cere-brum, and are, in part, causes of movements, in so far as the nerve excitations, by means of connecting fibers and intermediate ganglionic cells, reach the motor cen-ters of lower rank. Through this, the voluntary inhibi-tion of many reflexes also is then made possible. The simplest represented movement, viz., the first imitation, requires this co-operation of the cerebrum no less than it requires attention.

The *attention* of the child and of the adult is either compulsory—aroused by strong sense-impressions—or voluntary. In the first case—which happens in human beings only during the first three weeks—by means of a reflex movement after an unexpected stimulus of sound, of light, or other sensuous stimulus, a feeling is generated that is immediately, or after several repetitions, distinguished as a feeling of pleasure or of discomfort. The strong feeling leaves behind it a remembrance, and leads, after the perfection of the perceptive and then of the representative activity, to ideas (A) of the object of that movement—i. e., of the reflex stimulus. If, meanwhile, the co-ordination and separation of the muscular movements is sufficiently developed so that movements can also be brought to pass through motor ideas (B), then the latter (B) combine with the former (A) upon the object in question, and the attention is voluntarily directed to it. But we must not infer from the early, isolated symptoms of the later voluntary attention—like pouting of the lips, directing the gaze, cessation of crying or of uneasiness—an already existing concentration of attention; since this may be a case of the supplanting of one movement by another without will. The following of a moved light with the eye in the fourth week is possible, too, without the co-operation of the cerebrum (p. 45), whereas, later, it is precisely the fixation, for the purpose of seeing distinctly, that is voluntary. Not till the seventh week (pp. 54, 142) and the ninth week (pp. 55, 84) did I become convinced that my child was actually attentive—since his eye frequently showed a peculiar intensity of expression in hearing and seeing—after the operation of strong stimuli; but that he, of his own motion, turned to an object and lingered on it attentively, I observed first in the sixteenth and seventeenth weeks, when, of his own accord, he gazed at his own image in the glass. At this time, and much later still, an uninterrupted strain of his attention was impossible to the child. His attention lasted only for moments.

Every act of will requires attention, and every concentration of attention is an act of will. Hence an act of attention without an accompanying muscular contraction is unrecognizable. But those muscular movements that take place without any co-operation whatever of voluntary attention, are void of attention, either for the reason that will is still wanting—in the first weeks —or for the reason that will is no longer required to keep in operation the oft-repeated, voluntary movement —or, finally, because the will is inactive, as, e. g., in sleep.

In conclusion, in regard to education, which always has to control the motor ideas of the child, and, in case these are improper ones, to substitute better, we have especially to consider the *weakness of the will* even in the complete waking condition. The surprising credulity, docility, obedience, tractableness, the slight degree of independence of will in young children, that attests itself besides in many little traits of character, reminds one of the similar behavior of adults in the mesmeric sleep. For example, if I say to my two-and-a-half-year-old child, after he has already eaten something, but is just on the point of biting off a fresh piece from his biscuit— if I say categorically, without giving any reason at all, with a positiveness that will tolerate no contradiction, very loud, yet without frightening him, "The child has had enough now!" then it comes to pass that he at once puts away from his mouth the biscuit, without finishing his bite, and ends his meal altogether. It is easy to bring children even three or four years old to the opinion that a feeling of pain (after a hit) is gone, or that they are not tired or thirsty, provided only that our demands are not extravagant, and are not pressed too often, and that our assertion is a very decided one.

In this weakness of the child's will lies also the reason that little children can not be mesmerized. Their will-power does not suffice to keep their attention concentrated persistently in one direction, which is a necessary condition of hypnotism.

The weariness connected with the strain of attention makes intelligible also the rapid alternation of the plays of the child. Through too frequent yielding in this respect, which appears unobjectionable only in the first period of play, the later development of voluntary inhibitions, upon which most depends in the formation of character, is rendered essentially more difficult, and caprice is fostered. Exercises in being obedient can not begin too early, and I have, during an almost daily observation of six years, discovered no harm from an early, consistent guiding of the germinating will, provided only this guiding be done with the greatest mildness and justice, as if the infant had already an insight into the benefits of obedience. By assuming insight in the child, insight will be earlier awakened than by training; and by giving a true and reasonable ground for every command, as soon as the understanding begins, and by avoiding all groundless *prohibitions*, obedience is made decidedly more easy.

Thus, through cultivation of ideas of a higher order, the will may be directed even in the second year, and thereby the character be formed; but only through inexorable consistency, which allows no exception to a prohibition, is it possible to maintain the form once impressed upon the character.

[The third part of this work, treating of the Development of the Intellect, together with supplementary matter, is reserved for another volume of this series.— EDITOR.]

END OF VOL I.

*P*ICTURES FROM ROMAN LIFE AND STORY.
By Professor A. J. CHURCH, author of "Stories from Homer,"
"Stories from Virgil," etc. Illustrated. 12mo. Cloth, $1.50.

In the picturesque and graphic manner which distinguishes his work,
Professor Church has drawn a series of vivid pictures of the lives and times
of the Roman emperors. He brings up before the reader Horace and Mæ-
cenas and Seneca, and other contemporaries of the doomed line of Cæsars,
as well as the triumphs and tragedies and frantic excesses of the emperors
themselves. He is never didactic, but always readable, and his book is an
admirable example of history presented intelligently and judiciously in popular form.

"In the main, an anecdotic history of the twelve Cæsars, compiled from Tacitus,
Suetonius, Pliny, and Martial. The principal episodes of the first century are told
with some fullness, and descriptions of manners are introduced at suitable places. . . .
Mr. Church has a remarkable command of the literature of the period, and has used it
with his customary grace and deftness."—*London Athenæum.*

*W*ARRIORS OF THE CRESCENT. By the
late W. H. DAVENPORT ADAMS, author of "Battle Stories
from English History," etc. 12mo. Cloth, $1.50.

This story of Oriental magnificence, of glittering campaigns, fatalistic
heroism, and the pillage of the marvelous riches of India by the Sultans of
Ghazni and their followers, comes to the reader like new tales of the Arabian
Nights. Here we may read the exploits of Mahmud, Timur the Tartar, and
the Great Moguls. It is a splendid but little known chapter of history, and
Mr. Adams's graphic, vivid style clothes history with the garb of romance.
Many who reach the dazzling records of Shah Jahan, The True Star of the
Faith, or Auranyzib, the Conqueror of the Universe, will find a new world
opened to them in these pictures of magnificent Oriental despotism.

*E*L DORADO; OR, THE GILDED MAN. And
other Pictures of the Spanish Occupancy of America. By Prof.
A. F. BANDELIER, author of "The Social Organization and
Government of the Ancient Mexicans," "Studies among the
Sedentary Indians of New Mexico," etc. 12mo. Cloth.

In this book Prof. Bandelier tells the romantic stories of Cibola and Jean
l'Archevêque, and pictures other phases of the strange scenes when the mailed
Spaniards bore cross and sword northward and eastward from the land of
Montezuma in their thirst for exploration, gold, and conquest. These ro-
mances of Spanish discovery in America are fitly presented in this anni-
versary year.

New York: D. APPLETON & CO., 1, 3, & 5 Bond Street.

*A*BRAHAM LINCOLN : *The True Story of a Great LIFE.* By WILLIAM H. HERNDON and JESSE W. WEIK. With numerous Illustrations. New and revised edition, with an introduction by HORACE WHITE. In two volumes. 12mo. Cloth, $3.00.

This is probably the most intimate life of Lincoln ever written. The book, by Lincoln's law-partner, William H. Herndon, and his friend Jesse W. Weik, shows us Lincoln the man. It is a true picture of his surroundings and influences and acts. It is not an attempt to construct a political history, with Lincoln often in the background, nor is it an effort to apotheosize the American who stands first in our history next to Washington. The writers knew Lincoln intimately. Their book is the result of unreserved association. There is no attempt to portray the man as other than he really was, and on this account their frank testimony must be accepted, and their biography must take permanent rank as the best and most illuminating study of Lincoln's character and personality. Their story, simply told, relieved by characteristic anecdotes, and vivid with local color, will be found a fascinating work.

"Truly, they who wish to know Lincoln as he really was must read the biography of him written by his friend and law-partner, W. H. Herndon. This book was imperatively needed to brush aside the rank growth of myth and legend which was threatening to hide the real lineaments of Lincoln from the eyes of posterity. On one pretext or another, but usually upon the plea that he was the central figure of a great historical picture, most of his self-appointed biographers have, by suppressing a part of the truth and magnifying or embellishing the rest, produced portraits which those of Lincoln's contemporaries who knew him best are scarcely able to recognize. There is, on the other hand, no doubt about the faithfulness of Mr. Herndon's delineation. The marks of unflinching veracity are patent in every line."—*New York Sun.*

"Among the books which ought most emphatically to have been written must be classed 'Herndon's Lincoln.'"—*Chicago Inter-Ocean.*

"The author has his own notion of what a biography should be, and it is simple enough. The story should tell all, plainly and even bluntly. Mr. Herndon is naturally a very direct writer, and he has been industrious in gathering material. Whether an incident happened before or behind the scenes, is all the same to him. He gives it without artifice or apology. He describes the life of his friend Lincoln just as he saw it."—*Cincinnati Commercial Gazette.*

"A remarkable piece of literary achievement—remarkable alike for its fidelity to facts, its fullness of details, its constructive skill, and its literary charm."—*New York Times.*

"It will always remain the authentic life of Abraham Lincoln."—*Chicago Herald.*

"The book is a valuable depository of anecdotes, innumerable and characteristic. It has every claim to the proud boast of being the 'true story of a great life.'"—*Philadelphia Ledger.*

"Will be accepted as the best biography yet written of the great President."—*Chicago Inter-Ocean.*

"Mr. White claims that, as a portraiture of the man Lincoln, Mr. Herndon's work 'will never be surpassed.' Certainly it has never been equaled yet, and this new edition is all that could be desired."—*New York Observer.*

"The three portraits of Lincoln are the best that exist ; and not the least characteristic of these, the Lincoln of the Douglas debates, has never before been engraved. . . . Herndon's narrative gives, as nothing else is likely to give, the material from which we may form a true picture of the man from infancy to maturity."—*The Nation.*

New York: D. APPLETON & CO., 1, 3, & 5 Bond Street.

MISCELLANEOUS WORKS OF HERBERT SPENCER.

EDUCATION : Intellectual, Moral, and Physical.
12mo. Paper, 50 cents ; cloth, $1.25.

CONTENTS: What Knowledge is of most Worth ?—Intellectual Education.—Moral Education.—Physical Education.

SOCIAL STATICS. By HERBERT SPENCER. New and revised edition, including " The Man *versus* the State," a series of essays on political tendencies heretofore published separately. 12mo. 420 pages. Cloth, $2.00.

Having been much annoyed by the persistent quotation from the old edition of " Social Statics," in the face of repeated warnings, of views which he had abandoned, and by the misquotation of others which he still holds, Mr. Spencer some ten years ago stopped the sale of the book in England and prohibited its translation. But the rapid spread of communistic theories gave new life to these misrepresentations ; hence Mr. Spencer decided to delay no longer a statement of his mature opinions on the rights of individuals and the duty of the state.

CONTENTS: Happiness as an Immediate Aim.—Unguided Expediency.—The Moral-Sense Doctrine.—What is Morality ?—The Evanescence [? Diminution] of Evil. —Greatest Happiness must be sought indirectly.—Derivation of a First Principle.— Secondary Derivation of a First Principle.—First Principle.—Application of this First Principle.—The Right of Property.—Socialism.—The Right of Property in Ideas.— The Rights of Women.—The Rights of Children.—Political Rights.—The Constitution of the State.—The Duty of the State.—The Limit of State-Duty.—The Regulation of Commerce.—Religious Establishments.—Poor-Laws.—National Education.—Government Colonization.—Sanitary Supervision.—Currency Postal Arrangements, etc.— General Considerations.—The New Toryism.—The Coming Slavery.—The Sins of Legislators.—The Great Political Superstition.

THE STUDY OF SOCIOLOGY. The fifth volume in the International Scientific Series. 12mo. Cloth, $1.50.

CONTENTS: Our Need of it.—Is there a Social Science ?—Nature of the Social Science.—Difficulties of the Social Science.—Objective Difficulties.—Subjective Difficulties, Intellectual.—Subjective Difficulties, Emotional.—The Educational Bias.—The Bias of Patriotism.—The Class-Bias.—The Political Bias.—The Theological Bias.— Discipline.—Preparation in Biology.—Preparation in Psychology.—Conclusion.

New York: D. APPLETON & CO., 1, 3, & 5 Bond Street.

NEW EDITION OF SPENCER'S ESSAYS.

ESSAYS: Scientific, Political, and Speculative. By HERBERT SPENCER. A new edition, uniform with Mr. Spencer's other works, including Seven New Essays. Three volumes, 12mo, 1,460 pages, with full Subject-Index of twenty-four pages. Cloth, $6.00.

CONTENTS OF VOLUME I.

The Development Hypothesis.
Progress: its Law and Cause.
Transcendental Physiology.
The Nebular Hypothesis.
Illogical Geology.
Bain on the Emotions and the Will.
The Social Organism.
The Origin of Animal Worship.
Morals and Moral Sentiments.
The Comparative Psychology of Man.
Mr. Martineau on Evolution.
The Factors of Organic Evolution.*

CONTENTS OF VOLUME II.

The Genesis of Science
The Classification of the Sciences.
Reasons for dissenting from the Philosophy of M. Comte.
On Laws in General, and the Order of their Discovery.
The Valuation of Evidence.
What is Electricity?
Mill *versus* Hamilton—The Test of Truth.
Replies to Criticisms.
Prof. Green's Explanations.
The Philosophy of Style.†
Use and Beauty.
The Sources of Architectural Types
Gracefulness.
Personal Beauty.
The Origin and Function of Music.
The Physiology of Laughter.

CONTENTS OF VOLUME III.

Manners and Fashion.
Railway Morals and Railway Policy.
The Morals of Trade.
Prison-Ethics.
The Ethics of Kant.
Absolute Political Ethics.
Over-Legislation.
Representative Government— What is it good for?
State-Tampering with Money and Banks
Parliamentary Reform: the Dangers and the Safeguards.
" The Collective Wisdom."
Political Fetichism.
Specialized Administration.
From Freedom to Bondage.
The Americans.‡
Index.

---

* Also published separately. 12mo. Cloth, 75 cents.
† Also published separately. 12mo. Cloth, 50 cents.
‡ Also published separately. 12mo. Paper, 10 cents ; cloth, 50 cents.

New York: D. APPLETON & CO., 1, 3, & 5 Bond Street.

EVOLUTION SERIES, NOS. 1 TO 17.

Popular Lectures and Discussions before the Brooklyn Ethical Association.

EVOLUTION IN SCIENCE, PHILOSOPHY, AND ART. With 3 Portraits. Large 12mo. Cloth, $2.00.

CONTENTS.

Alfred Russel Wallace. By EDWARD D. COPE, Ph. D.

Ernst Haeckel. By THADDEUS B. WAKEMAN.

The Scientific Method. By FRANCIS E. ABBOTT, Ph. D.

Herbert Spencer's Synthetic Philosophy. By BENJAMIN F. UNDERWOOD.

Evolution of Chemistry. By ROBERT G. ECCLES, M. D.

Evolution of Electric and Magnetic Physics. By ARTHUR E. KENNELLY.

Evolution of Botany. By FRED J. WULLING, Ph. G.

Zoölogy as related to Evolution. By Rev. JOHN C. KIMBALL.

Form and Color in Nature. By WILLIAM POTTS.

Optics as related to Evolution. By L. A. W. ALLEMAN, M. D.

Evolution of Art. By JOHN A. TAYLOR.

Evolution of Architecture. By Rev. JOHN W. CHADWICK.

Evolution of Sculpture. By Prof. THOMAS DAVIDSON.

Evolution of Painting. By FORREST P. RUNDELL.

Evolution of Music. By Z. SIDNEY SAMPSON.

Life as a Fine Art. By LEWIS G. JANES, M. D.

The Doctrine of Evolution: its Scope and Influence. By Prof. JOHN FISKE.

"The addresses include some of the most important presentations and epitomes published in America. They are all upon important subjects, are prepared with great care, and are delivered for the most part by highly eminent authorities."—*Public Opinion.*

EVOLUTION SERIES, NOS. 18 TO 34.

MAN AND THE STATE. Studies in Applied Sociology. With Index. Large 12mo. Cloth, $2.00.

CONTENTS.

The Duty of a Public Spirit. By E. BENJAMIN ANDREWS, D. D., LL. D.

The Study of Applied Sociology. By ROBERT G. ECCLES, M. D.

Representative Government. By EDWIN D. MEAD.

Suffrage and the Ballot. By DANIEL S. REMSEN.

The Land Problem. By Prof. OTIS T. MASON.

The Problem of City Government. By Dr. LEWIS G. JANES.

Taxation and Revenue: The Free-Trade View. By THOMAS G. SHEARMAN.

Taxation and Revenue: The Protectionist View. By Prof. GEORGE GUNTON.

The Monetary Problem. By WILLIAM POTTS.

The Immigration Problem. By Z. SIDNEY SAMPSON.

Evolution of the Afric-American. By Rev. SAMUEL J. BARROWS.

The Race Problem in the South. By Prof. JOSEPH LE CONTE.

Education and Citizenship. By Rev. JOHN W. CHADWICK.

The Democratic Party. By EDWARD M. SHEPARD.

The Republican Party. By Hon. ROSWELL G. HORR.

The Independent in Politics. By JOHN A. TAYLOR.

Moral Questions in Politics. By Rev. JOHN C. KIMBALL.

"These studies in applied sociology are exceptionally interesting in their field."—*Cincinnati Times-Star.*

"Will command the attention of the progressive student of politics."—*Pittsburg Chronicle-Telegraph.*

Separate Lectures from either volume, 10 cents each.

*T*HE DIARY OF AN IDLE WOMAN IN CONSTANTINOPLE. By Frances Elliot, author of "The Diary of an Idle Woman in Sicily," "The Italians," etc. With Plan and Illustrations. Crown 8vo. Cloth, $3.50.

"Those who love the romance of history better than its dry facts will probably find 'The Diary of an Idle Woman in Constantinople' a book to their taste. The author has rebuilt and repeopled the romantic scenes of this essentially Eastern city, gathering her information largely from Gibbon, Von Hammer, and similar writers, and remolding its shape according to her own ideas of what is most interesting. Thus details of dynasties and statistics are thrown aside, and she dwells on the beauties, natural and human, of a long line of favorite Sultanas, and of Byzantium of old and the Golden Horn to-day. The author gives us material very much more difficult of access in the ordinary way." —*London Literary World.*

*A*N ATLAS OF ASTRONOMY. By Sir Robert S. Ball, F. R. S., Professor of Astronomy and Geometry at the University of Cambridge ; author of "Starland," "The Cause of an Ice Age," etc. With 72 Plates, Explanatory Text, and Complete Index. Small 4to. Cloth, $4.00.

"The high reputation of Sir Robert Ball as a writer on astronomy at once popular and scientific, is in itself a more than sufficient recommendation of his newly published 'Atlas of Astronomy.' The plates are clear and well arranged, and those of them which represent the more striking aspects of the more important heavenly bodies are very beautifully executed."—*London Times.*

New Popular Edition of Lecky's England and Ireland.

A HISTORY OF ENGLAND IN THE EIGHT-EENTH CENTURY. By William E. H. Lecky. Cabinet Edition, seven vols., 12mo. Cloth, $7.00.

A HISTORY OF IRELAND IN THE EIGHT-EENTH CENTURY. By William E. H. Lecky. Cabinet Edition, five vols., 12mo. Cloth, $5.00.

The "History of Ireland" was formerly included in the eight-volume edition of the "History of England." By a rearrangement of the contents the two histories now appear separately as above, each complete in itself, but bound uniformly. Important revisions have been made, and the work is in some respects practically new.

The well-known high character of this standard work needs no fresh commendation.

*T*HE POLITICAL VALUE OF HISTORY. By William E. H. Lecky, author of "History of England in the Eighteenth Century," etc. A Presidential Address delivered before the Birmingham and Midland Institute in October, 1892. Reprinted with Additions. 12mo. 57 pages. Cloth, 75 cents.

*T*HE HISTORICAL REFERENCE-BOOK, *comprising a Chronological Table of Universal History, a Chronological Dictionary of Universal History, a Biographical Dictionary.* With Geographical Notes. For the use of Students, Teachers, and Readers. By LOUIS HEILPRIN. Third edition, revised and brought down to 1892. Crown 8vo. 569 pages. Half leather, $3.00.

"One of the most complete, compact, and valuable works of reference yet produced."—*Troy Daily Times.*

"Unequaled in its field."—*Boston Courier.*

"A small library in itself."—*Chicago Dial.*

"An invaluable book of reference, useful alike to the student and the general reader. The arrangement could scarcely be better or more convenient."—*New York Herald.*

"The conspectus of the world's history is as full as the wisest terseness could put within the space."—*Philadelphia American.*

"We miss hardly anything that we should consider desirable, and we have not been able to detect a single mistake or misprint."—*New York Nation.*

"So far as we have tested the accuracy of the present work we have found it without flaw."—*Christian Union.*

"The conspicuous merits of the work are condensation and accuracy. These points alone should suffice to give the 'Historical Reference-Book' a place in every public and private library."—*Boston Beacon.*

"The method of the tabulation is admirable for ready reference."—*New York Home Journal.*

"This cyclopædia of condensed knowledge is a work that will speedily become a necessity to the general reader as well as to the student."—*Detroit Free Press.*

"For clearness, correctness, and the readiness with which the reader can find the information of which he is in search, the volume is far in advance of any work of its kind with which we are acquainted."—*Boston Saturday Evening Gazette.*

"*The geographical notes which accompany the historical incidents are a novel addition, and exceedingly helpful.* The size also commends it, making it convenient for constant reference, while the three divisions and careful elimination of minor and uninteresting incidents make it much easier to find dates and events about which accuracy is necessary. Sir William Hamilton avers that too retentive a memory tends to hinder the development of the judgment by presenting too much for decision. A work like this is thus better than memory. It is a 'mental larder' which needs no care, and whose contents are ever available."—*New York University Quarterly.*

A CHRONOLOGICAL TABLE OF UNIVERSAL HISTORY. Extending from the Earliest Times to the Year 1892. For the use of Students, Teachers, and Readers. By LOUIS HEILPRIN. 12mo. 200 pages. Cloth, $1.25.

This is one of the three sections comprised in Heilprin's "Historical Reference-Book," bound separately for convenience of those who may not require the entire volume. Specimen pages sent on request.

New York: D. APPLETON & CO., 1, 3, & 5 Bond Street.

APPLETONS' LIBRARY LISTS.

Libraries, whether for the school, home, or the public at large, are among the most important and wide-reaching educational factors in the advancement of civilization. Modern intellectual activity, keeping pace with modern invention, has added to the earlier stores of literature myriads of books, and a still greater mass of reading-matter in other forms. Unfortunately, much of the material put into print is not of an educational or elevating character. It is important, then, in the selection of books for public use, especially for the young, that great care be exercised to secure only such kinds of reading as will be wholesome, instructive, and intrinsically valuable.

For more than fifty years Messrs. D. Appleton & Co. have been engaged in the publication of the choicest productions from the pens of distinguished authors of the past and present, of both Europe and America, and their catalogue now comprises titles of several thousand volumes, embracing every department of knowledge. Classified lists of these publications have been prepared, affording facilities for a judicious selection of books covering the whole range of Literature, Science, and Art, for individual book-buyers or for a thorough equipment of any library.

Lists A, B, and C are of books selected especially for School Libraries. The other lists are of books grouped according to subjects. The classifications are as follows :

List A.—For Primary and Intermediate Grades.

List B.—For Grammar and High School Grades.

List C.—For College and University Libraries.

List D.—HISTORY.
" E.—BIOGRAPHY.
" F.—PHYSICAL SCIENCE.
" G.—MENTAL AND MORAL SCIENCE.
" H.—POLITICAL AND SOCIAL SCIENCE.
" I.—PHILOSOPHY AND METAPHYSICS.
" K.—HYGIENE AND SANITARY SCIENCE.
" L.—FINANCE AND ECONOMICS.
" M.—TECHNOLOGY AND INDUSTRIAL ARTS.

List N.—ANTHROPOLOGY AND ETHNOLOGY.
" O.—LITERATURE AND ART.
" P.—BOOKS OF REFERENCE.
" R.—TRAVEL AND ADVENTURE.
" S.—PEDAGOGY AND EDUCATION.
" T.—FICTION.
" U.—AMUSEMENTS AND RECREATIONS.
" V.—EVOLUTION.
" W.—ARCHÆOLOGY AND PALÆONTOLOGY.

Also, Special Lists of Legal, Medical, and Religious Works.

We respectfully invite the attention of public and private book-buyers everywhere to these lists, confident that they will be found of interest and profit. Either or all will be mailed free on request.

New York: D. APPLETON & CO., 1, 3, & 5 Bond Street.